Fodor's EXPLORING

AUSTRALIA

FODOR'S TRAVEL PUBLICATIONS

NEW YORK • TORONTO • LONDON • SYDNEY • AUCKLAND

WWW.FODORS.COM

Important Note
Time inevitably brings change, so always confirm prices, travel facts, and other perishable information when it matters. Although Fodor's cannot accept responsibility for errors, you can use this guide in the confidence that we have taken every care to ensure its accuracy.

Published in the United States by Fodor's Travel Publications, a unit of Fodors LLC, a subsidiary of Random House, Inc., and simultaneously in Canada by Random House of Canada Limited, Toronto.

Fodor's and Fodor's Exploring are registered trademarks of Random House, Inc.

Published in the United Kingdom by AA Publishing.

ISBN 1-4000-1498-0
ISSN 1098–7428

Sixth edition

Fodor's Exploring Australia

Author: **Michael Ivory**
Revision Verifier: **Anne Matthews**
Cartography: **The Automobile Association**
Cover Design: **Tigist Getachew, Fabrizio La Rocca**
Front Cover Silhouette: **Melinda Berge/Network Aspen**
Front Cover Top Photograph: **AA Photo Library**

Special Sales
This book is available for special discounts for bulk purchases for sales promotions or premiums. Special editions, including personalized covers, excerpts of existing books, and corporate imprints, can be created in large quantities for special needs. For more information, write to Special Markets/Premium Sales, 1745 Broadway, MD 6-2, New York, NY 10019 or e-mail specialmarkets@randomhouse.com.

A02140

Printed and bound in Italy by Printer Trento srl.
10 9 8 7 6 5 4 3 2 1

How to use this book

ORGANIZATION

Australia Is, Australia Was
Discusses aspects of life and culture in contemporary Australia and explores significant periods in its history.

A–Z
Breaks down the country into regional chapters, and covers places to visit, including walks and drives. Within this section fall the Focus On articles, which consider a variety of subjects in greater detail.

Travel Facts
Contains the strictly practical information vital for a successful trip.

Hotels and Restaurants
Lists recommended establishments throughout Australia, giving a brief summary of their attractions.

ABOUT THE RATINGS
Most places described in this book have been given a separate rating. These are as follows:

▶▶▶   **Do not miss**

▶▶   **Highly recommended**

▶   **Worth seeing**

MAPS
To make each particular location easier to find, every main entry in this book has a map reference to the right of its name. This comprises a number, followed by a letter, followed by another number, such as 176B3. The first number (176) refers to the page on which the map can be found, the letter (B) and the second number (3) pinpoint the square in which the main entry is located. The maps on the inside front cover and inside back cover are referred to as IFC and IBC respectively.

Contents

*Above: Palm Valley, Finke Gorge
National Park
Left: Yachts moored in Hobart*

Bright flowers of the bottlebrush

**Michael Ivory has
written extensively
about the lands of
Eastern Europe—his
books include AA
Essential Hungary,
AA *Essential Czech
Republic*, AA *Explorer
Prague* and AA
CityPack Prague. He
welcomed the chance
to write a guide to
Australia, a place that
has always intrigued
him. This book reveals
something of his
pleasure in
experiencing this
fascinating and
diverse country.**

*Top: Uluru (Ayers Rock);
Opposite: Kalbarri Gorge,
Western Australia*

My Australia

Crossing the interminable Nullarbor Plain aboard the
Indian Pacific train, I made the Englishman's mistake of
heading for an empty table in the dining car. The steward
was shocked: 'Hold on a minute, mate! Why don't you sit
over here with these folk? I'm sure you'll have plenty to
talk about.' He was right of course. Australia is a place
where human contact is easy. Indeed, Australian
friendliness is proverbial; first names are used freely and
'mates' are easily made, especially if you show yourself
ready to join in, say what a wonderful country it is (not
difficult!), and refrain from invidious comparisons with
wherever you come from.

I won't forget that train ride eastward from Kalgoorlie
across the Nullarbor Plain, where the scenery doesn't
change from one day to the next and it was a real relief
to have entertaining companions at the dining table.
Australians have long since overcome what one of them
called 'the tyranny of distance', the impossibly vast
spaces that faced early explorers. Nowadays half the
enjoyment of Australia lies in the many different ways
there are of getting around. It was a special thrill to get
up into the cab of the big truck heading for the Indian
Pacific, to marvel at the aching emptiness of the scene
and at the single track heading ruler-straight to the far
horizon. In utter contrast was the bumpy ride up the
Bloomfield Track in Far North Queensland, with rain forest to either side. Rather more relaxing was a trip through
the same kind of landscape aboard an amphibious
DUKW, which took jungle, rivers and snake-filled pools
in its stride. I also joined bushwalkers in their wander-
ings among the beautiful bush country and eucalypt
forest that surrounds most of the big cities. Here, perhaps
more than anywhere else, flying comes into its own. Not
by comfortable airliner, but in a light plane, tossed
around by the thermals bubbling upwards from the hot
surface of Uluru, or in a little seaplane skimming the surface of Tasmania's Gordon River gorge. And the most
sublime moment of all? Not in the air, but whizzing
across Sydney Harbour in a powerboat, 'tinnie' of lager
in hand, at the moment when the Opera House came into
sight beneath the great span of the Harbour Bridge, and I
felt I'd really arrived 'Down Under'.
Michael Ivory

Australia Is

Australia occupies a lonely place on the globe. Apart from the frozen Antarctic, it is the only continent to lie wholly within the southern hemisphere; Papua New Guinea is over the horizon across the Timor Sea, New Zealand is more than 1,984km (1,233 miles) across the Tasman Sea, and the Asian mainland at Singapore is 2,984km (1,854 miles) distant.

Girded by nearly 36,000km (22,370 miles) of coastline, the 'island continent' has a threefold structure.

THE WESTERN PLATEAU Almost two-thirds of the land surface belongs to the Western Plateau, a vast and arid tableland covering most of Western Australia, South Australia, the Northern Territory and part of Queensland. Mostly flat and low-lying, it is interrupted by spectacular individual features like Uluṟu (Ayers

Mount Warning National Park, New South Wales

Rock) and Kata Tjuṯa (the Olgas), by rocky strongholds like the Kimberley and Arnhem Land, and by rugged ridges like those of the MacDonnell, Flinders and Hamersley ranges.

The plateau is an ancient land whose fertility was leached away by rains that fell millions of years ago, leaving arid wastes with evocative names like the Nullarbor Plain or the Sturt Stony Desert. Similarly, winds that ceased to blow long ago left repetitive patterns of sand dunes. Except in the tropics, rainfall is not only minimal but also irregular; none may fall for years, then sudden downpours will fill the normally vacant river beds, though the rainwater soon disperses to the great salt lakes.

Much of the area is uninhabited or very thinly settled, with a population measured in hundreds of square kilometres per person. Only to the west of the Darling Range, on the relatively fertile coastal plains around the great city of Perth, are there extensive farmlands and a network of settlements linked by roads and railways. Elsewhere, settlements exist in isolation as ports, mining towns and staging posts along endless highways, or, increasingly, as areas for Outback tourism.

THE GREAT DIVIDING RANGE
This mountain range runs down the whole of the eastern coastline from Cape York in the far north to the hills and highlands of New South Wales and Victoria in the south, where it leaps the Bass Strait to reappear in the mountains of Tasmania. The continent's highest peaks are found here: Mount Kosciuszko in New South Wales (2,228m/7,310 ft),

Mount Bogong in Victoria (1,986m/6,516 ft) and Mount Ossa (1,617m/5,305 ft), Tasmania.

However, much of the area is not made up of mountains but of high plateaus, from which rivers run eastward across the coastal plain. The bulk of the country's population lives here, clustering for the most part in the metropolitan areas around the great coastal state capitals of Sydney (New South Wales), Melbourne (Victoria), Adelaide (South Australia) and Brisbane (Queensland). Rural settlement is relatively dense in the valleys between the uplands and all along the fertile strip extending into the tropics along the Queensland coast. The only inland city of any size is Canberra, the federal capital.

CENTRAL EASTERN LOWLANDS

Between the Western Plateau and the Great Dividing Range, the Central Eastern Lowlands slope down gradually from the east towards the interior. A series of broad basins succeed one another, from the southern rim of the Gulf of Carpentaria through Queensland's Channel Country to the area drained by the country's greatest river system, the Murray/Darling/Murrumbidgee.

Here in the Outback, grazing animals outnumber people by several hundred to one, and rural life depends as much on unreliable rainfall as on the state of world markets. Mineral wealth has created a small number of towns like Broken Hill and Mount Isa, which are linked by interminably long roads and railways to the coast.

South Australian opals

❏ The world's driest continent after Antarctica has a surprisingly small range of climates. The highest rainfall is in the tropical or subtropical north, where temperatures stay high all year round (29°C/84°F in summer and 24°C/75°F in winter). Unlike the north, where the rain falls during the summer, temperate southern Australia experiences its highest rainfall in winter and spring, and there is more variation in average temperatures (24°C/75°F in summer to 10°C/50°F in winter when snow falls on the higher peaks). Much of the interior is arid, with little rain, and temperatures here soar to scorching heights; a maximum of 53°C (127°F) was recorded at Cloncurry in Queensland in 1889, although nights can be very cold. ❏

11

Australia's 40 million years of isolation from the rest of the world resulted in plants and animals that are unique to the continent. Over this long period, both fauna and flora evolved in response to local conditions quite independently of developments elsewhere, resulting in the array of strange creatures and plants that so delighted Joseph Banks as he accompanied Captain Cook aboard the Endeavour *in 1770. Despite subsequent development that had little regard for environmental side effects, Australia was quick to create national parks, some 2,000 of which await today's visitor.*

12

FORESTS The richest habitat in Australia is that of the rain forest. Tropical rain forest is best seen in northern Queensland (see page 222), but also lies in parts of the northern coastlands in the Northern Territory and Western Australia. Temperate rain forest, of great fascination and beauty, spreads over much of the wild country of southwestern Tasmania. This is the domain of the **southern beech** and of one of the longest-lived trees on earth, the **Huon pine**.

Great forests still cloak some of the less accessible areas of the southeast and southwest, but all of Australia's woodland has suffered grievously at the hands of the timber-cutters. The majority of the country's trees are variations on the theme of **eucalyptus** (also referred to as eucalypts and gum trees); they include some of the tallest trees on earth, like the mountain ash of the Victorian coastal forests or the karri of southwestern Western Australia.

SCRUBLAND AND DESERT Away from the coast, the pioneers found impenetrable **mallee** (a dense scrub of low-growing eucalyptus) or more open, park-like woodland. Most of these original plant communities have been cleared for grazing land, while native grasses and herbs have given way to exotic, high-yielding varieties. The desert is perhaps the

The rainbow lorikeet

most intriguing of all Australian ecosystems, where **saltbush**, **spinifex** and the occasional **desert oak** provide shelter for creatures such as scorpions and spiders, themselves food for snakes, lizards and **goannas**. The seeds of many small plants lie in wait for the sparse rain, flowering spectacularly when nourished.

FROM POUCHES TO PLATYPUSES
Of all the marsupials that inhabit the island continent, the macropods—**kangaroos** among them—seem to need little introduction, having long

The kangaroo—one of Australia's best-known marsupials

been familiar as one of the country's best-known emblems. But there's a whole world of roos out there; as well as the red kangaroo (reaching 2m/6.5 ft), there are some 50 other varieties, ranging from the equally large Forester kangaroos to the quokkas (mistaken for rats by early explorers) and brush-tailed bettongs. Kangaroos live in most parts of the country, even occasionally on the fringe of towns.

After the kangaroo, it is the endearing **koala** that every visitor wants to see. Koalas spend most of their time asleep and the rest chewing on the leaves of certain eucalypts. The population is recovering after being hunted for its fur, but it is still subject to disease and loss of habitat. As a result, you're more likely to see them in one of the country's excellent wildlife parks than in the wild alongside **wombats**, burrowing marsupials and **possums**, some of which are actually able to glide from tree to tree, thanks to their flight membrane.

Another creature that you are more likely to see in an artificial environment is the **platypus**. This shy, egg-laying mammal with its soft bill was thought to be a hoax when a specimen was first sent to Britain for examination. The spiny anteater, or **echidna**, is less timid, being well defended by its ability to burrow below ground or present an attacker with its array of sharp spines.

NATIONAL PARKS Australia declared its first national park (Sydney's **Royal National Park**) as early as 1879. Today more than 2,000 such areas are protected and managed in order to conserve their natural beauty, protect their wildlife and make them accessible to visitors. The outstanding quality and global importance of the country's natural treasures has also been recognized by the designation of no fewer than 13 World Heritage Areas. Visitors to national parks will generally find a high standard of management in evidence, with good information services and lots of walking trails that have been created to encourage people to experience and explore the landscape. Always seek the advice of rangers about local conditions.

It's quite possible you'll meet a stereotypical Australian male while Down Under. You've probably imagined him already: tall, sun-burned, probably blond and blue-eyed, short on words but long on ability to sink the stubbies (get drunk) with his mates, unhurried, an enemy of pretentiousness, and unreconstructed in his chauvinism. The stereotype exists, of course, but few Australians can be quite so easily categorized these days.

14

For many thousands of years, the Aborigines alone inhabited this vast continent. They had possibly arrived during the Ice Age, before Australia became isolated from the rest of Asia by the rising sea levels. Then, in the 1770s, Captain James Cook reached Botany Bay and claimed Australia for the Western world.

EARLY IMMIGRANTS The story of Australia's earliest European settlement is bizarre, to say the least. After James Cook's 1770 voyage of discovery, the British government came up

A classic Aussie 'character'

❏ Although rather romantically called 'convicts', most of Australia's earliest immigrants were neither noble political prisoners nor dashing highwaymen. The majority of the First Fleeters were transported for relatively minor offences, such as receiving stolen goods, forgery and petty theft, that ranged from the pathetic (pilfering a packet of snuff) to the tragic (the hunger-driven crime of stealing two hens, worth a total of fourpence). ❏

with an ambitious—many would say outrageous—solution to the 'disposal' of its felons and criminals. In May 1787, 11 ships carrying over 1,400 people, including 759 male and female convicts, set sail from England for the long and arduous journey to the virtually unknown southern continent. On their arrival in Sydney in January 1788, they became Australia's first, albeit unwilling, immigrants.

The 19th- and early 20th-century non-British immigrants to Australia were very conspicuous and often resented, although the pious and hardworking Germans who helped settle South Australia fitted in well enough. Gold rushes brought thousands of Chinese, who were treated with extreme prejudice, and South Sea Islanders known as Kanakas were kidnapped and enslaved to work the sugar plantations of Queensland, until they were repatriated under anti-slavery legislation.

Greek deli in Melbourne

WAR REFUGEES The postwar boom led to a demand for more workers than Britain could supply, and the country opened its gates to a Europe crowded with 'reffos' (refugees) and displaced persons. Australia accepted hundreds of thousands of immigrants from northern and central Europe—Czechoslovakia, Germany, the Netherlands, Scandinavia and the Baltic states.

When this source of workers began to dry up, the emphasis changed to southern Europe, and the next wave of 'New Australians' consisted of Italians, Greeks, Maltese, Croats and Serbs. A tacit 'White Australia' policy was followed; non-Europeans were rarely admitted, excluded sometimes by means of the infamous dictation test that allowed an immigration officer to give the would-be immigrant a test in a language of his (the immigration officer's) choice. An undesirable applicant of Chinese origin could thus have been examined on his knowledge of Gaelic, and, not surprisingly, fail.

A MULTICULTURAL SOCIETY A continuation of this policy became unsustainable with an increasing awareness of Australia's geopolitical position and of its social ties with Asia. A continuing, though fluctuating, demand for workers resulted in a huge influx of Cambodian, Vietnamese, Filipino and other Asian immigrants, a fact that is instantly verifiable on the streets of any of the state capitals.

The total assimilation of the newcomers has been abandoned; today, immigrant culture is preserved. Of the two state-funded television channels, SBS specializes in broadcasts in a variety of different languages. Australia is now one of the most racially diverse countries in the world. More than half of all Australians were either born overseas themselves, or have at least one parent who was born overseas.

In the midst of multiculturalism, the Aborigines, who are, after all, the only Australians who are neither recent settlers nor descended from immigrants, strive to retain their traditions and culture (see pages 24–25). Only in recent times have Australians begun to accept their different way of life.

'No worries' seems to sum up much of the average Australian's attitude to life. Work doesn't play the central role here that it does in some societies around the Pacific Rim or even in Europe. Life is to be made the most of, preferably out in the open, enjoying food and drink, watching sports with passionate intensity, or swimming, surfing, bushwalking and simply lazing around in the great outdoors of the 'best country in the world'.

Celebrating at the Melbourne Cup

The founding period of convicts was once a source of shame but is now looked back on with pride. It can be seen as a positive factor contributing to the way Australians are today. Australian 'mateship' has its roots in shared oppression and in the importance of comrades in making a life in a harsh and empty land. The land posed a tough physical challenge, in which the conventional qualities of 'manliness' were directly related to success or even survival. Work was originally performed under duress and for someone else, after which you were free to lead your own life. Authority was exercised by prison wardens and governors, and consequently resented, but there was no old ruling class or complicated code of manners. Strangers were seldom seen, but if they needed help they could be sure of getting it.

EVERYONE IS EQUAL So Australia has long been a land where people feel themselves to be basically equal and as good as the next person. Money and the making of it are admired, but this does not mean that the monied become beings apart. There is an openness about social contacts that is surprising to many visitors. When Australians say 'How are you?' there's a good chance that they actually mean it, and will enjoy hearing your answer (especially if you reveal to them how much you like their country). If you expect to be deferred to, you could be in for an unpleasant surprise; Australians don't like pretension, and will prickle if they detect it.

THE OUTDOOR LIFE Given the character of the country, with its space, climate, the grandeur of its natural landscapes and the fact that the vast majority of the population lives close to a beach, it's hardly surprising that people seem obsessed with outdoor life and sport.

Everyone loves a 'barbie' (a barbecue) and a session on the beach, whether sunbathing or surfing. The great days of lifesaving clubs and parades are certainly not over, and neither is the allure of the beach; surfing is indeed a way of life for quite a number of people.

Gambling is also a national passion, taking place indoors in front of endless ranks of 'pokies', at the casino or

❏ Even though women got the vote at an early date, Australia was always a man's country. The male–female ratio among the transportees brought by the First Fleet was hardly a balanced one, and the scenes that took place when the first cargo of women was discharged were said to be 'indescribable'. 'Sheilas' (women) were 'kept in their place' longer here than in most other countries, both at home and behind the bar, where they filled the glasses while the men on the other side got on with the serious business of drinking. Big changes came during World War II, however, and then later with the growth of feminism, one of the key works of which, *The Female Eunuch*, was by the Australian writer Germaine Greer. ❏

Lifeguard at Bondi Beach

outdoors at the racetrack. On the first Tuesday in November, life stops across the nation for the big horse race, the Melbourne Cup.

SPORT Most Australians love sport, to watch if not to play. A passion for cricket is shared with other members of the British Commonwealth, and has been made more exciting by innovations like one-day matches, floodlighting and the move away from traditional cricket whites. Rugby Union and Rugby League are played primarily in NSW and Queensland. The really big ball game, however, and certainly in its Melbourne stronghold, is the one known as Australian Rules Football. It originated on the goldfields, a crude version of Gaelic football (soccer) played by prospectors taking time off from the diggings, and has been described as 'a kind of organized mayhem, remarkable for its lack of obvious rules'. Up to 100,000 spectators gather to watch the grand final at the MCG (Melbourne Cricket Ground) every September. The year 2000, however, placed Australia on the world's sporting map, thanks to Sydney's acclaimed hosting of the XXVII Olympiad.

Australian culture goes back far longer than the 200-odd years of white settlement. Visitors will be fascinated by the evidence of at least 40,000 years of uninterrupted civilization in both the dot and x-ray style rock- and cave-paintings, and in the haunting stories of the creation legends of the Aboriginal Dreamtime.

18

Australians today have a high regard for culture and talent, and take pride in the international success of Australian artists, filmmakers and writers. Most Aussies cannot resist a good performance, and visitors who demonstrate their enthusiasm will be much appreciated.

LITERATURE AND FILMS Drama has developed from such elegies for lost youth as Ray Lawlor's *Summer of the Seventeenth Doll* to the plays of David Williamson. Les Murray and the late Judith Wright are poets of world status, weaving together the personal and the public, while managing to capture the elusive character of the Australian environment.

Three classic Australian books are Robert Hughes's convict-era history, *The Fatal Shore*, Jill Ker Conway's childhood memoir, *The Road from Coorain*, and Bruce Chatwin's rendering of the Aboriginal relationship with the earth, *The Songlines*. Also

Tongue-in-cheek Crocodile Dundee

look for Barry Hill's *The Rock*, an illustrated multicultural history of Uluṟu (Ayers Rock).

Aussie novels that comment poignantly, sometimes humorously, on Australian life, history and landscape are Nobel Prize-winner Patrick White's *Voss*, Peter Carey's spirited *Oscar and Lucinda*, David Malouf's *Remembering Babylon* and Thomas Keneally's *The Playmaker*. Elizabeth Jolley sets her novels in her native state, Western Australia.

Since the 1970s, Australian filmmakers have produced an increasing variety of internationally known work. The tragic *Breaker Morant* and Peter Weir's *Gallipoli* and *Picnic at Hanging Rock* are in a class of their own. *My Brilliant Career*, about an aspiring young writer on a sheep station, is another knock-out. *Crocodile Dundee's* bushwhacking swagger has its place in Australian mythology, as does the apocalyptic *Mad Max 2/The Road Warrior*, for different reasons, of course. Other popularAussie films include *Strictly Ballroom, A Cry in the Dark, Muriel's Wedding*, the side-splitting *The Adventures of Priscilla, Queen of the Desert, Babe, The Castle* and *Shine*.

PAINTERS Marvellous light and scenery have contributed to a tradition of outstanding painting. The early dreamy landscapes of McCubbin and the Heidelberg School, lending the Australian scenery a European beauty, gave way to the more distinctively Australian works of painters like Sidney Nolan with his series of pictures depicting the fatal defiance of outlaw Ned Kelly. Arthur Boyd's and Brett Whiteley's enlargements of

The Sidney Nolan painting Dog and Duck Hotel

their own dreams and obsessions sometimes achieve a vast scale, and Fred Williams' wonderful evocations of the arid Australian landscape rival the originality of Aboriginal art, which is now much sought after by collectors all over the world.

Aboriginal paintings are well represented in museums and art galleries, and the outdoor rock art that can be found all over the country is an undeniable cultural achievement.

MUSIC Australia also has much to offer musically. The golden voice of Joan Carden makes her a worthy successor to Dame Nellie Melba and Dame Joan Sutherland ('La Stupenda'). Each state capital boasts an Australian Broadcasting Commission symphony orchestra of world standard, with internationally recognized conductors and repertoires including music by contemporary Australian composers such as Colin Brumby, John Antill and Peter Sculthorpe. Aboriginal music is increasingly entering the mainstream of the country's culture, and the growing international reputation of Yothu Yindi, the Aboriginal rock band, was recognized by the 1992 'Australian

of the Year' award given to its lead singer, Mandawuy Yunupingu. The country is also a hotbed of good jazz (James Morrison), folk (Archie Roach and Ruby Hunter), and country and western (Lee Kernaghan and Kasey Chambers).

THE MEDIA In contrast, most Australian newspapers and TV channels are owned by two media moguls —Murdoch and Packer. Their content is dominated by personality trivia, sports, sentimental 'bushwhacker' pap and investigations into the private lives of public figures, often making the Australian press as sensationalist as any other.

The Australian Broadcasting Commission's radio and television broadcasts, on the other hand, gain many international awards for quality and interest, particularly in the fields of science, environment and religion. Especially outstanding is the current-affairs weekly *Four Corners*, which for over 20 years has exposed big business and government scandals that have been ignored by the commercial media.

The six states that came together on the first day of the 20th century to create the nation of Australia had all developed outwards from the isolated footholds of their port-of-entry capital cities, with very different characteristics and cultures. In contrast with the slow evolution of a national consciousness, the states maintain a vigorous political and economic competition both with each other and with the Federal Government.

Since 1940, Commonwealth control of tax revenues and appointment of Supreme Court judges has guaranteed the Federal Government victory in most disputes with individual states. This included the 1983 prohibition of damming of the World Heritage-listed Franklin River in Tasmania and the 1990 exclusion of logging from the unique tropical rain forests of northern Queensland. In these matters, the Commonwealth Government has been influenced by a Green movement that commands a disciplined voting block—generally estimated at between 8 per cent and 15 per cent of the electorate.

THE POLITICAL PARTIES After 13 years in power (an unprecedented six terms of office), Australia's Federal Labor Government was heavily defeated by the right-wing coalition of the Liberal Party (representing the urban middle classes and employers) and National Party (the traditional voice of rural interests) in the March 1996 elections. The current Liberal Party Prime Minister is John Howard, who is best known for his extremely conservative approach.

A large proportion of the population was delighted by this transfer of power after Labor's long, and perhaps increasingly complacent, rule. But many Australians are concerned, for example, about the future of the proposed Australian republic, free of constitutional ties to the reigning British monarch, who is still the official head of the country. There is also an ongoing debate regarding a new and more appropriate flag.

Aboriginal, immigration and arts policies have also changed, with John Howard and his supporters expressing little interest in these issues, and there was strong opposition from many quarters to the government's introduction of a GST (Goods and Services Tax) in 2000. The challenge to the Liberal/National Party coalition will be spearheaded by the Leader of the Opposition, Mark Latham.

ECONOMIC DEVELOPMENT The 'Lucky Country' cannot now find enough markets for its wool, wheat, beef or mineral exports to pay for its insatiable appetite for expensive imports. The tariffs that previously protected small local industries from being swamped by European and Asian manufacturers have been drastically cut in the interests of economic rationalism, and the Australian dollar, although weak, represents very good value for most overseas visitors. However, unemployment has fallen to under 6 per cent and there has been substantial economic growth in recent years, aided by the boom in international tourism.

There is now bipartisan political agreement on the need to develop manufactured goods for export, though the current government policy of reducing tariff barriers has had the opposite result and has caused unemployment. However, there can be no argument about the need to integrate better with the economies of both Europe and Southeast Asia and the Pacific Rim, Australia's closest neighbours.

Australia Was

In some parts of the globe, vigorous land-shaping processes are obviously hard at work. Ice and snow attack alpine peaks, glaciers grind through valleys, torrents and waterfalls erode, while elsewhere geysers boil and lava pours from beneath the earth. In contrast, Australia is a quiet continent, much of whose active geological history ended long ago.

ANCIENT TECTONICS Some 50 million years ago, Australia was part of Gondwanaland, the great southern supercontinent that slowly split into the separate fragments we know today as Antarctica, South America, Africa and India, as well as Australia and New Zealand. But its geological evolution goes back much further. Precambrian rocks more than 600 million years old are exposed over much of the continent, among them the ancient iron ore deposits of the Pilbara in Western Australia. Subsequently, much of the heart of the continent was periodically submerged beneath the sea, leaving deposits of sands, shells and grits, or the limestone of the Nullarbor Plain. Great coral reefs were also formed, which, when uplifted, became the basis of the extensive cave systems of New South Wales and Queensland,

The Great Dividing Range

or the great bastion that today guards the southern rim of the Kimberley. The Great Artesian Basin came into being at this time too, and the water pumped from it continues to support life in much of the Outback.

MORE RECENT CHANGES About 2 million years ago, what is now the arid Red Centre of the continent enjoyed a far higher rainfall and carried a rich vegetation of tropical forest, traces of which can still be seen in the palms and other plants that have found a refuge in the gorges penetrating the area's harsh ranges. In the east, the Great Dividing Range was thrown up as the result of convulsive earth movements; its southern, alpine area, together with the Tasmanian highlands, is the only part of the continent to have been subjected to glaciation in the last Ice Age (10,000 years ago). As the ice melted, the sea level rose, creating a wonderful natural harbour for the future city of Sydney. At the same time, the land bridges with Tasmania and New Guinea were cut. Later still (some 5,000 years ago), an outburst of volcanic activity covered the plains of southwestern Victoria with lava, leaving a legacy of cones and crater lakes and of deep fertile soil.

Right: Tessellated rock formation on the Tasman Peninsula
Below: Australia in 1848; note the lack of information on the unexplored interior of the continent

European explorers and educated early settlers tended to romanticize the black people they encountered on the unknown continent. Aborigines were seen by some as typifying the 'Noble Savage' dreamed up by the imaginative powers of 18th-century thinkers. The first Australians, now often referred to as Kooris, were an endlessly fascinating subject for artists and were sometimes depicted in the heroic poses of ancient Greek statuary.

VICTIMS OF THE WHITE MAN The Aborigines failed to correspond to the European stereotypes. In what now seems an entirely appropriate response, albeit one doomed to failure, some groups put up a vigorous resistance to the encroachment of white settlement on the lands that had formed the basis of their lives since time immemorial. Others fell

24

Ritual and ceremony are central to Aboriginal culture

easy victim to the diseases and vices of their conquerors. Only a few decades after the arrival of the First Fleet, the Aborigines of the Sydney region had been decimated by drink and influenza, and before the 19th century had run its course, full-blooded Tasmanians had virtually disappeared. Since then, Aborigines have generally been seen as second-class citizens; it was not until after a referendum in 1967 that they were given the right to vote.

It is only in relatively recent times that white Australians have begun to appreciate the richness and subtlety of the life that their appropriation of the continent all but destroyed, but which sustained the first Australians in material and spiritual harmony with the Australian environment for at least 40,000 years.

DREAMTIME Aboriginals live on the land in a way that is remote from European concepts of ownership and property. Rather than 'own' land, they inhabit it in sacred trust on behalf of ancestral beings who created it during the Dreamtime. The land itself is part of the spiritual realm of the whole of creation, in which all creatures, animals as well as humans and the dead as well as the living, have their being. The landscape is venerated by individuals, large family groups or clans, with certain places— 'sacred sites'—having a particularly intense meaning.

A deep understanding of the spiritual significance of the land was passed on by highly refined and diversified traditions of song and dance. Never codified in writing, many of these oral traditions tragically have been lost. Ritual gatherings, sometimes known as *corroborees*, took up large amounts of time, with men and women often having strictly separate ceremonies. Visual arts, like cave- or wall-paintings, or designs executed on the ground, had a ceremonial or storytelling role, and were ephemeral or subject to periodic renewal.

LIFESTYLE Virtually all Aboriginal groups were nomads, living a Stone-Age lifestyle of hunting, gathering and fishing based on the seasonal availability of game, seeds and fruits. Controlled burning of the bush took place in order to encourage regrowth and thus attract animals to the area. Material belongings were kept to an absolute minimum, and consisted of baskets and nets, digging sticks, shelters of brushwood, weapons of carved wood and sharpened bone, canoes of bark and boomerangs. Clothes were also minimal, except in the colder, wetter areas of south-eastern Australia, where skins and furs were worn.

Each clan had its own distinct territory, defined orally by song rather than marked out on the ground. For another group to cross

Aboriginal rangers are happy to share their knowledge of the land with visitors to the national parks

such an invisible but nevertheless definite boundary might have involved complex negotiation.

The whole of Australia can now be mapped in terms of these traditional territories, but at the time of European settlement no such map existed, except in the hearts of its inhabitants. This allowed legalistic Europeans to appropriate the land with a more or less clear conscience.

❑ Some 200 Aboriginal languages existed, related to one another but not necessarily mutually intelligible. Most people were multilingual, speaking perhaps five or six tongues. The language of the Aborigines around the future site of Sydney was, of course, unknown to Europeans, and the cry of '*Warra! Warra!*' they were greeted with was not understood. Even if it had been, would they have taken any notice? '*Warra! Warra!*' means 'Go away!' ❑

The first people to explore Australia were the ancestors of today's Aborigines, who may have crossed the still intact land bridge linking the continent to New Guinea well over 40,000 years ago. At first they lived along the coasts and in other areas where food was easily obtainable, and eventually spread all over the country, learning to live even in those regions where survival seemed all but impossible to European explorers.

THE PORTUGUESE AND DUTCH EXPLORERS The European discovery of the island continent began in a tentative, almost accidental way in the 16th century, as Portuguese mariners looked for routes to the eastern Spice Islands. But the first definite landfall was made in 1606 by the Dutch ship *Duyfken* ('Little Dove') sailing out of the Dutch colony of Batavia (now Jakarta). Her captain, Willem Jansz, was unimpressed by what he saw of the desolate western coast of Cape York and what he called its 'wild, cruel black savages'.

A little later, Dutch skippers on their way to Java found that they could cut weeks off their journey by making use of the Roaring Forties until they made a northward turn well short of the coast of western Australia. Some sailed straight on, like Dirk Hartog in 1616 (who left an inscribed pewter plate nailed to a post on the island that bears his name), and Frederik de Houtman, who landed on the Houtman Abrolhos islands in 1619.

Under the command of a captain whose name is unrecorded, the *Leeuwin* ('Lioness') sighted the southwestern tip of the continent in 1622. Subsequently, more systematic attempts were made by the Dutch East India Company to survey the coastline. The most famous of them was the voyage of Abel Tasman in 1642–1643 in the *Heemskerck* and *Zeehaan*; put ashore on Tasmania's Blackman Bay, his pilot heard voices coming from the bush, but the natives failed to show themselves. Tasman had the flag run up, and named the island after the Governor

W. R. Stott's painting shows William Dampier being attacked by Aborigines when he landed in 1699

of the Dutch East Indies, Van Diemen, a name changed to that of the actual discoverer in 1855.

In the course of a second voyage, Tasman failed (as had all his predecessors) to find the gap between New Guinea and Australia, subsequently called the Torres Strait, but mapped 3,000km (1,865 miles) of the north coast instead. By this time, the coast had been explored by Dutchmen from the tip of Cape York around Western Australia to the archipelago in the Great Australian Bight. Although the Dutch did not take the continent under their control, they named it—New Holland.

26

THE BRITISH ARRIVE The first Englishman to set foot on the shores of New Holland was the adventurer William Dampier, who landed twice on its northwestern coast, first in 1688, then again in 1699. It was Captain Cook, however, who not only found the unknown east coast, but sailed the length of it and identified the spot where British settlement was to take place. He completed his mission in spite of the fact that his ship the *Endeavour* ran aground on the Barrier Reef (see page 214). The name that Captain Cook gave to the land he claimed for the British Crown was New South Wales.

Even after British settlement had been well and truly established around Sydney Harbour (by Captain Phillip in 1788), many uncertainties remained as to whether the three known fragments added up to a continent. Part of the answer was provided by two truly intrepid men, George Bass and Matthew Flinders, who by 1798 had confirmed the existence of a channel between the mainland and Van Diemen's Land. Governor Hunter, impressed by this great discovery, named the channel Bass Strait after the explorer.

Aboard the *Investigator*, Flinders went on to explore the south coast with great thoroughness, meeting the French survey ship *Geographe* in what came to be known as Encounter Bay.

Early settlers: Captain Phillip arriving at Sydney Cove in 1788

The master of the *Geographe*, Nicolas Baudin, behaved impeccably, though Flinders was suspicious of the intentions of a servant of France, a country with which Britain had recently been at war. His suspicions of the French were justified when, later, having sailed around Australia in 1802–1803, he was arrested by the Governor of French Mauritius on his way back to England, unaware that war had broken out again. Held for six years by the French, he returned to England a prematurely aged 40-year-old, barely able to complete his *A Voyage to Terra Australis* before dying in 1814.

❏ Non-Europeans also made contact with Australia. Chinese junks may have sailed to Australia's northern coast as early as the 15th century, and there were exchanges between the Aborigines and the warlike inhabitants of New Guinea. From about 1700 onwards, fishermen from Macassar in the Celebes frequented the north coast in search of trepang (sea-cucumbers), an activity that continues today. ❏

The map of Australia is scattered with surnames attached to natural features or to settlements, honouring governors and other leaders. But there are some, like the Sturt Stony Desert, which commemorate a different kind of fame—that earned by the inland explorers, a breed of men who explored, with varying degrees of success, the new country's uncharted interior.

28

Straightforward curiosity may have impelled some adventures into the interior, but another factor was the hunger for land as the colony grew and needed to be fed. In addition, industrial England developed an insatiable appetite for wool, which the merino crossbreeds so successfully developed by John Macarthur could satisfy only if enough pastures could be found. For many years, the Blue Mountains seemed to bar the way from Sydney to the interior, but in 1813 this obstacle was overcome by William Lawson, William Charles Wentworth and Gregory Blaxland. Governor Macquarie had a road built across the mountains in record time, and settlers rushed into the rich grazing lands beyond.

STURT'S JOURNEY For many years the puzzle of what became of the rivers flowing westward from the

Many lost their lives in the exploration of Australia's interior

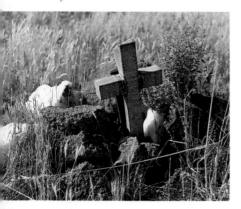

mountains perplexed authorities and explorers alike. Did they perhaps feed a great inland sea? A partial answer—no!—was given in 1829–1830, when Charles Sturt hauled a whaling boat over the hills and sailed down the Murrumbidgee to its confluence with the Murray. From there he continued downstream to wide Lake Alexandrina and the river mouth (in South Australia), which had so far been concealed from maritime explorers behind a sand bar. Sturt's return, rowing upstream against a swelling current, was an epic of endurance. It nearly ended in disaster as food for his party ran out and their strength ebbed.

❏ Explorers of several nationalities contributed to the exploration of Australia. In 1839–40, a Polish adventurer, self-styled 'Count' Paul Strzelecki, underwent hardships almost equal to those suffered by Sturt as he traversed the uplands to which he gave the name Gippsland, and from which he was only extracted by the skills of his Aboriginal guide. An impetuous and quarrelsome Prussian, Ludwig Leichhardt, was less lucky, though in 1844 his first journey succeeded in covering 4,800km (2,980 miles) from Brisbane to Arnhem Land. A more ambitious foray that was intended to carry him right across the country from Sydney to Perth failed. Leichhardt and his companions simply disappeared into the void. ❏

Above: Burke and Wills leave Melbourne in August 1860

BURKE'S EXPEDITION Another great failure, but a fully documented one, was the expedition that set out from Melbourne in 1860 under the impatient leadership of Robert O'Hara Burke. The expedition did reach its objective, the mangrove swamps of the Gulf of Carpentaria, but when the party returned to base camp at Cooper Creek, they found that it had been abandoned a mere seven hours previously by their support group. Both Burke and his deputy Wills perished, though another man, John King, was fed roots and fish by the Aborigines and survived to return and tell the tale.

Before successfully crossing the middle of Australia, Stuart had reached Alice Springs

EYRE AND STUART The names of highways spanning the great emptiness of the middle and the west commemorate the epic treks undertaken by two explorers whose persistence was almost legendary. In 1840–41, with the support of his Aboriginal guide Wylie, Edward Eyre reached Albany in Western Australia, having crossed the desert across the top of the Great Australian Bight. In 1862, John McDouall Stuart, almost blind and with hair turned white, finally reached the coast near what was to become Darwin. His previous attempts to cross the country from south to north had been frustrated by spinifex and scurvy, though he had planted the British flag on a hilltop near Alice Springs. His return to Adelaide, where he was mobbed by the ladies of the city, was made partly on a stretcher.

29

In the first half of the 19th century, Australia developed at a steady but unspectacular pace. Free settlers soon outnumbered convicts, and each colony won its right to a separate existence from New South Wales. But the discovery of gold transformed the country, drawing in a mass of enterprising folk who helped lay the foundation of Australia's essentially urban civilization.

GOLD FEVER The news of early gold finds was suppressed by the authorities, who were fearful of the disruption that such an announcement might cause. But there was no stopping Edward Hargraves, a veteran of the Californian gold rush of 1849, who struck gold near Bathurst in NSW in February 1851.

The rush began, draining the cities of population and making Melbourne so fearful for its prosperity that city officials offered a prize to whoever found gold within a certain distance of the city. One James Esmond obliged, and his find at Clunes in July 1851 was followed by others at Castlemaine, Bendigo and

Prospectors in the mid-19th century

Ballarat. Melbourne was emptied of able-bodied men and ships stood crewless in the harbour as sailors hurried inland to make their fortune.

Life in the goldfields was tough, raw and dangerous. Many of the prospectors longed for nothing more than solid respectability. They founded farms and businesses after striking lucky, or returned to seek their fortune among the seemingly limitless opportunities offered by 'Marvellous Melbourne'.

More rebellious spirits took a stand at the Eureka Stockade (see page 110), and even though this revolt failed, their gesture helped create a new democratic atmosphere in which representative government was to thrive. Victoria's population rose in ten years from less than 100,000 to more than half a million, and the whole country received an injection of energy that carried it through a boom lasting until the 1890s.

FORTUNE-SEEKERS Prospectors came flooding in from all over the world, including the gold miners of California and hopeful fortune seekers from Britain. The largest minority were the Chinese, many of whom disembarked in South Australia and walked overland to the Victorian goldfields rather than pay the £10 landing tax at Melbourne. They were much resented by the other settlers for their willingness to work hard, for keeping to themselves and for their sheer numbers. At the time of the Palmer River gold rush in the 1870s in North Queensland, Chinese diggers formed a majority of the male population in the state.

FROM BOOM TOWN TO GHOST TOWN

In Victoria, the rip-roaring days were soon over. By the late 1850s, most of the gold that was available on the surface or by shallow diggings had been worked out. Individual miners could not afford the equipment that was needed for the excavation and maintenance of deeper mines, and the initiative passed from the self-sufficient pioneer to companies able to raise the necessary capital. Ballarat ceased being a muddy chaos and turned itself into the most respectable of Victorian cities.

In the second half of the 19th century, gold strikes were made all over Australia, many of them ephemeral and leaving a poignant legacy of ghost towns. The last great rush was to the Eastern Goldfields of Coolgardie and Kalgoorlie-Boulder in Western Australia in 1892–93. This gave a similar boost to the languid economy of the colony, and transformed Perth into a real city. Large-scale operations continue in this area today, based on vast open-cast pits worked by huge machines, in total contrast to the primitive hand tools and hard manual work of the prospectors of early days.

Sovereign Hill at Ballarat in Victoria is a re-creation of gold-rush days

❏ Highway robbery had been practised in the colony for as long as highways had existed, and increased in appeal as the wealth created by the gold rush was moved around. Australia's bushrangers were just as fearsome as the legendary outlaws of the American West, their exploits winning them a heroic status among a population traditionally hostile to the police. The most notorious of them all, and a symbol of Australian defiance and sheer cussedness, was Edward 'Ned' Kelly, son of an Irish ex-convict. After a series of exploits, which included holding up whole towns, the Kelly gang was cornered in June 1880 at Glenrowan, a small town in north-eastern Victoria. Kelly emerged from the pub wearing his famous homemade suit of armour, but was shot in the legs, brought to trial and hanged in Melbourne on 11 November 1880. ❏

The Australian landscapes that the early European settlers first cast eyes upon lacked the ordered character of the scenes they had left behind. Much of the European effort in Australia was to impose a rational and productive discipline on this unfamiliar and seemingly chaotic scene. This was sometimes at a cost to habitats and natural beauty that is only now being calculated.

In Europe, the conversion of the forest into farmland began in neolithic times and took some 5,000 years to complete. In the wooded southeastern and western areas of Australia, the same process was virtually complete after only a single century. The replacement of the bush by productive fields was one motive, but in many areas the timber itself was highly valuable and logging quickly developed into a major industry.

The removal of the native forest or its replacement by exotic tree species like radiata pines continued into the 20th century, but a partial halt has now been called. Today, no visitor should miss seeing such glories of the Australian landscape as the tropical rain forest of Queensland, its temperate equivalent in the southeast and in Tasmania, the blue gums that have given their name to the Blue Mountains, or the splendid karri forests of Western Australia.

THE FARMERS MOVE IN Once the bush was cleared, squatters and sheep farmers divided up their land, erecting fences and planting European trees to give the place a more familiar look. They built themselves homesteads with whatever degree of architectural elaboration they could afford. Australian country properties ranged from elegant stone mansions to shacks that were made of corrugated iron.

This attempt to impose order often faltered in the face of the capricious nature of the land. Rainless years ruined many a farmer who had tried to push the frontier of agriculture too far inland. Australia has as many forgotten farmsteads as it has ghost towns abandoned by prospectors when mineral wealth ran out.

As settlement advanced, native animals retreated, displaced in many cases by flocks of sheep grazing on the imported grass species sown by farmers. Kangaroos and other animals, often shot as pests, sometimes profited by the irrigation of otherwise arid landscapes, and became a greater nuisance than ever.

CONFLICTS OF INTEREST The effect of these and other changes converted a seemingly formless scene into one that made economic and visual sense to the Europeans, and one that could be controlled and managed. It also meant that the landscape became uninhabitable by the Aborigines in any traditional way. Such basic differences of viewpoint probably contributed more than anything else to a conflict between settlers and the Aborigines, in which the latter were the inevitable losers.

❏ Rabbits were imported as game in the 1850s. Within a few years, the population exploded, and they advanced at the rate of 100km (60 miles) a year, destroying much of the native herbage for ever. Supposedly rabbit-proof fences were built, one running 2,000km (1,240 miles) across a large part of Western Australia. But the rabbits found ways round them, and were only curbed when myxomatosis devastated them in the 1950s and by the *calici* virus in the 1990s. ❏

How to tackle Australia

The first thing to remember about Australia is that it is a continent. Planning a holiday here is like taking a journey across Europe or the United States—Australia is comparable in size to the US, excluding Alaska, and approximately 24 times as big as the British Isles—you could get an overall idea of the country in one trip, but you need time and money if you want to get to know it really well.

THE EXTENDED VISIT An absolute minimum for an extended trip that takes in all major sights is three months. In this time you could visit all the states, including Tasmania, and cover most of the highlighted attractions of this guide, especially if you were able to do most of your journey, and some of your sightseeing, by plane. If you have more time, so much the better; you could stay in some places and absorb their atmosphere in a relaxed way rather than just hitting the principal sights. Now that you can drive right around the continent on paved roads, many retired Australians are getting to know their own country in a leisurely way, usually by driving an RV or camper van.

THE SHORTER TRIP Most visitors to Australia have only limited time at their disposal, and choices must be made. As well as seeing something of city life, if you want to enjoy what Australia has to offer you will need to get out into the country, drive along the unsurfaced roads of the Outback, leave your car behind and walk through the bush or along the beach, wander around an old goldrush

Camper vans are ideal for exploring the country, particularly for those on a tight budget

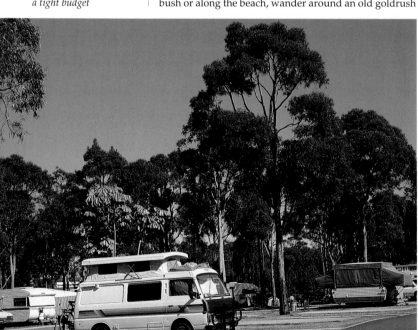

township, sit at the bar of an Outback pub or sample the excellent diving or snorkelling.

Australians take great pleasure in inviting you to join in: You can take part in all kinds of activities, from riding a camel in the desert to digging for witchetty grubs in the company of an Aboriginal ranger. Not only are there probably more museums per head than anywhere else in the world (ranging from the impeccably professional to the endearingly amateur), but all kinds of industries and enterprises also open their gates to visitors. Wineries without tastings are unheard of, farms make you welcome and there is plenty of accommodation available on country properties that offer the chance to take part in rural activities.

PLANNING AN ITINERARY Within the confines imposed by a conventional holiday of a few weeks, setting definite limits on what you can reasonably undertake is very important. Though vast, nearly all the Australian states are dominated by their respective capital city, each of which has its own character and attractions. This is where colonial life began and where its traces are thickest on the ground. Wild landscapes start just beyond the suburbs; no big city lies out of sight of the hills or mountains of a national park.

One solution would be to choose one city or town as a base and then make excursions, some involving overnight stays, in order to appreciate the extraordinary contrasts between city and rural life that are such a feature of Australia. An overland trip by rental car, train, bus or organized tour beginning at one point and taking your time to reach another is a good way of getting the feel of the country; your round-trip airline ticket can usually be arranged to accommodate this. If you only have a week in Australia, you could just about take in very short visits to Sydney, Cairns, the Barrier Reef, Darwin, Alice Springs and Uluṟu by flying between sites.

The Outback is uniquely rewarding, but before you head off in your rental car or camper van, stop and contemplate the distances involved. Remember that Cairns is 2,680km (1,665 miles) from Sydney, Alice Springs is 2,928km (1,820 miles) distant via Adelaide, Darwin 4,400km (2,735 miles) via Adelaide and Alice Springs and Perth a staggering 4,160km (2,585 miles) from Sydney. You don't have to go all the way out and back overland; if time is short, you can fly to one of the many bases for Outback tours and start from there.

Australia has a varied and well-developed tourist infrastructure, mostly staffed by people who go out of their way to be helpful. Apart from accommodation and restaurants to suit a range of budgets, there are also many tour operators. However, make sure that the tours offered are exactly what you want; the ingredients of a package may have been put together to suit the operator's convenience rather than yours.

AUSTRALIAN ISLANDS
Far out in the Pacific, Lord Howe Island (over 700km/435 miles north-east of Sydney) and Norfolk Island (another 1,000km/620 miles farther on) are popular with Australians in search of something different. Norfolk was a prison island where offenders from Sydney were sent to suffer under a notoriously brutal regime, and the remains of convict-era buildings give it something of the atmosphere of Tasmania's Port Arthur. The climate is subtropical and as well as rain forest, there are stands of the famous Norfolk pines and rolling pasturelands. Lord Howe Island is less than half the size of Norfolk Island and is dominated by mountain peaks, with unique vegetation and birdlife that have led to its designation as a World Heritage Area. There are hardly any cars, and when not snorkelling you will have to get around by bicycle.

Drivers: beware of camels!

Sydney

38

Walsh Bay

Dawes Point

Sydney Harbour Bridge

Wharf Theatre

Bennelong Point

DAWES POINT

Millers Point

SYDNEY HARBOUR TUNNEL

E

Garrison Church (Holy Trinity)

Sydney Visitor Centre

Overseas Passenger Terminal

Syd Ope Hou

MILLERS POINT

ARGYLE PLACE

Argyle Centre

Cadman's Cottage

Governme Hou

Sydney Cove

Observatory Hill & Sydney Observatory

Museum of Contemporary Art

Ferry Terminal

THE ROCKS

Circular Quay Station

CAHILL EXPRESSWAY

Justice & Police Museum

National Trust Centre SH Ervin Gallery

Customs House

Sydney Conservatoriu of Music

D

MACQUARIE PLACE

BRIDGE STREET

GROSVENOR STREET

Museum of Sydney

Darling Harbour

Australia Square

State Library of NSW

Jones Bay

Sydney Passenger Terminal

Wynyard Station

GEORGE STREET

State Parliame House

Pyrmont Bay

State Library of NSW

Sydney Hospital

ERSKINE STREET

MLC Centre

Martin Place Station

Martin Place

King Street Wharf

CLARENCE STREET

YORK STREET

GPO

Hyde Park Barrack Museu

St James Church

C

Metro Light Rail

Australian National Maritime Museum

KING STREET

Strand Arcade

Sydney Tower

QUEENS SQUARE

Star City

Sydney Aquarium

PITT ST

St James Station

PYRMONT

Pyrmont Bridge

MARKET STREET

State Theatre

Hyde Park

Harbourside

Cockle Bay

Cockle Bay Wharf

Queen Victoria Building

Great Synagogue

COLLEGE STREET

Sydney Convention Centre

DRUITT STREET

PARK STREET

Museum Station

IMAX Theatre

Sydney Town Hall

Town Hall Station

BATHURST STREET

St Andrews Cathedral

B

Wentworth Park

BRIDGE ROAD

WATTLE STREET

Sydney Exhibition Centre

Tumbalong Park

Chinese Garden

Metro Monorail

Anzac Memorial

PIER STREET

DIXON

HARBOUR ST

GEORGE STREET

LIVERPOOL STREET

ELIZABETH STREET

WENTWORGOULBU

PYRMONT STREET

HARRIS STREET

DAY ST

GOULBURN STREET

Sydney Entertainment Centre

Chinatown

WILLIAM HENRY STREET

Powerhouse Museum

HAY STREET

CAMPBEL

A

Harbourside and History Walk

Paddy's Markets & Market City

SURRY HILLS

City Centre and Darling Harbour Walk

MARY ANN STREET

HAYMARKET

Belmore Park

RAWSON PLACE

ALBION

ULTIMO

GEORGE STREET

Central Railway Station

EDDY AVE

FOVEAUX ST

1

2

3

0   500 m
0   500 yards

Sydney

Port Jackson

Fort Denison

Mrs Macquarie's Point

Garden Island

Mrs Macquarie's Chair

Farm Cove

Woolloomooloo Bay

Royal Botanic Gardens

Sydney Tropical Centre

The Domain

Andrew "Boy" Charlton Pool

Fleet Base

POTTS POINT

Elizabeth Bay

Art Gallery of New South Wales

Woolloomooloo Wharf

COWPER WHARF ROAD

Elizabeth Bay House

Beare Park

The Domain

LINCOLN CRESCENT

MACLEAY STREET

ELIZABETH BAY

GREENKNOWE AVENUE

WOOLLOOMOOLOO

Fitzroy Gdns

ROSLYN GARDENS

Mary's Cathedral

PALMER STREET

VICTORIA STREET

DARLINGHURST ROAD

WARD AVENUE

Rushcutters Bay Park

WARATAH ST

KINGS CROSS

Kings Cross Station

RUSHCUTTERS BAY

WILLIAM ST

KINGS CROSS ROAD

BAYSWATER ROAD

Australian Museum

CRAIGEND STREET

EAST SYDNEY

MCLACHLAN AVENUE

NEILD AVENUE

CROWN STREET

BOURKE STREET

DARLINGHURST

Sydney Jewish Museum

VICTORIA STREET

STREET

OXFORD STREET

TAYLOR SQUARE

STREET

BOUNDARY STREET

BROWN ST

GLENMORE ROAD

PADDINGTON

CROWN STREET

BOURKE STREET

FLINDERS STREET

SOUTH DOWLING STREET

STREET

OXFORD STREET

Juniper Hall

Victoria Barracks

Paddington Town Hall

4 Airport

5

SYDNEY Curling seductively around its harbour, Sydney has a superb setting. It is one of the world's great cities, with over four million people—nearly a quarter of the population in its metropolitan area, and still seems in the first flush of youth: enthusiastic, welcoming, vibrant and open to growth and change. Two of its famous landmarks, the Harbour Bridge and Opera House, became icons the day they were completed. Seen from across the water, the new glamorous buildings constructed in the city in the last 30 years add further drama and excitement, while all around the 240km (150 miles) of harbour foreshore, waterfront suburbs of dream homes mingle with the remains of wild bushland.

Sydney, then, is beautiful, almost extravagantly so. There is also a fair measure of what has been called 'the Australian ugliness'. The skyscrapers make no attempt to harmonize with their immediate surroundings; close up, much of the city appears chaotic. Beyond the often charming Victorian suburbs sprawls an almost horizonless sea of red-roofed bungalow suburbs. But the monotony of this urban sprawl is compensated for by magnificent natural surroundings: the heaths and forests of **Ku-ring-gai Chase** and **Royal National Park**, the high wall of the **Blue Mountains** and the string of beaches along many kilometres of Pacific coastline. The climate, despite a fair amount of rain, gives hot summers and bright winter days that enhance your enjoyment.

EARLY DAYS In January 1788, the climate played no part in Captain Phillip's choice of Port Jackson as a landing place for his motley cargo of convicts. The First Fleet had originally anchored in Botany Bay and it was the first site chosen for the colony. Subsequently it

40

THE FIRST SYDNEYSIDERS
The area around Sydney seems to have been inhabited by three main Aboriginal groups, numbering several thousand people, when the 11 ships of Britain's First Fleet sailed in. Large numbers of Aboriginal carvings survive in the sandstone plateaus to the north and south. The Aborigines' response to the invaders was a mixture of indifference, resentment and curiosity, but they were in no position to resist, and by the early 1800s those who remained in the area had been reduced to drunkenness and begging.

was found that the area around today's Circular Quay had fresh water, which Botany Bay did not. And so the British flag was run up. The name given to the landing place, Sydney Cove (after the British Home Secretary of the time), was soon transferred to the disorderly settlement that grew up around its shore.

As the colony became established, free settlers moved in, and the population of the city increased sharply when gold was found to the west of the Blue Mountains in the 1850s. Handsome villas were built on the outskirts, while in the later years of the 19th century, middle- and working-class suburbs like Balmain and Paddington unrolled their streets of humble cottages and superior terraces over the countryside nearby, leaving areas like The Rocks to a life of drink, vice and violence.

By the time the population of the city had reached the million mark in the late 1920s, Sydney was a confident, swaggering sort of place, where a strong trade union movement helped ensure one of the highest living standards in the world for its members.

UP TO DATE World War II brought the city into abrupt contact with a wider world, which came even closer in the postwar period, when Sydney became the recipient of waves of New Australians, first from devastated Europe and later from Lebanon, Vietnam, China, the Philippines and other Asian countries. Once resolutely Anglo-Celtic, it is now a thoroughly multicultural city.

Sydney is a great tourist destination: Its charms are not hidden away, but put boldly on display; its intriguing history is readily accessible; and it has all the museums, galleries, shops, restaurants and entertainment that you would expect in a metropolis.

PENETRATING THE DEFENCES
One of Sydney's earliest fortifications, on Observatory Hill, was built to protect the colony's Establishment against a possible convict uprising; later, it was potential foreign invaders who became the worry, and by the mid-19th century virtually every promontory had been fortified. In World War II, despite a boom across the harbour's mouth, a Japanese midget submarine crept up as far as Garden Island. Here it launched its torpedoes at the cruiser USS *Chicago*; they missed. Depth-charges dealt with the brave and ingenious sub-mariners; their vessel was recovered and is on display in the Australian War Memorial in Canberra.

41

Many consider Sydney to be 'the best address on earth'

PLAYGROUND OF THE PACIFIC

This was the name given to Bondi Beach, and the early days of Australia's exuberant beach culture are celebrated with gusto in the Australian National Maritime Museum. Within living memory, the sands were scoured by inspectors who insured that no male swimmer went topless. But what emerges from the posters, photos and videos here is the sheer joy Australians have always had in stripping down and letting sea and sun work on their bodies. A serious note is struck by recalling Black Sunday, 6 February 1938, when what was described as an avalanche of waves took five lives in spite of the efforts of 60 lifesavers.

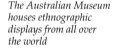

The Australian Museum houses ethnographic displays from all over the world

▶▶▶ Art Gallery of New South Wales   39C4

Art Gallery Road, The Domain (tel: 02-9225 1744 or 02-9225 1790 for recorded information). Open: daily 10–5. Admission free (varying charges for special exhibitions)

This dignified classical sandstone edifice was opened in 1887 and expanded several times over the years, including major extensions in the 1980s and 2003. Its generous interior houses the country's greatest art collection, even though the national collection is at Canberra. It covers the evolution of Australian art up to the present day, and has major sections on Aboriginal, Asian, American and European art; the collection of British 20th-century painting is outstanding. But it is the painters of Australia and their response to the people and places in this strange new land who most fascinate; they are all here, from John Glover's Tasmanian landscapes to Grace Cossington Smith's metamorphosis of the Harbour Bridge and Sidney Nolan's interpretation of the Ned Kelly saga.

▶▶▶ Australian Museum   38B3

6 College Street (tel: 02-9320 6000)
Open: daily 9.30–5. Admission: moderate

Australia's largest natural history museum is a lively place, expanded and altered in recent years so that its Victorian architecture almost becomes part of the intriguing displays on earth history, animals, insects and birds, and the life of the sea. Exhibits include human rituals and the evolution of Aboriginal culture over tens of thousands of years. There are also sections on biodiversity, skeletons, dinosaurs and Australia's ancient megafauna, as well as the superb Chapman Mineral Collection, showing Australia's extraordinary mineral wealth. There are stuffed animals, shown in context rather than as lifeless specimens, and plenty of 'hands-on' computer displays.

▶▶▶ Australian National Maritime Museum   38C1

2 Murray Street, Darling Harbour (tel: 02-9298 3777)
Open: daily 9.30–5. Admission: moderate–expensive

Looking more like a ship of the future than a museum, this extraordinary structure has displays of equally extraordinary objects that tell the story of the island continent's intimate relationship with the seas surrounding it.

There are many real vessels in the huge interior of this museum, from Aboriginal canoes to high-tech yachts, but the emphasis is as much on people as on things. There are displays on explorers, convicts, settlers, refugees and other immigrants, on whalers and wharfies who made their living from the sea, on swimmers and surfers who simply enjoyed it, and on maritime 'neighbours' like the Americans and Japanese. Tied up at the dock outside are more boats, including the Vietnamese *Tu' Do,* which arrived in Darwin in 1977, the 1874 tall ship *James Craig,* a submarine and the destroyer HMAS *Vampire.*

▶ Cadman's Cottage Historic Site   38E3

110 George Street, The Rocks (tel: 02-9247 5033)
Open: Mon–Fri 9.30–4.30, Sat–Sun 10.30–4.30. Admission free

This modest two-floor Georgian house, just 55m (60yd) from the shore, is the city's oldest surviving building, and is now a museum and the Sydney Harbour National Park information centre. It was erected in 1816, getting its name from the pardoned convict John Cadman who lived in it from 1827 to 1845. A lintel carries the initials GR for King George III in immaculately carved lettering.

▶ Chinatown   38B2

Immigrants from China first arrived as part of the gold rush and took up residence in The Rocks or around Botany Bay. Sydney's Chinese citizens are now scattered around the suburbs, but the city's Chinese heart beats strongest along Dixon Street, behind whose ornamental gateways is an array of exotic goods, food stores and restaurants. A few steps away is the **Chinese Garden of Friendship▶ ▶**, part of the redevelopment of Darling Harbour. Laid out by landscape architects from Sydney's sister city of Guangzhou in southern China, the gardens are a calm retreat of sensitively designed planting, lakes, bridges and waterfalls, with a traditional tea house overlooking a tranquil lily pond.

▶ ▶ ▶ Circular Quay   38D3

Sydney's chief people-watching site is also one of the city's most historic places, since it was here at Sydney Cove that the First Fleet dropped anchor on 26 January 1788. It is still the heart of daily life, with a continuous stream of people pouring out of the railway station, taxis, buses and the busy ferries that bustle in and out of the quays. Trains and traffic roar by overhead, ignored by those with time enough on their hands to stop and listen to the street performers on the broad promenade. Landward are the cliff-like buildings of the city, while towards the water are alluring and ever-changing glimpses of the Harbour Bridge and Opera House. A map on the quayside shows the colony in 1808.

Over 200 years on, Sydney Cove, the First Fleet's landing site, would be unrecognizable to those early pioneers

LOVELY HOMES
Not all Sydney's early houses were as unassuming as Cadman's Cottage, though the first Government House (see page 45) was damp and suffered from inexplicable smells. The aspirations of successful citizens were expressed in such delightful dwellings as Elizabeth Bay House, a splendid 1830s classical mansion in white stucco that turns its back on sleazy nearby Kings Cross (see page 59). Farther to the east is another highly desirable residence, Vaucluse House, whose battlements and verandas were created for the explorer William Charles Wentworth in the 1830s.

▶▶▶ Darling Harbour 38D1

The deep inlet on the western side of the city was called Cockle Bay by the early colonists. Like so many docklands of its kind around the world, it eventually lost its commercial functions but is now enjoying a vigorous new lease of life in tourism, with major exhibition and entertainment facilities.

The Harbour is an exciting place, an extraordinary medley of old and new, defined to the east by glittering office towers, with expanses of water and paving framing some of the city's most stimulating new buildings. The parkland at the southern end seems none the worse for its overhead expressways, while the whole area is linked to the heart of Sydney by a controversial monorail that glides over Pyrmont Bridge, the oldest swing bridge of its kind in the world.

For details on attractions in the area other than the Australian National Maritime Museum (covered on page 42), see panel.

▶▶ The Domain 39D4

The Domain extends inland from Mrs. Macquarie's Point to the large green space fringed by fig trees that serves as one of the city's most important parks. This is where orators challenge their audiences along the lines of London's Speaker's Corner, where joggers jog and office workers eat their sandwiches.

Open-air opera and classical music concerts are also held here, particularly during the January Sydney Festival. The Domain has, however, suffered from the incursions of the Cahill Expressway, the Eastern Suburbs Railway and from the construction of an underground parking garage.

▶ Garrison Church 38E2

Millers Point

Hacked through the central ridge of The Rocks area, **Argyle Cut** was one of the colony's early engineering feats. It leads to **Argyle Place**, which has been frequently described as Sydney's sole village green, though not many village greens benefit from such close proximity to a multiple-lane expressway (the Harbour Bridge approach). Nevertheless, it is a pleasant enough place, lined with attractive mid-19th-century cottages. Holy Trinity Church, near the entrance to the Cut, was given the name Garrison Church because of its use by the redcoats manning Dawes Point Battery. Built from the stone quarried from the Cut, its squat appearance isn't helped by its lack of a spire, but it has a spacious interior and some of the city's finest stained-glass windows.

▶ Hyde Park 38C3

Like its London namesake, this fine park once marked the very edge of town, but today it has become one of those central city oases where people retreat from the heat, fumes and noise of the street. Its avenue of majestic Moreton Bay fig trees is particularly fine, and there is a splendid imitation-baroque fountain, but the park's highlight is undoubtedly the **Anzac Memorial**▶▶ (see panel). This solemn but sumptuous essay in art deco forms the focal point of the Anzac Day (25 April) march.

DARLING HARBOUR ATTRACTIONS
Apart from the splendid Sydney Aquarium, there are the IMAX Theatre, outdoor entertainments, cruises on the harbour, the many shops of the Harbourside complex, the Cockle Bay Wharf dining precinct, a major convention centre and the Sydney Exhibition Centre, which hosts events like the Motor Show. The vast Saturday and Sunday Paddy's Market is just a step away, as is the King Street Wharf dining strip. The Star City casino complex is also in this region.

44

UNKNOWN SOLDIER
The Anzac Memorial in Hyde Park was designed by the Sydney architect Bruce Dellit 'to give an impression, not of the glory of war, but of its tragedy and horror'. It is a masterpiece of its kind. The external sculptures depicting the different branches of the services (including nursing) are by British-born Rayner Hoff. Inside, the dramatic central figure of the dead soldier can only be observed properly by bowing one's head. The vault above is pierced by 120,000 stars, each one representing a World War I volunteer.

▶▶ Hyde Park Barracks Museum   *38C3*

Queens Square, Macquarie Street (tel: 02-9223 8922)
Open: daily 9.30–5. Admission: inexpensive
This splendid three-floored edifice is one of the city's finest classical buildings. Standing in dignified seclusion behind its grand gates, it was designed for Governor Macquarie by the brilliant ex-convict Francis Greenway, whose architectural skills transformed Sydney. It provided accommodation for up to 1,000 convicts, who until then had had to find their own lodgings. It is now a museum of social history, with excellent displays on the colony's early history and its former inmates' lifestyle.

▶▶ Museum of Contemporary Art   *38D3*

140 George Street, The Rocks (tel: 02-9252 4033 or 9241 5892 for recorded information). Open: daily 10–5. Admission free (varying charges for special exhibitions)
This rather forbidding-looking building used to be the offices of the Maritime Services Board. Designed at the end of the art deco period, it is an incongruous setting for the country's major collection of contemporary art.

▶▶ Museum of Sydney   *38D3*

Phillip and Bridge streets (tel: 02-9251 5988)
Open: daily 9.30–5. Admission: inexpensive
Built on the site of the first Government House, this museum offers a portrayal of life in colonial Sydney. Using state-of-the-art technology, the museum takes you on a journey of discovery, from the story of the local Aborigines to the Sydney of the 19th century. One of the museum's highlights is outside in the forecourt. The 'Edge of the Trees' sculpture consists of poles, some of which 'speak', representing Sydney's original inhabitants and the early settlers.

OBSERVATORY HILL AND SYDNEY OBSERVATORY
With commanding views over the harbour, Millers Point was the site of a citadel, a windmill and then an observatory. The latter survives, established in 1858 to survey the hitherto unknown southern skies, and functioned until 1982. With its time-ball tower and domes, the observatory building has now been renovated as a museum of astronomy with plenty of intriguing hands-on features.

Sydney Observatory, a colonial building constructed from the local sandstone

One of the great privileges of life in Sydney is excellent access to the beaches of the Harbour and the Pacific Ocean. Astonishingly, until the beginning of the 20th century, swimming during daylight hours was prohibited by 'decency laws'. Then, finally, the flamboyant editor of a Manly newspaper strolled fully clad into the surf in the middle of the day, defying the prosecution that, in fact, was never made.

CHECK BEFORE YOU SWIM

Few big cities are entirely free of water pollution problems, and some of Sydney's beaches occasionally suffer contamination by sewage. Measures are taken to remedy the situation, and conditions can be checked locally.

THE HARBOUR BEACHES

These hardly compare with those on the ocean, but there are plenty of good spots for picnicking and sunbathing. On the south shore at Vaucluse are Nielsen Park and Parsley Bay; the north shore has beaches around Manly, as well as Mosman's Obelisk and Balmoral.

Surfers and surfboat crews make good use of Sydney's beaches

46

To the north, **Manly** is the city's shore resort *par excellence*, '7 miles from Sydney, but a thousand miles from care'. Lined with shops, take-away stands, cafés and pubs, a broad concourse called The Corso channels you from the ferry landing to the curving sandy beach with its double line of Norfolk pines facing the ocean. It was here, in 1915, that the art of surfing was born in Australia, and a big surf competition is held here every year. Manly has many other attractions, including the Oceanworld aquarium and the fascinating old Quarantine Station, once used to protect Sydney from contagious diseases, but now open for tours on most days.

World-famous **Bondi**, to the south, has another magnificent beach, stretching between two headlands, though its setting of cafés, pubs and apartment buildings has a tacky look about it. Bondi is suburban and popular, once connected to the city by a famous tramway whose cars would make the final descent to the beach at breakneck speed, giving rise to the expression 'to shoot through like a Bondi tram'.

Eighteen other beaches, equally fine if less famous, stretch north from Manly up the Warringah Peninsula to delightful Palm Beach. Some, like Narrabeen, are urban in character, while others, like Freshwater and Whale beaches, are still largely undeveloped. A string of beaches runs south from Bondi, ending at Cronulla, which is accessible by suburban train.

►►► Powerhouse Museum 38A2

500 Harris Street, Ultimo (tel: 02-9217 0111 or 02-9217 0444 for recorded information)
Open: daily 10–5. Admission: moderate
The cavernous boiler halls and other generous interior spaces of the old power station and tram depot on the edge of Darling Harbour are now home to the vast collections of Sydney's Museum of Applied Arts and Sciences, one of Australia's largest museums. The array of objects is quite astonishing. The decorative arts are strongly represented, as is social history, with stimulating displays on the life of the local Aborigines, traditional women's work and brewing. There are hands-on exhibits as well as audiovisual presentations, sound effects and holograms.

►► Queen Victoria Building 38C2

George Street
This many-domed, late-Victorian shopping gallery, occupying an entire city block, was completed in 1898; more recently a thorough renovation has restored all of its original features. With its many levels, stained glass and mosaics, it is a cathedral to conspicuous consumption.

►►► The Rocks 38D2

Named after the sandstone peninsula ending in Dawes Point, this is the site of Australia's first European settlement. For many years, it had a reputation as a place of brawling, hard drinking, whoring and villainy, but this murky past does no harm whatsoever to The Rocks' present status as a tourist mecca (see panel). In fact, the area has long since been tamed, first by wholesale demolition of many of its unsanitary dwellings after the outbreak of bubonic plague in 1900, and then by another swath of destruction preceding construction of the Harbour Bridge.

►►► Royal Botanic Gardens 39D4

Mrs. Macquaries Road, The Domain (tel: 02-9231 8125 or 02-9231 8111). Open: daily 7–dusk.
Admission: Gardens free, Tropical Centre inexpensive
These luxuriantly planted 30-hectare (74-acre) gardens are the perfect counterpoint to the high-rise buildings and bustle of the city. They benefit enormously from their proximity to the harbour, looking on to the long curving promenade of Farm Cove, which is set between twin promontories, one crowned by the Opera House and the other by Mrs. Macquarie's Point. Once the site of the first government farm, the gardens contain a visitor centre, a restaurant, the National Herbarium (with more than a million plant specimens), a fernery under a slatted steel dome and the **Sydney Tropical Centre►►** which shelters tropical plants from many countries.

► State Parliament House 38C3

Macquarie Street (tel: 02-9230 2047)
Open: Mon–Fri 9.30–4. Admission free
Like the nearby Mint building, the home of the New South Wales legislature was once part of the 'Rum' Hospital that was built in 1816. The Legislative Council Chamber is a prefabricated iron structure, sent out from England to serve as a goldfields church. State Parliament House is open to the public, even when in session.

The highly entertaining Powerhouse Museum is one of the best places for kids to visit

THE ROCKS TODAY
The area is now a place to wander at leisure and enjoy the almost medieval atmosphere, quite absent elsewhere in Australia. You may wish to start your visit at the informative Sydney Visitor Centre, in the Old Sailor's Home at 106 George Street.

Sydney

DE GROOT'S DARK DEED
The opening of the Harbour Bridge on 19 March 1932 was the excuse for the biggest carnival Sydney had yet known, attended by one million people. As the crowds waited for the Labor Premier of NSW, Jack Lang, to cut the tape, a uniformed horseman darted forward and slashed the tape with his sword. Irishman Francis de Groot couldn't bear the thought of a socialist politician getting all this glory.

THE BRIDGE EXPERIENCE
There are several ways to 'experience' the bridge; take the footway from Cumberland Street in The Rocks and visit the southeastern pylon's observation platform and museum, or take a thrilling guided walk to the very top with a company called BridgeClimb.

SYDNEY TOWER
The view from the observation deck of this 300m-high (985-foot) structure—Australia's tallest building—is nothing short of spectacular. With a 360-degree vista that takes in the entire metropolitan area, it's the ideal place to familiarize yourself with Sydney's layout.

A DRAMA OF AN OPERA
In spite of the brilliance of its design, the Sydney Opera House is not an ideal building for opera, with acoustics inferior to those of Melbourne's Arts Centre. A local joke has it that Australia has the world's best opera house, the outside in Sydney, the inside in Melbourne.

The Sydney Harbour Bridge, completed in 1932, still functions as a major link between north and south

▶▶▶ Sydney Harbour Bridge   *38E3*
Not just a symbol of Sydney but of Australia itself, the Harbour Bridge leaps in a great arch between its granite pylons to span the narrows between Dawes Point and Milsons Point to the north. Opened in 1932, after almost nine years of complicated construction, the bridge carries eight traffic lanes, a double-track railway, a cycleway and a footpath. Its broad deck is the widest in the world and rises 60m (195ft) above water level (the top of the arch is 134m/440ft up). Since the early 1990s the congestion-prone bridge has been supplemented by the Sydney Harbour Tunnel, which passes beneath the harbour.

▶▶▶ Sydney Opera House   *38E3*
Bennelong Point (tel: tours 02-9250 7250, box office 02-9250 7777). Open: tours daily 8.30–5, performances most days
Admission: tours moderate–expensive
Once the site of a ramshackle tram terminus, since 1973 Bennelong Point has been crowned by this building, which is the inspired creation of Danish architect Joern Utzon, born in 1918 and educated at the Royal Danish Academy. The construction of this world-famous landmark was plagued by both technical and political problems, leading Utzon to resign from the project before the building's completion. The complex curving shapes of the exterior are spectacular and have been compared to billowing sails, shells or the hoods of nuns' habits. The elegant, soaring roofs are covered in over a million Swedish ceramic tiles. The interior houses the auditorium of the opera and four other performance spaces, including a concert hall and three theatres, plus restaurants, bars, gift shops and a library. Outside are large-scale steps and a promenade around the point. A variety of guided tours of the interior and exterior is available on most days.

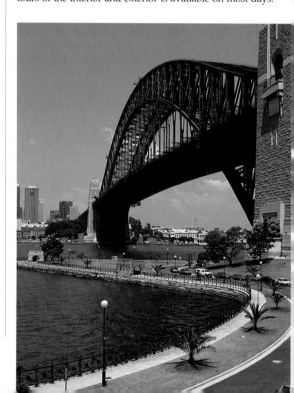

Walk

Harbourside and history

See map on pages 38–39.

This 5km (3-mile) walk gives magnificent harbourside views, leads through the splendid botanic gardens and then returns to Circular Quay past many fine early buildings.

The landward approach to the **Opera House** may lack some of the drama of the waterside approach but is still impressive, past modern apartments, hotels and cafés, then up gigantically scaled flights of steps. The fine trees of the **Royal Botanic Gardens** and Government House sweep down to the path leading around Farm Cove to the promontory of Mrs. Macquarie's Point, a popular harbourside viewpoint. Do not miss the Botanic Gardens Tropical Centre with its 'Arc' and 'Pyramid' greenhouses.

The bridge leading to the **Art Gallery of New South Wales,** over the Cahill Expressway, has good views over the city and east suburbs. Macquarie Street leads northwards, bounded to the west by mostly modern structures, and to the east by a sequence of fine historic buildings. Bridge Street penetrates westward, with modern buildings vying with the old. Macquarie Place makes a green interlude before you reach the **Customs House** (dating from 1885), opposite Circular Quay. This beautifully renovated building is now the home of shops, cafés, bars, and exhibition and performance spaces.

Walk

Darling Harbour and the heart of Sydney

See map on pages 38–39.

This walk takes you through built-up streets to the revitalized Darling Harbour and back through Hyde Park.

From Martin Place Station, walk to Martin Place, Strand Arcade and Pitt Street Mall, pedestrian-friendly in their different ways. As you cross Pyrmont Bridge look up to see the monorail—a costly and unpopular initiative—and back to enjoy the city skyline.

An amazing array of new and varied facilities clusters around **Darling Harbour**. A rest in the **Chinese Garden** could precede the final leg of this walk: across Dixon Street leading to **Chinatown**, then up into **Hyde Park**, with its splendid avenues of fig trees and the imposing **Anzac Memorial**, from where a visit to the nearby **Australian Museum** is recommended.

The Chinese Garden, designed by landscape architects from China

Sydney

WHERE TO STAY?

In many ways, it's an advantage to be right in the city centre, but Sydney's suburbs offer some excellent alternatives. Kings Cross has a wide range of hotels and price brackets, and is just one train stop from the city. You can stay on the beach at Bondi, Coogee and Manly, and the inner east suburb of Double Bay offers sophisticated surroundings, albeit at a price.

The London Hotel in downtown Balmain

Accommodation

There is a tremendous variety of accommodation in the Sydney area, though the city is not renowned for being cheap, except in the area of backpacker-style lodges. Hotels range from first-rate, like the super Park Hyatt or The Observatory, to modest, and there are also serviced apartments, motels, hostels, campsites and bed-and-breakfast accommodation. An important factor is location, since there are places that are extremely remote unless you have a car, and others whose distance from the sights is compensated for by good public transportation links. Advance reservation is advisable for peak holiday periods like Christmas and the January school holidays.

Hotels The city has an excellent range of first-class hotels, as do a number of inner suburbs like Manly, Kings Cross and Double Bay. Whatever your price bracket, Manly is worth considering for its vacation atmosphere and its link to the city—by conventional ferry in 30 minutes or in about half that time by JetCat. The heart of town also has medium-priced and budget hotels, with a particular concentration around the Central Railway Station; Kings Cross also has a variety of such places, many of them in streets of relative tranquillity.

Budget Kings Cross is a backpacker's paradise, with many lodges in Victoria Street. The scene here is in constant flux, so it is wise to check at the time whether a particular establishment is for you. Demand is often heavy, and it might be a good idea to start your tour of inspection early in the day. There is another cluster of accommodation at Bondi and Coogee—intriguing temporary addresses! The emphasis here is on affordable lodgings, with plenty of places offering rooms with cooking facilities. Bed-and-breakfast establishments are scattered all over the city, and you can get details from a number of agencies (see also Hotels and Restaurants on pages 268–281). Again, accessibility is a key factor. Camping sites are a long way out of the city.

Food and drink

Eating out Even more so than in the rest of Australia, eating in Sydney has been revolutionized in recent years, largely because of the huge influx of immigrants. *The Sydney Morning Herald's Good Food Guide* covers no fewer than 40 categories of cuisine, beginning with African and ending with Vietnamese. New restaurants continue to open, ingredients are good and chefs are increasingly skilled, particularly in the popular, internationally acclaimed style of cooking known as 'Modern Australian', a fusion of culinary styles and ingredients. Prices are extremely reasonable. The better restaurants often offer a fixed-price lunchtime menu at a considerable saving. Prices are kept even lower because of the Bring Your Own phenomenon (this, though primarily a feature of cheaper, unlicensed restaurants, is sometimes available at licensed establishments). Remember that a small corkage charge may be made. The highest prices are reserved for restaurants that offer something extra, like a harbourside setting or a panoramic view.

Ethnic restaurants These are scattered all over the city, though there are concentrations in particular districts that have been settled by different nationalities. Thus **Greek** restaurants cluster around Elizabeth and Liverpool streets, **Chinese** restaurants are found in Chinatown, **Italian** in Leichhardt and Newtown, and **Vietnamese** in the southwestern suburb of Cabramatta. Restaurants of different kinds keep company in certain parts of town, along Darlinghurst's Oxford and Victoria streets, in Kings Cross, or to the west of the city, along Glebe Point Road, in King Street, Newtown, or Darling Street, Balmain. Manly and Bondi have many restaurants, cafés and take-away facilities.

Drink There is no shortage of places to drink in Sydney. The basic 'hotel' or pub is still much in evidence, while others have been renovated and offer a more varied experience, which might well extend to food and entertainment. Further up the scale of sophistication are the many hotel and cocktail bars; the locally famous **Marble Bar** can be found at the Hilton hotel.

Sydney's excellent brasseries and bistros are deservedly popular

EXCLUSIVE EATING
Given Sydney's extensive shoreline, there are plenty of expensive restaurants with harbourside settings, from The Rocks to Watsons Bay near South Head. The most stunning view is from the two restaurants on top of Sydney Tower.

REFRESHMENTS
Sydney has plenty of cafés offering excellent Italian-style coffee. Visitors may also be pleasantly surprised at the quality of food and refreshments available at the various museums and galleries.

Queen Victoria Building: shopping in historic surroundings

THE ROCKS MARKET
A visit to The Rocks on a Saturday or Sunday has the added bonus of the lively market, held in Upper George Street. In addition to the 150 or so stalls that sell jewellery, homewares and unusual gifts, you'll find free entertainment and a carnival atmosphere.

DUTY FREE
Duty- and tax-free merchandise is available to those with an international air ticket, with substantial discounts on electrical goods, jewellery and watches, liquor and perfume. Outlets in the city are sometimes even cheaper than those at the airport.

Shopping

Sydney's CBD (Central Business District) has all the temptations a shopper might reasonably expect in a metropolitan city. There are department stores like **David Jones** and elegant 19th-century galleries like the **Strand Arcade**, or its modern equivalent, the shopping complex inserted into the lower floors of an office block. With its 200 boutiques and cafés on several levels, the immaculately restored **Queen Victoria Building** (see page 47) is a visitor attraction in its own right.

Souvenir hunting Souvenirs are plentiful in places where tourists congregate. Faced with the problem of what to bring home from Australia (apart from the inevitable stuffed koala or kangaroo, often made in China), you might consider a stylish Akubra hat or tough outdoor clothing to go with it, like a bush shirt or an oilskin coat. Sheepskin products, opals or surfing gear are other possibilities. Australians are great readers, and bookstores are well-stocked with a good range of Australiana, albeit quite expensive, while newsagents sell an incredible range of periodicals catering to every taste.

For maps, a visit to the **Travel Bookshop** (175 Liverpool Street) or **Dymocks** (424 George Street) will be helpful. Aboriginal objects of varying quality— paintings, carvings, boomerangs, fabrics and didgeridoos (a large wooden wind instrument)—are widely available, but are better bought from a specialist shop than from a souvenir stall. Try the souvenir shops run by the museums and galleries; the **Australian Museum's** stuffed platypus actually looks like the real thing!

Markets Outside the heart of the city, the more vibrant suburbs such as Paddington and Balmain are good places to browse, while Sydney's markets offer a memorable shopping experience. Usually held on a Saturday or Sunday, they take place in The Rocks, Bondi Beach, Balmain, Glebe, Manly and in Paddington. The famous **Paddy's Market** in the Chinatown area is good for fresh produce, and the vast and lively **Sydney Fish Market** at Pyrmont is a daily spectacle worth watching.

Nightlife

Concerts and theatre With several auditoriums, the **Opera House** is a major site for classical concerts, ballet and drama. Classical music can also be heard at the **Town Hall** and, performed by student musicians, at the **Conservatorium of Music**. Some 20 theatres give you a choice of musicals, mainstream or alternative plays in a variety of locations, some—like the **Wharf Theatre** (near The Rocks) or **Ensemble Theatre** (on the north shore)—in an attractive waterside setting. A visit to the beautifully restored 1928 **Capitol Theatre** in the Haymarket area is highly recommended. The exciting **Sydney Dance Company** and the **Aboriginal and Islander Dance Theatre** appear at various venues.

Film The city's cinemas show the latest blockbusters, and there are a number of houses specializing in second runs and foreign films in Paddington (Palace Academy) as well as in the heart of town (the two Dendy cinemas). The **State Theatre**, with its extravagant decoration, is the home of the city's June Film Festival.

Music Sydney has a lively jazz scene; the best venue is the long-running **Basement**, near Circular Quay. Rock is also well represented, with mammoth concerts held in the **Entertainment Centre**. Discos, cabarets and nightclubs abound, catering to all tastes and pockets. There are probably more gays in Sydney than in the rest of Australia put together, with the bars, clubs and pubs of Darlinghurst's Oxford Street the main focus of the gay scene.

INFORMATION
The wealth of distractions available in this exhilarating city is detailed in the Wednesday *Sydney Live Magazine* from the *Daily Telegraph*, and the Friday edition of *The Sydney Morning Herald*, while various free publications also provide comprehensive entertainment listings.

STAR CITY
Sydney's first, temporary, casino opened in the mid-1990s, and has since moved to its permanent site to the west of Darling Harbour. This vast complex includes a hotel and theatre, as well as restaurants, bars, 1,500 poker machines and 200 gaming tables that offer roulette, blackjack, baccarat, Asian games such as pai gow and two-up, a home grown game, which is essentially betting on which way two coins will fall.

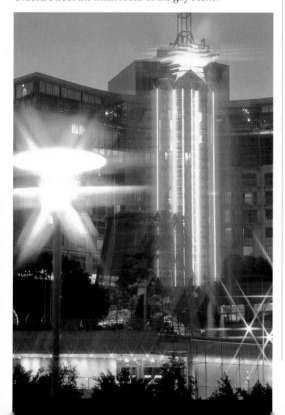

The bright lights of Sydney's Star City casino

Sydney

THE SYDNEYPASS

This combined ticket gives unlimited bus (including Airport Express, Sydney Explorer and Bondi Explorer), train and ferry travel for three, five or seven days, and is a bargain well worth thinking about.

TAXIS

Taxis are numerous and can be hailed on the street, picked up at a taxi stand or ordered by telephone. Don't get worried if the driver has to consult his street directory!

SYDNEY METRO LIGHT RAIL

Sydney's newest transportation system re-creates the days of trams. The Light Rail track runs from Central Station to Chinatown, Darling Harbour, the casino and the Sydney Fish Market, then on to the inner west suburbs of Glebe and Leichhardt. At peak times trams run every 10 minutes.

The Metro Monorail

Practical points

Tourist information Contact **Sydney Visitor Centre**, 106 George Street, The Rocks (tel: 9240 8788 or visit www. sydneyaustralia.com); **Transport Infoline** (tel: 13 1500) for all metropolitan bus, rail and ferry enquiries.

Getting around Probably the best way of familiarizing yourself with the layout of the city is to take a guided bus tour, most of which pick up and drop off at central hotels. Alternatives are the bright red **Sydney Explorer**, which trundles around a 28km (17-mile) circuit of the principal attractions, allowing you to get on and off at will for a set fare, and the blue **Bondi Explorer**, which travels to the harbourside Eastern Suburbs, Bondi, Bronte and Coogee beaches, and Paddington on the same basis.

Buses run a comprehensive scheduled service in both the city and the suburbs. They connect with ferries and trains at Circular Quay and with trains at Wynyard and Central stations. Airport Express buses run from Circular Quay, Central Station and a few stops in the city, as well as from Kings Cross.

Ferries travel at frequent intervals between Circular Quay and a number of destinations such as Manly and Taronga Zoo on the north shore, or Balmain and Hunters Hill upriver. There are also daily ferries east to Double Bay, Rose Bay and Watsons Bay, and west to Parramatta.

Double-decker electrified **trains** run on an extensive network of suburban lines (including to the airport) as well as on a City Circle linking a number of stations in the CBD such as Town Hall, Central Station and Circular Quay. There's a useful spur from Central Station and Town Hall to Kings Cross and Bondi Junction (continue by bus to the beach). The line to North Sydney includes a trip over the Harbour Bridge. A novelty is the overhead **Metro Monorail**, which runs between the southwestern part of central Sydney and Darling Harbour.

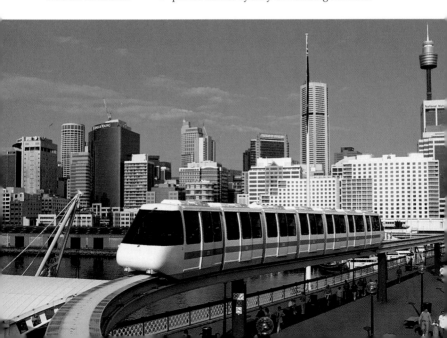

What Captain Cook named Port Jackson and Captain Phillip called 'the finest harbour in the world' is still alive with freighters, ferries and pleasure craft. The glorious stretch of water forming the harbour is Sydney, the reason for the city's existence, the source of its distinct identity and special renown.

One of the world's largest harbours Sydney Harbour has a complex outline of inlets, tributary rivers, bays, coves and promontories, so that many city residents have some sight of the water from where they live, though competition is fierce and prices astronomical for those dwellings that enjoy the best views. Much of the 240km (150 miles) of shoreline has been preserved as reserves or national park land. Added interest is given by an array of islands, including Fort Denison, where the skeletons of the executed once swung, and Goat Island with its old shipyards west of the Harbour Bridge.

How to explore Undoubtedly, the best way to explore the harbour would be an unhurried cruise, taking all day, on a friend's yacht! Water taxis would do the same kind of job, albeit expensively. The variety of commercial cruises are a more realistic choice. But perhaps the most authentic way, enjoyed every day by many city commuters, is the ferry. Now that the tramcar has all but vanished from the streets, the ferry is the city's only remaining traditional means of conveyance.

An assortment of vessels plies Sydney Harbour from the central hub of Circular Quay. In a matter of minutes you can slip across the water in the shadow of the Harbour Bridge to Kirribilli, or chug upstream in the afternoon with uniformed schoolchildren returning to their pleasant suburban homes on the promontory of Hunters Hill. Or you could take the 50-minute journey by RiverCat upriver, via Sydney Olympic Park, to the historic city of Parramatta, where you can see some of Australia's very first buildings (see page 61).

The magnificent harbour and its twin symbols of Sydney, and Australia

A STROLL AROUND THE ROCKS
The Museum of Contemporary Art contrasts with Cadman's Cottage of 1816 and the other old buildings above it in well-restored George Street, where the visitor centre dispenses useful information. Old and new come together around Campbells Cove, while Dawes Point Park, crouching at the feet of the Harbour Bridge, was the first fortified position in Australia. The way back is via the high-level Gloucester Walk and Argyle Street.

Sydney

The Blue Mountains Drive

Palm Beach and West Head Drive

E

Ebenezer

Cattai National Park

Cattai

Hawkesbury Heritage Farm

Freemans Reach

Wilberforce

Maraylya

Glenorie

Arcadia

Hawkesbury

Butterfly Farm

Pitt Town

North Richmond

Richmond

Galston

Windsor

Mulgrave

Agnes Banks

John Tebutt Observatories

Box Hill

Vineyard

Round Corner

D

Rouse Hill

Castlereagh

South Creek

Schofields

Kellyville

Castle Hill

Marsden Park

Quakers Hill

Baulkham Hills

HILLS MOTORW

Featherdale Wildlife Park

Doonside

Seven Hills

Emu Plains

Penrith

St Marys

Rooty Hill

Eastern Creek

Blacktown

Northmead

Panthers World of Entertainment

GREAT WESTERN

HIGHWAY

Pendle Hill

Old Government House

Parramatta

Blue Mountains, Wentworth Falls, Cliff Drive, Echo Point, Govett's Leap Lookout

C

4

WESTERN

MOTORWAY

Prospect Reservoir

Experiment Farm Cottage and Elizabeth Farm

Merrylands

Erskine Park

Prospect Creek

Guildford

Smithfield

Fairfield

Ches Hill

Cecil Park

Kemps Creek

Cabramatta

31

Wallacia

Bonnyrigg

Warwick Farm Racecourse

B

Warragamba

Luddenham

Badgerys Creek

Milperra

Liverpool

Hoxton Park

SOUTH WESTER

East Hills

Bringelly

Rossmore

Glenfield

Harris Creek

Nepean

HUME HIGHWAY

5

Ingleburn

Military Reserve

A

Gledswood Homestead

31

Minto

Minto Heights

Georges

Lucas Heights

Australiana Park

SOUTH WESTERN FREEWAY

Southern Highlands

Campbelltown

0   5   10 km

0   5 miles

1   2   3

Palm Beach
Whale Beach
Bangalley Head
Avalon
Newport Beach
Bungan Head
Church Point
Mona Vale
Turimetta Head
Narrabeen
Collaroy
Long Reef Point
Dee Why
Manly
Oceanworld
North Head
Sydney Harbour National Park
South Head
Watsons Bay
Vaucluse
Vaucluse House
Rose Bay
Double Bay
Bellevue Hill
Bondi
Bronte
Tamarama Bay
Coogee
Maroubra
Malabar
La Perouse Monuments
Bare Island Fort
Cape Banks
Captain Cook's Landing Place
Botany Bay National Park
Potter Point
Cronulla
Bate Bay
Port Hacking Point
Port Hacking

Brisbane Water National Park, Old Sydney Town
Cowan Creek
Ku-ring-gai Chase National Park
Broken Bay West Head
Pittwater
Berowra Waters
PACIFIC HIGHWAY
SYDNEY NEWCASTLE FREEWAY
Akuna Bay
Hornsby Heights
Bobbin Head
Ku-ring-gai Wildflower Garden
Terrey Hills
Hornsby
St Ives
Garigal National Park
Belrose
Oxford Falls
Narrabeen Lakes
Turramurra
Frenchs Forest
Beacon Hill
Tennant Hills
Lane Cove National Park
Koala Park
PACIFIC HIGHWAY
Gordon
Killara
Middle Harbour
Balgowlah
Epping
Macquarie University
Carlingford
Eastwood
West Ryde
Chatswood
Willoughby
Cremorne
Mosman
Taronga Zoo
Sydney Harbour National Park
Dundas
Ryde
Vienna Cottage
Greenwich
Crows Nest
Waverton
Neutral Bay
Pt Jackson
Rosehill Racecourse
Hunters Hill
Misons Pt
Kirribilli
Vaucluse House
Sydney Olympic Park
Drummoyne
Balmain
SYDNEY
Sydney Harbour Bridge
Elizabeth Bay
Lidcombe
Leichhardt
Glebe
Kings Cross
Darlinghurst
Paddington
Strathfield
Burwood
Enfield
University of Sydney
Central Station
Bondi Junction
Regents Park
Cooks
Sydenham
Redfern
Erskineville
Centennial Park
HUME HIGHWAY
Bankstown
Lakemba
Canterbury
Sydney Airport
Kingsford
Blue Gum Farm
Rockdale
Brighton-le-Sands
Botany
Banksmeadow
Riverwood
Hurstville
Beverley Park
Botany Bay
La Perouse
Penshurst
picnic point
Georges River National Park
Sans Souci
Kurnell
Lugarno
Como Bridge
Captain Cook Bridge
Kurnell Peninsula
Georges
Como
Sylvania
Jannali
Menai
Sutherland
Gymea
Caringbah
Sydney Tramway Museum
EG Waterhouse National Camellia Garden
Loftus
Woronora
Engadine
Audley
Heathcote NP
Heathcote 4
Royal National Park
Woronora
Dee Why

Drive

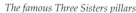

The famous Three Sisters pillars

58

The Blue Mountains

See map on pages 56–57.

The truly spectacular cliffs, canyons and forests of the World Heritage-listed Blue Mountains can be seen in a day trip.

The fastest exit from Sydney is via Parramatta Road, which connects to the Western Motorway (M4) near

Strathfield. The route then crosses the plain past Penrith to begin the climb up into the mountains, running parallel to the railway. Several places of interest are marked by signs off the freeway; **Wentworth Falls** are probably the grandest waterfalls in the region. Pretty little Leura marks the start of the **Cliff Drive**, which skirts the 300m (985-ft) drop into the valley below. **Echo Point** is, deservedly, the most famous view-point in the mountains. Not far from the visitor centre, viewing platforms offer panoramas over cliffs, eucalyptus forest and the Three Sisters sandstone columns. There are designated walks from here, or you can ride the Scenic Railway or Sceniscender farther along the Cliff Drive.

Stops can be made at **Katoomba**, 'capital' of the Blue Mountains, and northeast of Blackheath at the Blue Mountains Heritage Centre. **Govett's Leap Lookout** offers amazing views of the canyon.

Return on the Western Motorway, via Parramatta and Homebush Bay, where you will see the main venue for the 2000 Olympics—**Sydney Olympic Park**. The International Aquatic Centre and some of the other sporting facilities are open to the public, and informative bus and walking tours of the site and its venues are available.

Drive

Palm Beach and West Head

This drive goes from Sydney to the splendid Northern Beaches and head-lands. *See map on pages 56–57.*

Beyond the Harbour Bridge, Route 10 (Military Road) leads northeastward, crossing Middle Harbour by the Spit Bridge. A detour can be made to **Manly** (better visited by ferry from Circular Quay), or continue northward past the fine beaches of Long Reef, Collaroy, Narrabeen and Whale Beach.

The road narrows and winds as it approaches **Palm Beach**. To the west are fine views over the Pittwater inlet, a contrast to the crashing surf of the ocean beach to the east. On its head-land to the north is the **Barrenjoey Lighthouse**. Return to Mona Vale and follow the road around the southern end of Pittwater, turning right through the greenery of the **Ku-ring-gai Chase National Park** to **West Head**.

The head offers a completely different but equally spectacular view over Pittwater and Broken Bay. There are many well-marked trails through this section of the national park, and it is a short walk to see bushland, Aboriginal paintings and perhaps some wildlife.

Return via Mona Vale Road (Route 3) and the Pacific Highway.

The suburbs

There is a great deal to see and do in the various historic inner suburbs of the city.

The red-light district of **Kings Cross▶** has its fair share of hookers, strip joints and adult bookshops. But there are also lots of places to eat and drink and plenty of shops for the local community. A stroll along Darlinghurst Road between Kings Cross Station and Fitzroy Gardens with its El Alamein Fountain is entertaining day or night. The genteel suburb of Elizabeth Bay next door holds a contrasting attraction—1830s **Elizabeth Bay House▶**. This elegant mansion, built for the NSW Colonial Secretary, is a reminder of the area's 19th-century opulence.

Built in the heady days of the Victorian-era gold rush, then proletarian and now gentrified **Paddington▶▶**, or 'Paddo', has had a varied career as it has passed in and out of popularity. Its glory is its delicious terraced houses with their fine ironwork and their subtle adaptation to the contours of the slopes falling northward towards the harbour. Built between the 1860s and 1890s, most have been carefully restored. Also here are **Juniper Hall** (1824), the **post office** (1885) and **Paddington Town Hall** (1891). Opened to mark Sydney's 100th birthday, **Centennial Park** supports a varied birdlife as well as offering many outdoor activities.

The whole population of **Balmain▶▶** used to work in its shipyards, but its delightful terraces and little detached timber cottages have been colonized by a middle-class population generally more left-leaning and artistically inclined than Paddington's inhabitants.

Hunters Hill▶ is a tranquil place of expensive, fine stone houses and humbler cottages. Many of the former were built in French style in the 1850s. One of the 19th-century tradesmen's abodes, **Vienna Cottage**, has been restored by the National Trust and houses a local museum.

SYDNEY JEWISH MUSEUM
A short stroll from Kings Cross brings a very different experience. The excellent Sydney Jewish Museum (corner of Darlinghurst Road and Burton Street, Darlinghurst) traces Australia's Jewish connections, from the First Fleet convicts to post-World War II arrivals, and serves as a poignant memorial to the millions of Jewish people who perished in the Holocaust.

EASTERN SUBURBS
Sydney's Eastern Suburbs contain the country's most desirable and expensive real estate and at Double Bay it shows, with plenty of designer labels and a discreet lack of price tags in its exclusive shops. There are lots of pleasant cafés too, where shoppers can be seen relaxing after making their choices.

See how the other half lives in exclusive Hunters Hill

Sydney

UP THE HAWKESBURY

The area around Richmond and Windsor along the upper reaches of the Hawkesbury River was settled within a few years of the arrival of the First Fleet. The winding lower river is best explored in a leisurely way; a unique experience is to board the mail boat at Brooklyn and accompany the letters, packages and much more on their journey to isolated little places along the tranquil river.

THE LOSS OF LA PEROUSE

Jean-François de Galaup, Comte de La Perouse, had brushed with the British before his meeting in Botany Bay with Captain Phillip. He was taken prisoner after the battle of Quiberon Bay in 1759 and later fought in the American wars. His ships *Astrolabe* and *Boussole* had reached Australia after a long search for the elusive Northwest Passage. On quitting Botany Bay, La Perouse disappeared forever, though wreckage assumed to be that of his ships was discovered off the New Hebrides in 1826.

Captain Cook's landing place memorial

Excursions

The easy-to-reach sights from Sydney are covered alphabetically on these two pages.

Broad **Botany Bay▶** (11km/7 miles south of the city), where Captain Cook's *Endeavour* dropped anchor on the 28 April 1770, was given its name in recognition of the array of Antipodean plants collected here by Joseph Banks. Oil installations, industry and the airport now dominate the scene, but to commemorate Cook's historic landing on the Kurnell Peninsula, the national park contains monuments, a visitor centre and a museum. At the northern edge of the bay, La Perouse, named after the commander of the French expedition that arrived just after the First Fleet, is the site of a museum and one of Sydney's principal Aboriginal settlements.

Starting just 75km (46 miles) north of the city, the **Central Coast▶** provides a natural playground for Sydney residents; although so close, this region of surf and uncrowded sandy beaches, bushland and forest, waterways and national parks, is a very different world. There are few man-made attractions here, but the Australian Reptile Park, with its native fauna and fascinating snake venom milking, is well worth a visit.

With splendid coastal and river scenery, Brisbane Water National Park resembles Ku-ring-gai Chase, its sandstone foundation supporting the same spectacular range of flowers and wildlife. There are woodlands of eucalyptus and pockets of rain forest, and Aboriginal carvings can be viewed at the Bulgandry site.

A visit to Parramatta, by road (see page 61) or RiverCat, can easily encompass a tour of **Sydney Olympic Park▶▶** at Homebush Bay, the main site for the 2000 Olympic Games (see page 58).

Ku-ring-gai Chase National Park▶▶ (30km/19 miles north of Sydney) remains in its wild state thanks to its designation as a national park as far back as 1894. The rugged sandstone plateau is deeply incised by the deep sheltered waterways of the Hawkesbury River. From West Head there are spectacular views across Broken Bay and the broad expanse of Pittwater. The Ku-ring-gai (Guringai) Aborigines who once lived here traced many carvings in the sandstone. There is a visitor centre at Bobbin Head, with interesting displays on the area's varied animal and bird populations.

At the very tip of the Warringah Peninsula, 40km (25 miles) north of the city, lies the exclusive residential area of **Palm Beach▶▶**. To the east, the ocean surf crashes on the beach, and to the west, the tranquil surface of the beautiful **Pittwater▶** inlet is a windsurfer's paradise. The lighthouse on Barrenjoey headland offers a terrific view over Broken Bay and inland up the drowned valley of the Hawkesbury River.

Parramatta▶▶ was founded only a matter of months after Sydney itself, because of the fertility of the surrounding area. Now the focal point of the sprawling western suburbs 24km (15 miles) from the city, it has been redeveloped, although traces remain of early days, including some of the nation's very first buildings.

Beyond the mock-Tudor gatehouse to Parramatta Park stands Australia's most venerable public edifice, **Old Government House**, which was built in 1799 though much expanded early in the 19th century. For many years the official Vice-Regal residence, it contains early Australian furniture. **Elizabeth Farm** in Alice Street is even older, begun in 1793 by the agricultural pioneers John and Elizabeth Macarthur. Its veranda is the prototype of countless others that adorn dwellings all over Australia. It too has been refurnished in the style of that period, as has the interior of **Experiment Farm Cottage** in Ruse Street. The land on which this house stands belonged to one of the few convicts with any farming experience; in 1789, James Ruse was the first man in Australia to sow a crop of wheat successfully.

Australia's first national park, proclaimed in 1879, the **Royal National Park▶▶** consists mostly of a rugged sandstone plateau with a varied vegetation of heathland (which has a brilliant show of wildflowers in spring), fine forests of blue gum and patches of rain forest. Eaten into by the sea, the park has a coastline of spectacular cliffs interspersed with sandy coves. About 35km (22 miles) from Sydney, it has long been popular with serious bushwalkers, and is now *the* place to go for weekend outings of all kinds.

Reached by ferry from Circular Quay, the splendid **Taronga Zoo▶▶** benefits from its superb site almost directly opposite the city and is worth visiting for the view alone, particularly if you take the cable-car ride. Taronga doesn't limit itself to native animals, but it is the Australian fauna that most visitors want to see.

A room inside 1835 Experiment Farm Cottage, Parramatta

THE ROAD TO PARRAMATTA
A road was built from Sydney to Parramatta as early as 1794, but for years it was easier to bring people and goods up the river than along the highway. Partly superseded by an expressway, today's Parramatta Road is neither lovely nor efficient, though a trip along it reveals a cross-section of Australian suburbia. In spite of interminable traffic lights and shabby shopping malls, there remains something indefinably romantic about it, a whiff of the days when it alone pointed to the interior of the unknown continent.

New South Wales and the ACT

Sunset on Black Mountain, Canberra, capped by the Telstra Tower

NEW SOUTH WALES This state *was* Australia in the early days of European settlement. Today, with almost 6.7 million citizens, it is still the country's most populous state, and its capital, Sydney, is the country's greatest city. If time is short, some travel planners advise visitors to concentrate on this state alone; a holiday spent entirely within New South Wales' far-flung borders can be very rewarding for both urban pleasures and the delights of wild nature.

THE COASTAL LOWLANDS The 'Premier State' can be divided into four regions, which encompass many facets of the Australian experience. Most of the population lives in the Coastal Lowlands, a fertile strip of country of varying width running some 1,400km (870 miles) from Victoria to Queensland. Apart from glamorous Sydney,

64

WHAT'S IN A NAME?
Between 1768 when he set out for Tahiti, and 1779 when he was killed on a Hawaiian beach, Captain Cook probably named more places than anyone else in history. Some recall people (Port Jackson), some are a lively evocation of events (Cape Tribulation, where Cook's ship was holed by a reef), some characterize a quirk of topography (Mount Dromedary in Tasmania has two humps). Inspiration seems to have failed him when confronted with the task of finding a suitable name for the whole of the eastern coast of Australia, even given the supposed resemblance of part of it to the coastline of southern Wales. But perhaps New South Wales, as a name, is one up on such masterpieces of inventiveness as South Australia.

the region is home to the beachside industrial cities of **Newcastle** and **Wollongong**, as well as a glorious chain of little ports and shore settlements like Ulladulla (directly east of Canberra). White Australia's history began here, when Captain Cook's charts led the First Fleet to Botany Bay, and where, after a shaky start, the process of colonization gradually got under way with the founding of townships and the clearing of the bush for farmland.

The area has also been the focus of much of the country's modern history, its industrial heartland and stronghold of the Labor movement that has played an often decisive role in Australian government and politics. It is here that the foundation was laid for Australian beach culture, as love of the sun, surf and sheer physical well-being overcame the remnants of Victorian prudery in the early decades of the 20th century, a process that owed much to the incomparable beaches, which are still one of the state's main tourist attractions.

THE GREAT DIVIDING RANGE In places, the Great Dividing Range drops almost directly into the sea. It provides a constant backdrop to the coast, with its hill peaks and tablelands also running the length of the state. Despite their low altitude, the forested hills remained an impregnable barrier to exploration until 1813, when the spectacular **Blue Mountains** were successfully crossed for the first time.

The highlands are as wonderfully varied as the coast: To the south, in the Snowy Mountains, they include the country's highest peaks and most extensive snowfields; to the north lies the high-level plateau of New England, named after the old country for its misty coolness and vivid green. In places, as in the **Southern Highlands**, the

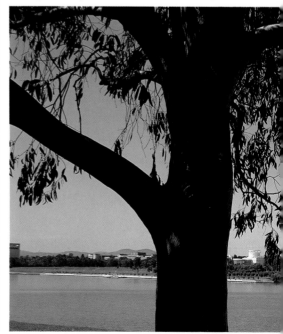

ranges are interspersed with broad plains that were converted early on into attractive farmland. Here there is a wealth of old buildings in town and country, as well as a 2,500sq km (965-sq-mile) tract carved out of the state to form the Australian Capital Territory (ACT), the site of the nation's capital, Canberra.

Most of the rivers of southeastern Australia have their source in the uplands, with their relatively abundant rain and snowfall. Some, like the Hawkesbury and Hunter, are quite short, running east to the Pacific; others, much longer, form part of the huge Murray/Darling system, flowing slowly westwards.

THE WESTERN SLOPES Beyond the mountains and tablelands, the Western Slopes fall gradually towards the interior. Settled in the early 1800s, the area today consists mostly of unspectacular wheat and wool country, and there are several substantial towns and even small cities in this region such as Moree, Dubbo, Orange, Wellington, Bathurst and Wagga Wagga. To the south, in the Riverina, the waters of the Murray and Murrumbidgee have been used to create huge irrigated areas that now support a variety of crops.

THE WESTERN PLAINS This area stretches to the borders with South Australia and Queensland. It is the New South Wales Outback, with vastly more sheep than people. Here the township of **Bourke** has given its name ('back of Bourke') to utter remoteness, the Outback beyond the Outback. In the harsh landscape, the city of **Broken Hill** has grown up based on the world's richest lode of silver, lead and zinc; it is a place that attracts many visitors for its sheer strangeness.

CLINGING TO THE COAST
Between them, the cities of Sydney, Newcastle and Wollongong are home to over 4.9 million people, a very large proportion of the state's 6.7 million. The remainder of the population lives mostly in coastal towns, far from the inhospitable interior.

65

Attractive Canberra, a modern planned city that is like nowhere else in Australia

The home of foreign embassies

Canberra

Australia's capital comprises the prestigious buildings that house the nation's central institutions, all in a setting of broad boulevards and intimate districts and framed by glorious mountain scenery. As well as being the country's only major inland city, Canberra is unique in having been planned in every detail from the start.

At the time of Federation, in 1901, the dispute between Sydney and Melbourne about which should become the capital was finally resolved by choosing neither. Instead, the new Constitution stipulated that a site should be found in New South Wales, no closer than 160km (100 miles) to Sydney. After much debate the present location was chosen, and in 1911 some 2,500sq km (965sq miles) of land south of Goulburn Plains became the Australian Capital Territory. Over 130 hopefuls took part in the international competition for the design of the new city, the American landscape architect Walter Burley Griffin, a pupil of Frank Lloyd Wright, emerging as winner.

Griffin had never seen Canberra when he drew up his plans for a new city thousands of kilometres from his Chicago base, but his experience enabled him to interpret maps and diagrams, and to appreciate the potential of the chosen location. His design is very much of his period, a combination of great vistas framing noble buildings, and self-contained residential districts.

The target population for the country's capital was 25,000, but Canberra's growth was painfully slow and this total was only reached in the years following World War II. Growth took off in the 1960s, and today the city is home to over 320,000 people. Around 40 per cent of its workforce consists of public employees, not necessarily a sound basis for a satisfactory social balance. In its infancy and adolescence, the city was seen as a place of exile, populated by bored civil servants longing for the fleshpots of Sydney or Melbourne. Nor is its contemporary image among Australians a particularly happy one; many think of it as a privileged place of parasitic politicians and cosseted bureaucrats. In recent years, though, Canberra's dining, entertainment and nightlife scene has become far more lively than it used to be.

The city of Canberra has been described with some truth as a collection of suburbs in search of a city, but what it lacks in urbanity it more than makes up for with easy access to national parks, wildlife, wineries, sheer spacious beauty and convenience (there are no gridlocks!). It certainly is nothing like any other city in Australia and is well worth visiting for that reason alone, with an array of splendid modern buildings in the immaculately landscaped setting planned for them in the early years of the nation's foundation.

The extraordinary Parliament House (completed in 1988) is rich in national symbolism

The 81m (265-ft) flagpole on top of Parliament House and Capital Hill

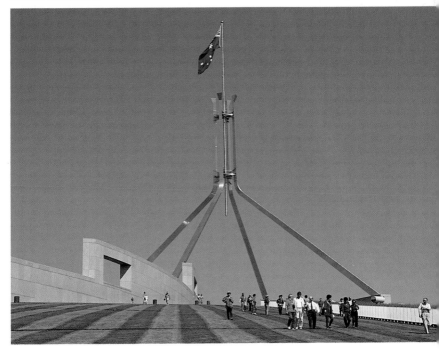

▶▶ Australian National Botanic Gardens   66C1
Clunies Ross Street, Acton (tel: 02-6250 9540)
Open: daily 9–5 (later in Jan–Feb). Admission free
These attractive gardens on the lower slopes of Black Mountain present a wonderful range of native Australian plants—over 7,000 species in all. A network of paths leads through a series of contrasting environments, each with its fully labelled array of trees, shrubs and other plants. This is *the* place to appreciate Australia's flora.

▶▶▶ Australian War Memorial   66C3
Treloar Crescent, Campbell (tel: 02-6243 4211)
Open: daily 10–5. Admission free
The dome of the War Memorial stares somberly from the lower slopes of Mount Ainslie, down Anzac Parade towards Capital Hill on the far shore of Lake Burley Griffin. With its great courtyard containing the Roll of Honour and the Eternal Flame, it was opened in 1941 and redeveloped and expanded in 1998–2001. It is not just a great monument, but a world-class museum that attempts to make some sense of the senselessness of war. Beyond the carefully crafted symbolism of the exterior are extensive galleries and displays evoking the many conflicts in which the country has been involved, from the Maori Wars of the 1860s to 1970s Vietnam. As well as the hardware of war, such as guns and planes, there are superb paintings, photographs, huge dioramas, film and sound recordings, and documents and papers.

▶ Diplomatic Missions   66B2
A fascinating Canberra tour is to the suburb of Yarralumla, where many foreign countries have built their embassies. National self-expression takes a variety of forms: The American embassy is a handsome, Williamsburg-style edifice, Greece's has classical columns, that of Papua New Guinea has an exuberantly gabled longhouse, and Indonesia has a Balinese temple.

▶▶ Lake Burley Griffin   66B2
Burley Griffin included a beautiful lake in his plan for the new city, but it was not until 1964 that the great body of water bearing his name came into being, with an area of more than 704ha (1,740 acres) and a varied shoreline 35km (22 miles) long. A number of islands enliven the scene, which is further enhanced by lakeside landscaping, as in **Commonwealth Park**. The **Captain Cook Memorial Jet▶** waterspout reaches 140m (460ft) in calm weather.

Dating from 1860, **Blundell's Cottage▶** near the lakeshore is one of the few old buildings in Canberra. Rising over the weeping willows on Aspen Island are the crisp white concrete shafts of the **National Carillon**, a gift from Britain to mark Canberra's 50th anniversary in 1963. Its 53 bells play Australian melodies as well as hymns and popular songs. Designed to be the focal point of this city, the lake makes a splendid setting for many of its most prominent buildings; an excursion aboard one of the cruise vessels is a pleasant way to make the most of it.

The slender **Australian-American Memorial**, close to the lake's eastern shore, commemorates the role that American forces played in the defence of Australia during World War II.

A CAPITAL LIBRARY
In addition to several million books, the neo-classical-style National Library of Australia houses other unique collections relating to the history and evolution of Australia. The interior is adorned with fine tapestries and stained glass.

An Aussie 'digger' (soldier) runs up the flag outside the Australian War Memorial

▶▶ National Capital Exhibition   66C2

Regatta Point, Commonwealth Park (tel: 02-6257 1068)
Open: daily 9–5 (6 in summer). Admission free
Boasting 'the best view of the national capital', this is the place to appreciate the meticulous and sometimes controversial planning of the city. The exhibition has audiovisual displays, laser map, photographs and objects.

▶▶ National Gallery of Australia   66B3

Parkes Place, Parkes (tel: 02-6240 6502). Open: daily 10–5
Admission free (varying charges for special exhibitions)
The National Gallery has an excellent array of Australian art, beginning with Aboriginal objecs and ending with canvases on which the paint seems hardly dry. There is much else besides, displayed to advantage in well-lit and varied spaces, including a good selection of European and American art—particularly of the 20th century—as well as works from Asia and the Pacific. Sculpture benefits from the attractive setting of the Sculpture Garden, which also serves as a venue for outdoor events.

▶▶▶ National Museum of Australia   66B2

Lawson Crescent, Acton Peninsula (tel: 02-6208 5000). Open:
daily 9–5. Admission free (charges for special exhibitions)
This extensive museum explores the key issues, events and people that have shaped Australia. Focusing on five main themes—indigenous peoples, the symbols of Australia, the peopling of the nation, personal stories of ordinary and famous Australians, and the land and its people—the museum uses state-of-the-art design and technology to express its message. The ultra-modern

The National Botanic Gardens are renowned for their splendid collection of Australian native plants

CAPITAL VIEWS
Canberra's ring of uplands provides splendid viewpoints over the carefully planned city in its superb setting. The spike of Telstra Tower rises from the top of Black Mountain (779m/2,555ft), giving panoramic vistas from its viewing galleries. Mount Ainslie (841m/2,760ft) rises through bushland behind the War Memorial and has equally spectacular views, as does Red Hill, which is 2km (1.2 miles) south of Parliament House.

Parliament House, one of Canberra's most popular attractions

CAPITAL COINAGE
As well as a gallery enabling visitors to see the country's money being made, the Royal Australian Mint has a public coining press where you can mint your own coins or tokens.

CAPITAL PUNISHMENT
Justice has moved on in Australia since the early days when the jail was sometimes the most prominent building in town, but modern Australians are second only to Americans in their fondness for litigation. The imposing High Court has an exhibition explaining the workings of the country's legal system.

A SPORTING CAPITAL
Sports fans should not miss a tour of the Australian Institute of Sport (AIS) in the northern suburb of Bruce. The institute, set up in 1980, has top-class facilities and the fascinating Sportex complex with displays and entertaining hands-on exhibits. Tours are conducted by the AIS's élite athletes.

lakeside building includes cafés, a restaurant with water views and a well-stocked shop.

▶▶ Old Parliament House 66B2
King George Terrace, Parkes (tel: 02-6270 8222)
Open: daily 9–5. Admission: inexpensive
This beautifully renovated 1927 building is now the home of the **National Portrait Gallery▶**, a collection of likenesses of famous and lesser-known Australians.

▶▶▶ Parliament House 66B2
Capital Hill (tel: 02-6277 5399). Open: daily 9–5 (later when Parliament is sitting). Admission free
Home to the Senate and the House of Representatives, this truly spectacular structure has become a major visitor attraction in its own right, rich in artworks and national symbolism. Over 85,000cu m (3 million cu ft) of soil was removed to make way for the new building, then replaced to form its green roof. This superb viewpoint over the city is topped by an 81m (265-ft) stainless steel flagpole, flying what must be the biggest flag in the world. Inside a complex of beautifully designed internal spaces is adorned with the creations of Australian artists like Arthur Boyd. The 48 marble columns of the foyer recall the country's eucalyptus trees, whose green colour appears again in the chamber of the House of Representatives.

▶▶ Questacon 66B2
King Edward Terrace, Parkes (tel: 02-6270 2800
Open: daily 9–5. Admission: moderate
The National Science and Technology Centre has around 200 hands-on displays in six galleries. This informative and interactive centre brings the world of science alive, even to the most non-technical, and is well worth a visit.

▶ ScreenSound Australia 66C2
McCoy Circuit, Acton (tel: 02-6248 2000)
Open: Mon–Fri 9–5, Sat–Sun 10–5. Admission: moderate
Australia was an early leader in the development of the motion picture; exhibits here present an intriguing selection from the nation's contribution to the delights of the silver screen, including a short film of the 1896 Melbourne Cup. Radio, TV and music are also represented.

How to travel

By air A comprehensive network of international and domestic air services operates from Sydney's Kingsford Smith Airport, 11km (7 miles) south of the city. Buses and taxis link the separate domestic and international terminals, as does the Airport Link Railway, which continues to Central Station via several stops in the middle of town. The service takes around 15 minutes to reach the city. The frequent Airport Express buses are the most economical way to reach the city and its inner suburbs. There are flights to the NSW Outback and many coastal resorts, to Cooma (for the Snowy Mountains) and to Canberra.

By bus Schedules can be inconvenient to remote townships. On the main routes there is likely to be a choice of operator and times. Many places can be visited by organized bus tours from Sydney. Major cities and some larger towns have a good network of local bus services.

By train NSW has a widespread rail network, and of those towns that have lost their train service, many are connected to a railhead by buses operated by the State Rail Authority (Countrylink). Multiple-unit express trains (XPTs and XPLORERS) ply between many major towns. Interstate trains run to Brisbane and Melbourne, and the legendary *Ghan* now runs from Sydney to Alice Springs and Darwin via Adelaide. Broken Hill is visited by the *Indian Pacific* on its way to and from Western Australia, and has its own weekly XPLORER link to Sydney. The Greater Sydney region is well served by frequent CityRail services, which extend as far as Newcastle and Dungog in the north, the Blue Mountains in the west, Goulburn and the Southern Highlands, and Nowra on the south coast.

By car Driving is not recommended in the Sydney area, unless you are heading out of town to places like Palm Beach or the Royal National Park. Public transport and the taxis are the best option. However, many remote parts of the state are accessible only by car.

SAVE TIME AND FLY
Unless you have plenty of time to spare and are happy to drive, flying to the more distant parts of the state is highly recommended. Regional Express, along with Qantas and its subsidiaries cover most major NSW destinations.

A LONG WAY BY CAR
New South Wales is crisscrossed by a web of named highways, very helpful in planning an itinerary, though they tend to be of variable quality. Driving the Pacific Highway north along the coast can get tedious, and many prefer the inland and more scenic New England Highway.

Renting a 4WD makes sense if you plan to go off road

One of the grand old buildings in the pleasant city of Bathurst

72

THE WAY TO THE WEST
Just visible from Sydney, the dark escarpment of the Blue Mountains, which rises abruptly (the highest point, near Mount Victoria, is 1,069m/3507ft) from the Sydney plains, blocked the way westward to the early colonists. Some convict escapees were convinced that China lay just beyond the mountains as they headed towards what they hoped would be freedom. The puzzle of how to cross the mountains, by keeping to the ridges rather than to the valleys, was solved by Blaxland, Lawson and Wentworth in 1813, and within two years Governor Macquarie had a road built by a convict workforce on the route still followed by the modern road and railway. This marked a great leap forward in the development of the colony, promising an opening up of the immense potential of the then unknown interior.

►► Armidale   63C4

Unofficial capital of the cool uplands of New England in the northeast of the state, Armidale is the nearest thing Australia has to a university city. There are a number of higher education colleges and several private schools as well as the University of New England in its parkland campus. A couple of cathedrals, plus a number of venerable public buildings and delightful old houses further enhance the refined atmosphere. The modern **New England Regional Art Museum►** has a reputation as the best provincial collection of Australian art, and there is a Folk Museum housed in a building dating from 1863.

Armidale is the ideal base for exploring this part of New England (whose Scottish settlers tried and failed to make the name New Caledonia stick); within easy reach are a number of spectacular waterfalls, including the highest in Australia, **Wollomombi Falls►** in the World Heritage-listed Oxley Wild Rivers National Park.

► Batemans Bay   63A4

This fishing port and popular tourist resort on the estuary of the Clyde River is the closest ocean beach to Canberra, only 149km (92 miles) away over the mountains. There are fine oysters and lobsters, and a penguin colony on the Tollgate Islands Nature Reserve.

►► Bathurst   63B4

At the end of the Great Western Highway from Sydney, Bathurst was founded by Governor Macquarie in 1815, making it the country's oldest inland settlement. It was the point of departure for many expeditions farther into the interior, and in 1851 this area was the scene of Australia's first gold rush. Those days are re-created in the open-air museum called **Bathurst Goldfields►**, and the town itself is full of interest. The scenic drive around Mount Panorama forms part of what is considered to be Australia's finest motor-racing circuit.

►►► Blue Mountains National Park   63B4

Sheer cliffs dropping into deep canyons and glorious eucalyptus forests make up some of the most spectacular landscapes to be seen in Australia. The grandeur of this World Heritage-listed natural scene is all the more impressive because of the proximity of the manicured residential and retirement areas clustered along the main road and railway from Sydney, 90 minutes away.

The Blue Mountains are not really mountains, but a vast sandstone tableland, deeply incised by watercourses like the Nepean and Cox's rivers. However, they really are blue; a vaporous emanation from the leaves of the eucalypts hangs in the air as a haze. Since the early part of the 20th century the mountains have attracted serious bushwalkers as well as sightseers, and they offer all kinds of pleasures today, from antique hunting in sophisticated little townships, to real escape into wild country. The following main sights could just about be seen in the course of a day-trip from Sydney, but it would be far better to stay at least a couple of days.

A good place to start is at the excellent **National Parks and Wildlife Service's Heritage Centre►►**, 2km (1.2 miles) to the east of the main highway at Blackheath. A

73

Dramatic sandstone cliffs and densely forested valleys around Katoomba in the Blue Mountains

short distance away is one of the most spectacular lookouts in the whole national park, **Govett's Leap▶ ▶**, with views of the Grose Valley and Bridal Veil Falls. A panoramic walk leads along the clifftop to other vantage points, while a steep track (for experienced hikers) descends into the forest of blue gums far below.

The other great viewpoint in the park is **Echo Point▶ ▶**, just to the south of **Katoomba**, the 'capital' of the municipality known as City of the Blue Mountains. Here there is another visitor centre whose glass wall looks straight out into the treetops, while projecting platforms give giddy views of the famous sandstone pillars of **The Three Sisters▶ ▶ ▶**. A number of popular walks fringe the clifftop or descend into the valley. Just to the west are two exciting forms of transport; the Scenic Railway, an inclined plane dropping steeply into the valley bottom; and the much newer Sceniscender cable car.

To the east are the famous **Wentworth Falls▶**, the highest in the area with a drop of 270m (885ft); nearby Faulconbridge is the home of the **Norman Lindsay Gallery and Museum▶**, which commemorates this well-known artist and writer. The charming village of **Leura▶ ▶** has historic houses, antiques and craft shops, cafés and the National Trust-listed **Everglades Gardens▶**. Westward are the truly spectacular **Jenolan Caves▶ ▶** and the late-Victorian guest house associated with them, while one of the country's great feats of railway engineering, the **Zig Zag Railway▶** (see panel) can be experienced first-hand at Clarence, near Lithgow.

THE GREAT ZIG ZAG
In 1866, the engineers building the railway line to the west were faced with the problem of how to lower it from the top of the Blue Mountains down the sheer cliff face into Lithgow. Their solution was to construct a line in the form of a letter Z down the cliff face, with reversing stations at two points. This was replaced by the present main line, which takes a long way round but eliminates the need for reversing. The Zig Zag has been restored as a tourist railway, an impressive spectacle as powerful engines haul their coaches up the steep slope.

Wentworth Falls lookout in the Blue Mountains

WORLD HERITAGE SITES
Four of the World Heritage sites in Australia lie within New South Wales. The most accessible are the Greater Blue Mountains Area and the lush rain forests of Dorrigo National Park, inland from Coffs Harbour. The others are Lord Howe Island, out in the Pacific, and the Willandra Lakes region, in the state's far southwest.

NOT JUST PARKS
The NSW National Parks and Wildlife Service manages a number of sites whose interest is primarily human, rather than natural. These include places like Mutawintji Historic Site, with its wealth of mysterious Aboriginal relics, and sites of significance in the early European settlement of the country like Captain Cook's Landing Place at Botany Bay. Sydney's oldest dwelling, Cadman's Cottage, is a National Parks and Wildlife Service information centre.

National parks

New South Wales, with its long coastline, mountains and extensive Outback, has wonderful examples of many of the continent's characteristic natural landscapes.

In the far west On the fringes of Australia's Red Centre and well over 1,000km (620 miles) from Sydney are two superb arid wildernesses. In **Sturt National Park** summer temperatures can reach 50°C (122°F) for days on end; grassy plains alternate with claypans and pebbly desert from which rise flat-topped *mesas* (rocky tableland). In the extreme west are the ruddy sand dunes of the Strzelecki Desert. **Kinchega National Park** has vast plains of red sand as well as the strange saucer-shaped overflow lakes of the Darling River. Both areas are home to emus and large red kangaroos.

To the east The land gradually rises through the western slopes of the Great Dividing Range to the range itself, the backbone of the state. On the border with Victoria is one of the world's great national parks, focused on Australia's highest peak, 2,228m (7,310-ft) **Mount Kosciuszko**, after which the park itself is named. Glacial lakes, wild heathlands, alpine flowers and glorious forests of snow gums make a superb setting for summer hiking, while the area is at its most popular in winter, during the ski season, from early June to early October each year. The forested highlands that extend from near Newcastle through New England to the Queensland border have a rich vegetation that includes much undisturbed rain forest; here over 50 separate parks and reserves have been grouped together to form one of Australia's World Heritage areas, the **Central Eastern Rainforest Reserves**. Old volcanoes give rise to dramatic landforms here and at **Warrumbungle National Park** farther inland, a weird world of rocky crags and natural skyscrapers. **Bald Rock National Park**, near the Queensland border in the far north, is another extraordinary landform, a great granite dome rising 200m (655ft) out of the bush.

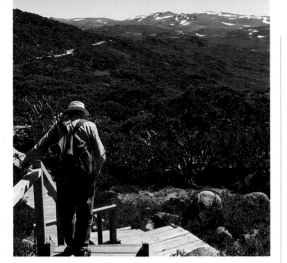

Mount Kosciuszko: good walking country

WHAT TO SEE
'OUT BACK'
From Broken Hill you can travel to many Outback locations. Lying within the relatively small distance of 290km (180 miles) are the opal-mining village of White Cliffs and Mutawintji National Park, Kinchega National Park and the Menindee Lakes, and Wilcannia, a quiet Darling River town with a large Aboriginal population.

▶ Bourke 62C2

This Outback town 776km (482 miles) northwest of Sydney seems utterly remote. It is the middle of a vast and semi-arid area supporting large numbers of sheep and cattle as well as some crops on land irrigated with water from the Darling River. Originally a wooden stockade built in 1835 against Aboriginal attack and then a major inland port, Bourke has a number of buildings dating from the latter part of the 19th century. Its main attraction, however, lies in its usefulness as a base for penetrating farther into the New South Wales Outback.

▶▶ Broken Hill 62C1

Founded on a 6.5km (4-mile) lode of silver, lead and zinc, the richest of its kind in the world, the unique 'Silver City' is still a thriving mining town, with metals extracted in large quantities despite low world prices for its products.

Thanks to the water that is piped in from its recreational reservoir at Lake Menindee 108km (67 miles) away, Broken Hill is a surprisingly green and leafy spot in what is one of the world's harshest environments: bitterly cold in winter, intolerably hot in summer, with a negligible rainfall that is only a tiny fraction of the evaporation rate. Nearly dead from thirst, the explorer Sturt gave the hump-backed ridge its name in 1844, but it was not until the 1880s that a German-born boundary rider, Charles Rasp, founded the Broken Hill Proprietary Company (see panel), which exploited the underground wealth in uneasy partnership with the workforce for many years. A great strike of 1919 ended in a historic compromise; the companies were ensured their profits and the workers granted conditions far in advance of the time, such as a 35-hour week. A confederation of workers unions effectively ran the town, not always on what today would be regarded as progressive lines. Broken Hill has always been a long way from the government in Sydney, and its ties are closer to South Australia, with smelters at Port Pirie, union beaches at Adelaide, clocks that keep South Australian time—half an hour behind that of Sydney—and a South Australian region telephone prefix code. *Continued on page 78.*

Continued on page 78.

BROKEN HILL
PROPRIETARY COMPANY
BHP, now known as BHP Billiton since its merger with Billiton, one of the world's leading mining companies, had its roots in Charles Rasp's discovery in 1883 of the immensely rich silver, lead and zinc lode at Broken Hill. It is now Australia's largest company, having long since diversified into iron and coal, gas and oil, and steel-making. Its profits are taken by many as an index of the prosperity of the country as a whole.

75

Born the son of a farm worker at Marston in Yorkshire in 1728, James Cook became the greatest explorer of his age. He was educated at the expense of his father's generous-minded employer, then learned seamanship aboard a Whitby coal vessel. In 1755, he joined the Royal Navy, where he refined his navigational and other skills in the course of the Seven Years' War. His charts of the St. Lawrence River helped Wolfe in the conquest of Quebec. The achievement for which Cook is best remembered is his voyage of exploration along the previously unknown east coast of Australia in 1770.

AHEAD OF HIS TIME
Cook was well in advance of his time in seeing beyond his own culture and background to the deeper harmony of the Aborigines' way of life. He wrote: 'they are...wholly (sic) unacquainted...with the superfluous...Conveniences so much sought after in Europe...the Earth and sea of their own accord furnishes them with all things necessary for life.'

1770: Cook takes possession of NSW for Britain...

As Cook had documented an eclipse of the sun off the coast of Newfoundland, he was a natural choice when the Royal Society wished for an accurate observation to be made from Tahiti of the transit of Venus across the face of the sun. Accompanying him on this mission aboard the barque *Endeavour* was an astronomer, Charles Green, together with two eminent botanists, Daniel Solander and the young Joseph Banks, who was only 25 years of age.

East coast sighting On 3 July 1769, the transit of Venus was duly observed and Cook opened the sealed orders given him by the Admiralty. These instructed him to investigate the existence or otherwise of a great southern continent and to survey and take possession of New Zealand. Having completed a thorough exploration of the New Zealand coast, Cook decided to return via the hypothetical 'East Coast of New Holland'. This was sighted on 19 April 1770, when Cape Everard in Victoria, originally called Point Hicks after Cook's sharp-eyed second in command, came into view.

Sailing northward along the coast, Cook found a convenient harbour where the ship could drop anchor and he and

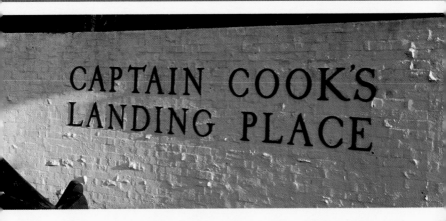

his men could investigate local conditions. The crew feasted on fresh fish, and the delighted botanists discovered an extraordinary array of plants, birds and animals previously unknown to science. In deference to their serious purpose, Cook altered his original name for the anchorage, Stingray Harbour, to Botany Bay.

Grounded on the Barrier Reef Farther north, Cook noted the existence of what seemed to be a fine natural harbour and named it Port Jackson. The wonderful setting for the future city of Sydney had to await full discovery until the arrival of the First Fleet 18 years later. Feeling his way into 'the labyrinth of coral islands, shoals, rocks and lee shores' of the Barrier Reef, even Cook with his superb seamanship couldn't fend off a grounding, and the *Endeavour* struck a reef.

Although the crew re-floated the vessel at high tide by jettisoning some of its equipment (including a cannon that is now in the Australian National Maritime Museum in Sydney), the barque needed repairs and was beached for a month near today's Cooktown at the base of Cape York. Once more the scientists had a field day, making their first acquaintance with kangaroos and turtles. When the *Endeavour* was seaworthy again, Cook sailed north to the tip of the cape where, on Possession Island, he hoisted the flag and formally declared the whole of eastern Australia to be British, giving it the unremarkable name of New South Wales.

The end of the road Promoted to captain, Cook went on between 1772 and 1775 to become the first to sail within the Antarctic Circle, finally putting paid to the idea of the great southern continent. In the course of an attempt in 1779 to find the elusive northern passage between the Atlantic and Pacific, he landed on Hawaii. As he was mediating in a relatively trivial dispute with the islanders, one of his men stupidly discharged his firearm; enraged, the islanders fell upon Cook, who had turned his back on them to restore order, and he collapsed beneath blows from clubs and daggers.

BANKS THE BOTANIST
Australia's 73 species of *Banksia* commemorate Joseph Banks, the wealthy botanist who sailed with Cook and who has been described as 'the father of Australian botany'. On the voyage out he listed 230 plant species at Madeira, 316 at Rio, 104 at Tierra del Fuego and 400 in New Zealand. Later, Banks was president of the Royal Society for 32 years.

77

...having made his mark in Botany Bay

Guess what grows at this Coffs Harbour plantation!

SILVER SCREEN SILVERTON
About 25km (15 miles) west of Broken Hill is the ghost town of Silverton, whose population moved to the bigger town when mining became unprofitable in the late 1880s. With its restored buildings seeming to typify the spirit of the Outback, it has taken on a new lease of life as a stage set for a number of films, including *A Town Like Alice* and one in the *Mad Max* series.

OUR BANANA'S THE BIGGEST
The improbably oversized fruit known as the Big Banana dominates the scene on the Pacific Highway just to the north of Coffs Harbour. Made of concrete it marks the entrance to a banana plantation and entertainment complex. Here you can see bananas growing, eat bananas in every imaginable form, buy banana-shaped souvenirs, and find out everything you always wanted to know about bananas but never dared to ask.

Continued from page 75.
  Protected from dust storms by extensive tree belts, Broken Hill is laid out on a grid of streets with names like Chloride, Mica and Cobalt. The excellent Visitor Information Centre is close to the old Sulphide Street Station, now a mineral and train museum. **The GeoCentre▶▶** is an interactive earth sciences museum, but it's more exciting to go down a former mine, like Delprat's Mine or Daydream Mine. The town is also a base for the **Royal Flying Doctor Service▶** and the **School of the Air▶**, both of which are open to the public. The strange environment of the city and its surroundings seems to have acted as a stimulant to a number of artists, and there is a sculpture reserve and several galleries, of which the best known is that run by Pro Hart.

▶▶ Byron Bay   63D5

Cape Byron is the easternmost point of the Australian mainland, capped with a powerful lighthouse. Byron Bay itself, with wonderful beaches and a gloriously scenic hinterland of forests and mountains, has been a focal point of alternative lifestyles since the late 1960s. A major attraction here is the town's lively dining, shopping and nightlife scene, as well as adventure activities such as sea kayaking and hang-gliding. The beaches on either side of the headland vary in character, from secluded coves to great stretches of sand. Surfing is well established; the first lifesaving club was founded here as early as 1907.

▶ Cobar   62C2

This copper-mining town on the fringe of the Outback straddles the Barrier Highway on its way west to Broken Hill. Founded in the early 1870s as a typical mining city of tents and huts, it soon reached its peak population of some 10,000. Among the buildings that date from the town's early days are the Great Western Hotel with its extraordinarily long veranda and the mining company's office, now the **Cobar Outback Heritage Centre▶**. After a long decline, the place prospered again in the 1960s.

▶ Cockington Green, ACT off 66D3

Gold Creek Village, 11 Gold Creek Road, Nicholls
(tel: 1800 627 273 or 02-6230 2273)
Open: daily 9.30–5 (last entry at 4.30). Admission: moderate
The original Cockington in the southwest of England, a
picture-postcard village with thatched cottages, a pub,
a forge and other items of rusticity, is reproduced on the
outskirts of Canberra in miniature form. A new display
has buildings from around the world, including scale
models from South Africa, Ireland and Germany.

▶▶ Coffs Harbour 63C5

Roughly halfway between Sydney and Brisbane, this old
timber port is famous for its beaches and banana plantations (see panel on page 78). A string of fine beaches runs
northward from the town's Park Beach, some with good
surf. There is rafting on nearby rivers, while man-made
attractions include the Pet Porpoise Pool, with seals,
sharks and penguins, as well as amiable dolphins. The
harbour is protected by a headland to the south, and by
Muttonbird Island, named after the species of burrowing sea birds that nest there. The town, with its **Historical
Museum▶** and **North Coast Regional Botanic
Garden▶▶**, is some distance inland.

▶ Dubbo 62C3

At the junction of the Newell and Mitchell Highways,
Dubbo is the flourishing hub for a large part of
NSW's Central West area. First settled in the 1840s, it
became a stopping point for those in search of 'better
land, further out'. Overlanders driving their cattle
southward to the markets of SA and Victoria used to
cross the Macquarie River near here. There are a number
of fine old buildings in the town, among them the 1876
bank, which now houses a good local museum and the
jail, complete with gallows. But most visitors come here
for the **Western Plains Zoo▶** which has animals from all
over the world roaming freely across its parkland.

▶ Eden 63A4

The last place of any size on the NSW coast before the border with Victoria, this little port and resort began life as a
whaling station, recalled in the **Killer Whale Museum▶**
and the fascinating Davidson Whaling Station Historic
Site on the southern side of Twofold Bay. Also on
Twofold Bay are the remains of Boydtown, begun around
the 1840s by the English entrepreneur Benjamin Boyd and
vaingloriously intended to rival Sydney as the colony's
capital.

▶ Forbes 62B3

Almost deserted after the gold rush of the 1860s, Forbes
survived as the focus for a rich agricultural area. The
Town Hall and other late 19th-century buildings still
grace the wide streets. Just outside town is a re-created
settlement of pioneer days, **Lachlan Vintage Village▶**,
where you can pan for gold or watch sheep being shorn.
The bushranger Ben Hall met his end in Forbes in 1865,
an event recalled in some detail in the old music hall that
houses the town's **Historical Society Museum▶**.

WHALE AND CHIPS
The first whaling station
on the Australian mainland
was established at Eden
in 1818, and whaling con-
tinued to be based here
until the 1930s. A revival
of Eden's economy took
place in the late 1960s
with the building of the
Harris Daishowa Chipmill,
designed to turn the
forests of the area (some
of the finest in the state)
into woodchips for the
Japanese paper industry.
The project aroused the ire
of the growing Australian
conservation movement,
whose members saw in it
the export of part of the
country's irreplaceable
natural heritage.

*Cape Byron's lighthouse
overlooks the beaches of
Byron Bay*

WATERING THE WILDERNESS

The explorer John Oxley reckoned no white man would ever want to take up residence in the 'barren and desolate' country he glimpsed from Mount Binya in 1817. But in the early 1900s, the NSW government, enthused by private successes with irrigation experiments, built the Burrinjuck Dam and encouraged settlement in the Murrumbidgee Irrigation Area, in the state's south. Many settlers were out-of-work miners from Broken Hill; later, returned servicemen and Italian immigrants with important agricultural skills moved in, and in spite of many disappointments and technical difficulties, the area produces crops of fruit (including grapes), vegetables, cotton and rice. Together with similar projects in the region, a total of 6,000sq km (2,317sq miles) of near desert has been made to bloom.

All of the 100 or so wineries in the Hunter Valley welcome visitors; most are around Cessnock and Pokolbin

▶ Glen Innes   63D4

This high-altitude town in northern NSW is in the middle of a prosperous farming area, once named the 'Land of the Beardies' after two pioneers. The region is well known for the sapphires and other gemstones that are extracted commercially (amateur fossicking or searching is also possible). The town has several well-cared-for late 19th-century buildings; the old hospital houses the **Land of the Beardies History House Museum▶**, one of Australia's most comprehensive small historical museums.

▶ Goulburn   63B4

The second oldest inland town in Australia straddles the Hume Highway some 200km (124 miles) southwest of Sydney and is the focal point of the well-tended farmlands all around, whose speciality is proclaimed by another of those Australian 'big ones'; 15m (50 feet) high, the Big Merino sheep guards the town's western approach. Goulburn is a 'real' city, with two cathedrals, a long main street and a number of imposing 19th-century buildings. On the edge of town is Riversdale, a coaching inn dating from the late 1830s, authentically restored and furnished.

▶ Grafton   63D5

The middle of the Clarence River district, Grafton was 'green' before its time. The town council initiated a policy of tree-planting as early as the 1860s, and today's citizens are benefiting from the many jacarandas and other flowering species that grace its broad streets. The bend of the Clarence was only bridged in 1932, by the double-decker structure you see today. Grafton is a good base for tours, with several national parks within easy reach.

▶ Griffith   62B2

Designed by Walter Burley Griffin, the American architect responsible for the planning of Canberra, this model township was built to act as the main urban focus for the

Murrumbidgee Irrigation Area. Its conception on the drawing board can be seen in its radial street pattern and in the decorative use of irrigation water in its gardens.

▶ Gundagai · 62B3

The name of this township along the Hume Highway is derived from an Aboriginal word meaning 'up-river'; in spite of warnings from the local Aborigines, the first settlers built their houses on the floodplain of the Murrumbidgee, and were duly swept away when the river broke its banks in 1852, causing the country's worst-ever flood disaster. The Murrumbidgee is crossed here by the longest wooden viaduct in Australia.

▶▶ Hunter Valley · 63C4

The broad valley of the Hunter River, which ends in the sea at Newcastle, has contrasting landscapes created by mines and wines. The coalfield has been exploited for a century and a half, and has been the making of the city of Newcastle. The vineyards were first planted here in the 1820s and, after periods of decline, are flourishing once more. A day-trip or, better still, one lasting a couple of days is a popular outing for Sydneysiders, not least because of the excellent food offered in the area.

The landscape of the Hunter is one of its attractions, in its framework of wooded hills running down from the Brokenback Range to the southwest of the valley. Grapevines benefit from the rich soil, which has its origin in the outpourings of ancient volcanoes. The wineries range from family-sized concerns to large-scale commercial enterprises. Australia's oldest wine-press is on display at the **Golden Grape Estate**. The vineyards of the Wyndham and Rothbury Estates are well worth visiting, while the **McGuigan Cellars ▶▶** has a superb cheese shop and the **Hunter Valley Gardens Village** has shops, cafés and a cellar door. Other wineries are in the Upper Hunter Valley, some 90km (56 miles) farther on.

A DOG'S LIFE
As teamsters made their way along the rough roads of early Australia, they were inevitably accompanied by various breeds of dog, one of which seems to have committed an unspeakable act while sitting on his master's tuckerbox (lunch box) by the side of the road. This and other deeds were recorded in the crude ballads of the time, refined somewhat in a version by the poet Jack Moses, and commemorated in a sculpture just outside Gundagai. This is the work of one Frank Rusconi, who was also responsible for the amazing model cathedral of marble on show in the Tourist Information Centre.

This part of the Great Dividing Range is the roof of Australia, much of it a highland plateau from which rise a number of peaks more than 1,980m (6,500ft) high. Parts of it have several well-equipped ski resorts. But the mountains are glorious in summer as well as in winter; a carpet of alpine wildflowers unrolls as the snow retreats, and there are superb paths and trails offering some of the most exhilarating hiking in the whole of Australia.

The region is popular with winter sports enthusiasts

82

THE SNOWY MOUNTAINS SCHEME
This was a visionary project to alter the course of rivers to irrigate the parched agricultural areas farther west and generate hydroelectric power in the process. Many dams were built, of which the largest, at Lake Eucumbene, holds back more water than is contained in Sydney Harbour. There are 80km (50 miles) of aqueducts, 148km (91 miles) of tunnels and seven power stations, the latter providing a good proportion of the electricity consumed in southeast Australia. Some of the impressive installations (like Murray 1 on the Alpine Way, or Tumut 2 north of Cabramurra) are open to the public.

History Aboriginal interest in the mountains was more recent than in many parts of Australia, dating only from the end of the last Ice Age some 10,000 years ago. This is one of the few Australian landscapes with glacial lakes, cirques and moraines, all the result of the action of the ice sheets that were absent throughout most of the country.

The mountains attracted graziers (sheep farmers) from early on in the days after white settlement, and a few determined bushwalkers between the two world wars, but it was only after the start of the Snowy Mountains Scheme in the late 1940s, when roads were driven through the wilderness and many other facilities created, that the area became accessible and visitors were able to come here in large numbers.

A popular starting point for exploring the mountains, which include the Kosciuzko National Park, is the town of **Cooma** at the junction of the Monaro and Snowy Mountains highways. It was from here that the Snowy Mountains Authority oversaw what was to be one of the greatest 20th-century engineering projects in the world. There are two tourist offices that provide information on the mountains and the great project that transformed them: the visitor information centre in town, and the Snowy Scheme Information Centre on the Canberra road.

The resort town of **Jindabyne** on its lake provides plenty of lodgings for winter sports enthusiasts and the National Parks and Wildlife Service has a useful visitor centre here, at Kosciuszko Road, before visitors head for the skiing areas in the heart of the mountains.

Popular resorts include the delightful alpine-style village of Thredbo on the southern side of the range, and the mega-resort of Perisher Blue, which encompasses the ski regions of Smiggin Holes, Blue Cow Mountain, Guthega and Perisher Valley—the latter reached by the underground railway known as the Ski Tube.

At the end of the northern road is Charlotte Pass, with superb views of the mountain peaks. This is the starting point for a number of wonderful walks, including the Summit Walk to the top of **Mount Kosciuszko**, at 2,228m (7,310ft) the highest peak in Australia.

Jindabyne is also the terminus of the **Alpine Way**, the splendid scenic highway that leads to the 1,582m (5,190-ft) pass at Dead Horse Gap. From here the partly unsurfaced road descends into the valley of the Murray River and on to Khancoban. This is the starting point for a fair-weather highway leading to **Mount Selwyn**, a winter sports resort on the north side of the peaks, and to the remains of the old gold-mining township of Kiandra.

Farther north are **Yarrangobilly Caves**. Of the dozens of caves so far discovered, six are open to the public.

SKIING

Although the snow isn't always as abundant as resort operators would like, the Snowy Mountains offer ideal conditions for cross-country skiing and some excellent downhill facilities. The main resorts are in the vast Perisher Blue region, which incorporates four ski areas and offers 50 lifts and T-bars, and the smaller and more charming alpine village of Thredbo. The ski season runs from early June to early October.

Murray 1 hydroelectric power station

New South Wales

A souvenir of your visit to Kangaroo Valley

THE KIAMA COAST
Kiama's beaches are pleasant enough—and excellent for surfing. Farther south lie Gerroa and Gerringong (which also offer great surfing), and then the spectacular wave-pounded expanse of Seven Mile Beach, part of a national park.

BLACK IS BEAUTIFUL
The Lightning Ridge black opals are not quite unique, but this is the only place in the world where this unusual stone occurs in quantity. It has been described as combining 'the iridescence of the dewdrop with the colour of the rainbow, set in the blackness of night'. The biggest stone ever found was given the name 'Queen of the Earth'.

MUTAWINTJI HISTORIC SITE
Within Mutawintji National Park, this extraordinary site represents one of the state's greatest collections of Aboriginal art and cultural relics. Some of the 20 rock shelters and 15 engraving sites can be visited in the company of an Aboriginal ranger.

► **Kangaroo Valley**   *63B4*
This is a delightful old township tucked away in an upland valley on the beautiful scenic road leading inland from Nowra, 100km (62 miles) south of Sydney. Apart from being the starting point for bushwalks, its main attraction is the **Pioneer Settlement Reserve**, a faithful reconstruction of a dairy farm of the 19th century.

► **Kiama**   *63B4*
The most famous feature of this popular and pleasantly situated port and resort on the 'Kiama Coast' south of Wollongong is the **Blowhole**, which gushes a waterspout up to 60m (195ft) into the air. To the west is the **Minnamurra Rainforest Centre►** (part of Budderoo National Park), with palms, fig trees and other rain-forest plants, rare red cedars and exquisite lyrebirds. The reserve can be explored via its two marked and interpreted walking tracks.

►►► **Kosciuszko National Park**   *62A3*
See pages 74 and 83.

►► **Lanyon Homestead, ACT**   *off 66A3*
Tharwa Drive, Tharwa (tel: 02-6237 5136)
Open: Tue–Sun 10–4. Admission: inexpensive
This fine building on the Murrumbidgee River was built in 1859 and extended a few years later. Now in the care of the ACT Government, both buildings and gardens have been sympathetically restored. There is a gallery housing a collection of the works of Australian artist Sir Sidney Nolan.

►► **Lightning Ridge**   *62D3*
Just off the Castlereagh Highway before it quits NSW for Queensland, this far northwestern township is famed for its black opals, mined here since 1902, in recent years by machine rather than by hand. Amateur fossickers (searchers for gold or gemstones) are welcome, provided they don't trespass on professionals' rights, and there are many old mines to visit and cutting demonstrations to watch, as well as artesian baths to relax in.

►► **Mount Warning National Park**   *63D5*
This 1,157m (3,796-ft) peak is the plug of an ancient volcano, given its name by Captain Cook to mark the reefs

off Point Danger, on which the *Endeavour* almost came to grief. It is the first place on the Australian mainland to receive the rays of the rising sun, and the view is worth the 750m (2,460-ft) climb from the visitor centre, where you can leave your car. The steep but well-made path rises through splendid woodlands that change from subtropical rain forest to temperate rain forest and finally to open bush.

▶▶ Mutawintji National Park   62C1

Beyond Broken Hill, in NSW's farthest northwest, are the rugged sandstone ranges of this remote national park, which is nevertheless accessible on gravel roads. Arid sandy plains and pebble deserts contrast with pools and watercourses fringed with river red gums and other lush vegetation. Aborigines occupied the area for countless years, leaving a wealth of rock paintings and engravings.

▶▶ Myall Lakes National Park   63B4

These tranquil lakes, 60km (37 miles) north of Newcastle and separated from the Pacific Ocean by windswept sand dunes, are best reached from the township of Tea Gardens by boat up the Myall River. There is little development along the shores, though the fishing village of Seal Rocks on the coast at the eastern end of the park is popular with visitors who want to get away from it all. You can rent everything from canoes to houseboats to explore the magnificent lakes.

▶ Nambucca Heads   63C5

Subtropical crops now grow in this attractive and popular resort, 50km (31 miles) south of Coffs Harbour, where the cedar forests were cleared last century. There are fantastic views from various lookout points, of which Yarrahapini is the most spectacular. You can take tours inland to the rugged ridges and deep forested valleys of the New England and Dorrigo national parks.

MYALL LAKES FLORA AND FAUNA
The Myall Lakes, fringed by splendid forest, that includes rain-forest species such as cabbage palms, make up the largest such lake system in the state. The lakes are also famous for the prawns (shrimp) that breed in them. Waterbirds abound, as well as sea eagles, and the area is rich in other wildlife, too.

85

Swim or surf from the beach at Nambucca Heads

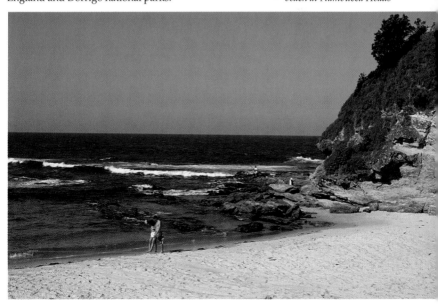

Attractive Lake Macquarie, Australia's largest saltwater lake, near Newcastle

AUSTRALIAN COUNTRY
Far inland from Port Macquarie, halfway between Sydney and Brisbane on the New England Highway, is the town of Tamworth. This sizeable place claims fame as the capital of Australian country music. An annual festival, held in January, draws thousands of fans to hundreds of performances; other attractions are the Australian Country Music Foundation Museum and the Hands of Fame Park (handprints).

▶ **Newcastle**   *63B4*

Dominated by its docks and the now closed BHP steelworks, industrial Newcastle is the largest city in Australia that is not a state capital. Its fortunes, like those of its namesake in England, were founded on abundant coal reserves that were discovered in the Hunter Valley; Newcastle coal constituted the country's first export.

But there's much more to Newcastle than industry. The Foreshore Park, Queen's Wharf and Customs House Plaza make a fine setting for festive occasions. **Fort Scratchley▶** is one of the few forts in Australia to have seen active duty—soldiers stationed there in 1942 fired on a Japanese submarine. The old stronghold gives a good panorama over the city in its setting, and houses the **Maritime Museum▶** and **Military Museum**. The city has some imposing 19th-century buildings and more museums and galleries. The 'Bogey Hole' on the city beach below beautiful King Edward Park was built as a saltwater bath in convict days. To the south of the city, **Lake Macquarie▶** offers all kinds of watersports. The country's largest saltwater lake, four times the size of Sydney Harbour, it is also the home of a koala colony and a delightful flora and fauna reserve.

▶ **Nimbin**   *63D5*

Set among the natural splendours of northern NSW, Nimbin developed as a hub for artists and bohemians in the early 1970s. Today, its crafts shops and cafés attract the curious as well. It is close to **Nightcap National Park▶ ▶**, whose 900m (2,953-ft) peaks form part of the outer walls of the huge extinct volcano of which Mount Warning is the core. The park, with its glorious rain forest and diverse wildlife, is now part of NSW's World Heritage Area protecting the temperate and subtropical forests of the north.

► Nowra   63B4

Nowra is just upstream from the mouth of the Shoalhaven River. It is an extremely busy tourist resort, largely because of the beaches that extend north and south along the coast, one of them (Hyams Beach on **Jervis Bay►►**) boasting the whitest sand in the world.

► Orange   62B3

Lava flows from the extinct volcano of Mount Canobolas, the highest point between the Great Dividing Range and the Indian Ocean, have broken down over the millennia into fertile soils that today support great tracts of orchards growing apples, pears, cherries and grapes for wine—but no oranges! The town of Orange has prospered from the fertility of its surroundings and is a busy but pleasant place, leafy with parks and trees. The first goldfield to be exploited in Australia was at nearby **Ophir**, where two prospectors made a sizeable strike in 1851. You can try your luck at searching for gold today in picturesque surroundings along Summer Hill Creek.

► Port Macquarie   63C5

At the mouth of the Hastings River, Port Macquarie has turned from trade and commerce to tourism and retirement with considerable success. **St. Thomas' Church** is a reminder of these early days; one of the first churches to be built in Australia (1824–28), it has box pews and a view from its tower. The **Hastings District Historical Museum►** has good displays on the evolution of the town and its hinterland, and nature is on show at the **Billabong Koala and Wildlife Park►**, and **Sea Acres Rainforest Centre►►**, with a boardwalk through the rain forest. Good beaches stretch southward from the town.

►► Southern Highlands   56A2

Easily accessible by train and by the Hume Highway, this is one of the great rural playgrounds of Sydneysiders. The district was opened up early in the colony's history, in the 1820s, and much of it has a pleasant air of maturity, with lush landscapes recalling those of Tasmania. Recreational facilities cater for every possible desire.

Among the towns in the area, **Bowral** is a leafy place with a number of fine old buildings along its main street. **Berrima►►** retains even more of its past; founded in the 1830s, it still has many sandstone buildings dating from that period, though the inns have dwindled in number from the original 13. The 1834 Surveyor General Inn claims to be the oldest continuously licensed premises in the country. Popular **Bundanoon►** acts as the gateway to the Morton National Park, a starting point for energetic bushwalks or casual strolls up Glow Worm Glen.

►► Tidbinbilla, ACT   off 66A1

There are two important visitor attractions at Tidbinbilla, 40km (25 miles) southwest of Canberra. The **Canberra Deep Space Communication Complex►** is a combined US/Australian deep-space tracking station; it is not open to the public, but the visitor centre has multimedia displays and model spacecraft. Back on earth, **Tidbinbilla Nature Reserve►►** is a vast tract of countryside with bushwalks and an array of Australian wildlife.

MORTON NATIONAL PARK
This high sandstone plateau into which rivers have cut deep gorges is one of the most beautiful attractions of the Southern Highlands. Waterfalls pour into the depths from high cliffs, as at Fitzroy Falls, where there is a visitor centre. Scenic highways connect the area to the coast (one of them goes via Kangaroo Valley), making an interesting round trip from Sydney possible.

87

Rugged Morton National Park is popular with Sydneysiders

The long list of Australian creatures able to cause you harm, in some cases fatal, is particularly impressive. Still, you are much more likely to come to grief at the hands of a local driver or suffer sunburn than you are to fall victim to the wildlife.

SPIDERS AND INSECTS
Spiders can reach an alarming size, and their bite can be unpleasant. Avoid the redback (or black widow), a small black spider with red patches on its back, and the larger funnel-web at all costs—tourist information centres can give further information on how to recognize them. The funnel-web, unlike most of its kind, is aggressive and rears up for the attack. It's also a Sydneysider, so be wary in Sydney gardens and parks. Insects abound in Australia, but flies, wasps, mosquitoes, ticks, ants and even scorpions are more of a nuisance than a real hazard.

Marine hazards Of the 85 species of **sharks** around the coast of Australia, a few are man-eaters. Attacks are extremely rare, and the average number of fatalities per year is just one person. The highest risk occurs in summer when the water temperature is in excess of 22°C (72°F), and during this time it might be advisable to swim only from one of the many beaches protected by systems of netting. More dangerous are **saltwater crocodiles** (salties—see page 183), and on no account should you swim (or stand close to the water's edge) in the northern areas frequented by these formidable creatures. Their numbers have also increased dramatically since they have been given the status of protected species.

Box jellyfish breed in river estuaries and infest the coastal waters of Queensland and the NT from October to May. Practically invisible, they deliver a sting that can be fatal. Stay out of the sea at this time! Some of the beautiful corals can also deliver a mild sting, as can the crown-of-thorns starfish that is attacking the Barrier Reef. Much worse, however, is the **stonefish**, which looks like a rock as its name suggests; wear shoes when walking on a reef, and avoid rockpools. There are also sea snakes, which become active at the same time as the box jellies.

Terrestrial hazards Snakes also inhabit the land, and there are some 170 species, the venomous ones outnumbering the harmless—in Tasmania, for example, *all* snakes are venomous. Rangers and bush folk are fond of detailing their degree of poisonousness in terms of the number of mice a bite could kill; this figure can get into the hundreds of thousands, and is quite enough to fell the strongest human. However, even the most lethal of snakes—like the taipan, tiger snake, death adder or brown snake—will get out of your way if it possibly can.

Steer clear of the deadly taipan

▶ Wauchope 63C5

Among the forests of the Hastings River district, Wauchope has long been a hub of the logging industry, a fact made much of in **Timbertown▶ ▶**. This ambitious re-creation of a late 19th-century pioneer settlement has a whole range of buildings (shops, houses, a church and sawmill), demonstrations of all the activities associated with logging and processing, as well as rides around the area aboard a cart or a steam train.

Kempsey▶, 25km (16 miles) north of Wauchope, is home to the world-famous Akubra hat. Akubras (believed to be an Aboriginal word for hat) are made from rabbit pelts—as imported rabbits pose a serious environmental threat, many see this as a good use for them.

▶ West Wyalong 62B3

In the harsh countryside at the junction of the Mid-Western and Newell highways, West Wyalong was NSW's busiest goldfield at the turn of the 20th century. Now the heart of an extensive wheat-growing area, it also produces and exports that quintessential Australian fluid, eucalyptus oil. However, visitors may be more interested in the model of a gold mine in the Historical Museum.

▶ White Cliffs 62C1

This old opal-mining settlement more than 1,000km (620 miles) northwest of Sydney is a place to experience life in the Australian Outback. A small, highly individual population of opal miners lives here, some of them underground, where they won't need air-conditioning—elsewhere a must because of the sometimes intolerable climate. There are plenty of opportunities to see opals in their various states, as well as one of Australia's largest solar power stations, which can be toured.

▶ Wollongong 63B4

The life of New South Wales' third largest city is based on heavy industry and there are few tourist attractions. But the nearby rugged Illawarra Coast has wonderful beaches while inland there are splendid hills and forests. Mount Keira and Mount Kembla in the **Illawarra Escarpment State Recreation Area▶** offer fantastic vistas.

Australia's famous Akubra hats are made in Kempsey, near Wauchope

WAGGA WAGGA OR WOGGA WOGGA?
More famous for its name (pronounced Wogga) than for its tourist amenities, Wagga (240km/150 miles south of West Wyalong) is a fair-sized town that has profited from its location on the Murrumbidgee River and Sydney–Melbourne railway line to become the thriving hub of NSW's Riverina district.

Victoria

Map

D Lake Victoria • Wentworth • Mildura
Murray • STURT HIGHWAY • Red Cliffs
20

Sunset Country
Hattah • Kulkyne Nat Park • Robinvale
Hattah
16
Ouyen • Manangatang

C OUYEN HIGHWAY
12
Nyah West • Swan Hill • Lake Boga
Lake Tyrrell
Wyperfeld Nat Park • Koondrook
Hopetoun • Sea Lake • Kerang • Murray • Cobram • Lake Mulwala
Lake Albacutya
79 • Loddon • Cohuna • Nathalia • Yarrawonga
Big Desert • Birchip • Pyramid Hill • Echuca • Numurkah
16
Lake Hindmarsh
Wycheproof
Warracknabeal • Charlton • Rochester • Shepparton • Wangaratta
Nhill • Dimboola • Donald • Wedderburn • Elmore • Kyabram • Benalla
WESTERN HIGHWAY • Murtoa • Inglewood • Tatura • Rushworth • Murchison
39

B Little Desert National Park • Horsham • St Arnaud • CALDER HIGHWAY • Euroa • FREEWAY
Little Desert • Wimmera • Avoca • Bendigo • Heathcote • Mansfie
Wimmera • Stawell • Maryborough • Maldon • 75 • Seymour • Alexandra • Lake Eildon
Halls Gap • Avoca • Clunes • Castlemaine • Kilmore • Eildon
Edenhope • Mt William 1167m • Ararat • Daylesford • Kyneton • Woodend • Yea • Marysville
Grampians (Gariwerd) Nat Park • Beaufort • Creswick • Kinglake NP • Healesville
Casterton • Coleraine • Dunkeld • 8 • Ballarat • 79 • Sunbury • Warburton
Glenelg • Skipton • Organ Pipes NP • MELBOURNE • Baw Baw Nat Park
Wannon • Hamilton • Lake Bolac • Bacchus Marsh • Dandenong Ranges • La Trobe
PRINCES HWY • Brisbane Ranges NP • Werribee • Dandenong • Drouin

A Lower Glenelg Nat Park • Mt Eccles Nat Park • You Yangs • Port Phillip Bay • Warragul • Mo
Discovery Bay • Heywood • Mortlake • Lake Corangamite • Geelong • Bellarine Pen • Strzeleck
Mt Richmond NP • Port Fairy • Camperdown • Queenscliff • Hastings • Korumburra • Coral Creek
Cape Bridgewater • Warrnambool • Colac • Mornington Pen • Heritage Village
Cape Nelson • London Bridge • Otway Ranges • Lorne • Cape Schanck • Phillip Island • Wonthaggi • Foster
Port Campbell • GREAT OCEAN ROAD • Inverloch
Loch Ard Gorge & 12 Apostles • Port Campbell Nat Park • Apollo Bay • Otway Nat Park • Cape Otway
Tidal Rive
B a s s   S t r a i t

NEW SOUTH
Lachlan • Murrumbidgee • Murray

SOUTH AUSTRALIA

90

1 • 2 • 3

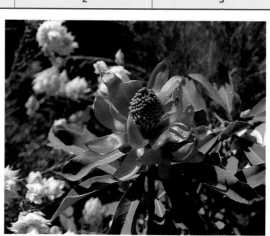

The Dandenong Ranges are famous for their profusion of native flora

VICTORIA What used to be known as the Garden State is the smallest of Australia's mainland states. However, it is comparatively densely populated and highly industrialized, with about a quarter of the country's inhabitants living on what amounts to only 3 per cent of its land surface, a substantial proportion of which is agriculturally productive. Out of the state's total of over 4.9 million people, 3.5 million live in the metropolitan area of Melbourne, whose area of more than 6,000sq km (2,300sq miles) makes it one of the largest cities in the world.

Beyond the metropolis, Victorians live in a variety of settlements, many of considerable charm and historic interest. There are delightful little ports and several well-established resorts along the 1,200km (745-mile) coastline, a multitude of places founded in the mid-19th-century rush for gold such as charming Bendigo, old river ports along the Murray, and prosperous agricultural areas quietly getting on with their own lives.

▶▶▶ **REGION HIGHLIGHTS**

Old Victorian building in Melbourne

The state's landscapes are diverse; with varied and spectacular coastal scenery, high mountains and extensive forested uplands, rich farmlands and semi-desert, Victoria has been described as a microcosm of Australia, though true Outback lies beyond its border. Agriculture takes many forms. The rolling hills of Gippsland feed dairy cattle, sheep graze on the vast pastures of the plains stretching to the west and fruit grows in profusion along the Goulburn and Murray rivers, thanks to irrigation works carried out on a huge scale at the turn of the 20th century.

For the tourist, the presence of such variety in close proximity to the state capital makes a stay particularly rewarding; few places are more than half a day's drive from Melbourne.

AS IT WAS Victoria belonged to a new phase of European colonization of the continent. The coast had been sighted from aboard the *Endeavour* in the course of Captain Cook's 1770 voyage; in 1803, Lieutenant David Collins attempted to found a settlement on the shores of Port Phillip Bay but gave up and went on to Tasmania instead. For decades, only whalers and sealers landed along the coast. Then, in 1835, one John Batman from Tasmania sailed into the bay again and signed a treaty of dubious legality with the local Aborigines that gave him title to 243,000ha (600,450 acres) of land. In spite of official attempts from Sydney to discourage settlement on the bay, Batman and others persisted; his famous phrase 'This will be the place for a village' marked the founding of Melbourne.

The new settlers wanted nothing to do with the convict system, sending any ships that arrived with prisoners on

BUCKLEY'S CHANCE

One of the members of Lieutenant Collins' party, which tried and failed to establish a settlement at Sorrento on the Mornington Peninsula in 1803, was the British-born convict William Buckley. Taking a chance, he decamped and fled around Port Phillip Bay to the Barwon area, where he lived with the local Aborigines. Decades later, in 1835, some of John Batman's associates were amazed at the emergence of 'a wild white man' at their encampment, hardly able to speak English any more. Buckley earned a pardon, a government pension and a place in the language ('Buckley's chance' means no chance at all).

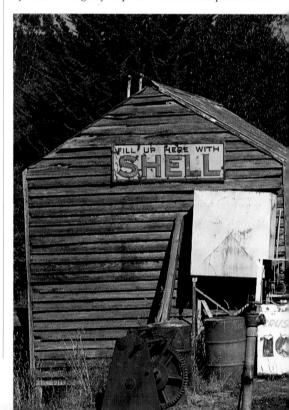

to Sydney, and petitioning for separation from New South Wales. This was granted in 1851, and the new colony was given the Queen of England's name. It was only weeks after this event that gold was found at Clunes and near Ballarat; other finds followed, the rush was on, and Melbourne and Victoria changed utterly in the process. Handsome new towns arose from the tent cities erected by the prospectors, and Melbourne boomed, fitting itself out with fine new buildings paid for by the profits made from the precious metal.

Melbourne has been eclipsed by Sydney as the financial capital of the nation; Sydney gets more migrants and has a more racially diverse character. But Melbourne is now one of the most cosmopolitan of Australia's major cities, while other places within the state retain a pleasing atmosphere of more stately and sedate times.

OUTDOOR VICTORIANS In spite of (or is it because of?) their unpredictable weather, the people of Victoria embrace the outdoors with enthusiasm, igniting the barbecue or flocking to the beaches at the slightest opportunity. The big event in the racing calendar is the Melbourne Cup, which takes place on the first Tuesday of November, when not only Victoria but the whole country comes to a stop. Australian Rules football is followed with passion by people of all ages and both sexes.

The accessibility of fine scenery brings out bushwalkers in summer, while in winter the roads to the snowfields of the Alps are crowded with the cars of skiers. Skiing began in the 1930s, when the first lift started taking people up to the plateau country beneath Mount Buffalo.

SKIING IN VICTORIA
Mount Donna Buang and Mount Baw Baw are accessible to day-trippers from Melbourne. Mount Buller, farther on in the Alps, is one of Australia's most popular winter resorts. The resort at Mount Hotham is the highest in the country, with its own airport and direct flights from Melbourne and Sydney, while Falls Creek in its sheltered bowl in the Alpine National Park has slopes suitable for every kind of skier.

Morning Star Creek, still with one foot in the past

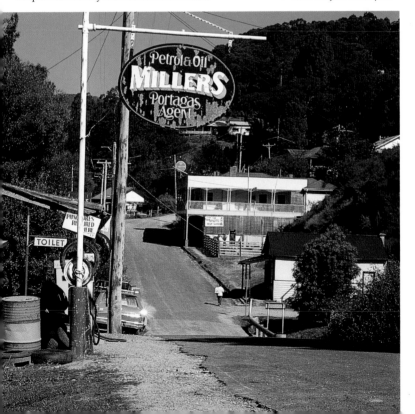

CARLTON

Imax Theatre,
Melbourne Museum

Carlt

Royal Park and
Melbourne Zoo

VICTORIA STREET

VICTORIA STREET

City Baths

Victorian
Police
Station

E

Queen Victoria
Market

Mac's
Hotel

Old
Melbourne
Gaol

Latrobe
Library

Wesley
Church

FRANKLIN STREET

State
Library

FRANKLIN ST

M

St James'
Old Cathedral

Melbourne
Central

Museum of
Chinese
Australian
History

Flagstaff
Gardens

St Francis'
Church

Chinatown

D

LATROBE STREET

Myer

Myer

David
Jones

Baptist
Church

Georges

Uni
Chu

Law
Courts

GPO

Centre
Point

The
Walk

Manchester
Unity Building

Town
Hall

Scots
Church

Royal
Arcade

City
Square

Regent
Theatre

McKillop
Street

Block
Arcade

Athenæum
Theatre

St Pau
Cathedr

St Augustine's
Roman Catholic
Church

ANZ
Bank

Victour &
Sportsgirl

C

Young &
Jackson's
Hotel

Le Meridien
at Rialto

Flinders Street
Railway Station

Melbourne
Observation Deck

Hellenic
Antiquities Museum
Immigration Museum

PROMENADE

Banana
Alley

SOUTHBANK

Melbour
Concert H

Spencer Street
Railway Station

Park

Melbourne
Aquarium

Southgate
Precinct

The
Arts Centre

B

Enterprize

Crown
Entertainment
Complex

SOUTH BANK BOULEVARD

World
Trade
Centre

Melbourne
Convention
Centre

Crown
Entertainment
Complex

POWER STREET

Yarra

Melbourne
Exhibition &
Convention
Centre

'Polly Woodside'
Melbourne Maritime
Museum

LORIMER STREET

Port Melbourne
and Williamstown

WEST GATE FREEWAY

SOUTH
MELBOURNE

A

0   200   400   600 m

0   200   400   600 yards

1   2   3

Completed in 1899, Flinders Street Station is a popular meeting place

GOOD FOR A LAUGH
The most popular of the city's many festivals, the hilarious Melbourne International Comedy Festival takes place in March and April each year. Along with similar festivals in Edinburgh and Montréal, this is one of the world's largest such events.

BATMAN'S BARGAIN
In exchange for 243,000ha (600,450 acres) of Aboriginal land, John Batman delivered 40 blankets, 30 tomahawks, 100 knives, 50 pairs of scissors, 30 mirrors, 200 handkerchiefs, 100 pounds of flour and 6 shirts. The understanding that a similar quantity of useful items would be handed over annually was soon consigned to oblivion.

Outside the 1856 Parliament House

Melbourne

Australia's second great metropolitan city sprawls around the head of Port Phillip Bay at the outlet of the muddy Yarra River. Hardly a generation ago, Melbourne was almost a synonym for dull respectability of a peculiarly British manner, but since the 1960s, the city and its population have undergone a startling transformation. Much of the city has been redeveloped with glittering office towers, to which the remaining treasures of 19th-century architecture act as a wonderful foil. Massive immigration, from southern Europe and Asia, has enlivened the city's social scene. In addition to countless galleries, museums, theatres and movie houses, the city now has a thriving nightlife of bars and discos, cabaret and comedians, jazz, rock and a casino. Melbourne offers a multitude of different types of cuisine, from 'Mod Oz' to Vietnamese. The shopping is a treat, too.

THE EARLY YEARS Once John Batman's illegal treaty of 1835, by which he acquired 243,000ha (600,450 acres) of land, had been accepted as a *fait accompli* by the authorities in Sydney, his 'village' above the Yarra soon became a city, laid out on the usual grid pattern by an army surveyor. Within a few years, the wealthy were buying estates to the southeast of the river where they could set themselves up as country gentlemen and build elegant houses. Due to gold and land speculation, Melbourne boomed for most of the second half of the 19th century, leading a roistering kind of life that was then characterized as 'American' in contrast to Sydney's staid 'Britishness'. A great slump in the 1890s ended the era of 'Marvellous Melbourne', and the city entered the long period of middle-aged respectability from which its recent renaissance has so triumphantly rescued it.

ATTRACTIONS TODAY Melbourne is a wonderfully green metropolis with an abundance of parks and trees, but it is also renowned for its dining, shopping and excellent 19th-century architecture. The best view of the city—and probably one of the finest panoramas in Australia—is from the south bank of the Yarra, particularly from Alexandra Gardens or the Southgate Precinct.

The Suburbs

The city's inner suburbs have a strong and varied identity that makes them well worth exploring.

Carlton, just north of the city, is home to Italian restaurants, the University of Melbourne and the huge 1870s Royal Exhibition Building. The adjacent Carlton Gardens area includes an **IMAX theatre** and the **Melbourne Museum**, which opened in 2000 (see page 100).

Once regarded as 'rough', **Fitzroy** has now turned Bohemian, its original inhabitants supplemented by students and artists. Brunswick Street is a fascinating mixture of cheap restaurants and alternative bookstores.

East Melbourne is a charming enclave of carefully restored terraced houses within walking distance of the city via Fitzroy Gardens.

The suburb of **St. Kilda** became Melbourne's seaside in the 1880s, when the pier and the substantial villas of the rich were built. These days, St. Kilda is vibrant, and Acland and Fitzroy streets are hard to beat as restaurant strips. The beach that stretches from here to Port Melbourne is still popular, and the bay has been cleaned up in recent years. On Sundays, St. Kilda hosts a big arts and crafts market.

South Melbourne has one of the most attractive of all inner city residential areas; in St. Vincent's Place Square, fine houses in a variety of styles were laid out around central gardens from the 1860s onward.

One of the wealthiest inner suburbs east along the Yarra, **Toorak** is synonymous with trendiness, and nearby South Yarra, where you'll find the historic **Como House**, is famous for its restaurants, shopping and nightlife.

Beyond the Yarra to the west, historic **Williamstown** has a superb view of the city across the water. A stroll along the Strand is well worthwhile, and railway buffs enjoy the Railway Museum. On the way here, at Spotswood on the western side of the Westgate Bridge, is the highly entertaining **Scienceworks**, an annexe of the Melbourne Museum. It has a planetarium and an amazing array of interactive exhibits on the theme of science and technology in the past, present and future.

Melbourne is the only Australian city with an extensive system of tramways

MELBOURNE'S TRAMS
One of the city's emblems, the network of mostly green and yellow trams covers much of the Melbourne metropolitan area. The older trams are classified by the National Trust, while a newer line speeds commuters and workers between the city and Port Melbourne. You can make good use of the free City Circle Tram service, and can even dine aboard a vintage model; the Colonial Tramcar Restaurant.

DOCKLANDS
Immediately west of the city, the vast Docklands development is transforming a former industrial area into a new suburb. When completed it will house waterfront restaurants, shops and entertainment precincts, as well as residential accommodation and office blocks.

Victoria

COLLINS STREET
This has always been the best address in town, ever since professional men set up here in the late 1840s. The upper, eastern end of the street, tree-planted and close to parklands and government buildings, was more salubrious than the western end, down by the railway tracks of Spencer Street Station. Not quite all the buildings from the era of 'Marvellous Melbourne' have been replaced by developments like twin-towered Collins Place (No. 45) or the harsh precast concrete panels of Nauru House (No. 80); the Melbourne Club, most exclusive of such institutions, still stands (No. 36), as do a number of dignified banks, office buildings, churches and theatres.

98

The gateway to Chinatown

▶▶ ANZ (Australia and New Zealand) Bank　　94C2

380 Collins Street (tel: 03-9558 8522)
Open: Museum Mon–Fri 9.30–4. Admission free
One of the finest examples of Gothic revival architecture in the country, this building is more Venetian than the Doge's Palace in Venice, with a magnificently elaborate interior whose blue, cream and pale green decoration is enhanced by lavish use of gold leaf.

Downstairs, the **ANZ Banking Museum▶** has exhibitions on the history of Australian banking.

▶ Chinatown　　94D3

Melbourne's Chinatown, around Little Bourke Street, has existed ever since Chinese prospectors joined the rush to the goldfields in the 1850s. It expanded later in the 19th century as the goldfields contracted and miners drifted back to the big city. Today it still flourishes as a haven for the Chinese community and for diners in search of cheap and excellent food and groceries, and has been fitted out with the usual archways that boldly proclaim its identity.

An interesting addition to the area is the **Museum of Chinese Australian History▶▶** in an old warehouse in Cohen Place, just off Little Bourke Street. Its displays bring alive the considerable Chinese contribution to Australian history. Star exhibits include a life-size replica of a warrior-general of the 2nd century BC and Dai Loong, the 100m (328-ft), 100-legged dragon that emerges for the Chinese New Year parade. Guided heritage walks of the Chinatown area depart from the museum.

▶▶ Como House　　*off 95A6*

Corner Williams Road and Lechlade Avenue, South Yarra (tel: 03-9827 2500). Open: daily 10–5. Admission: moderate
Begun in 1847, this delicious white mansion crowning the rise in the middle of its richly landscaped gardens is a wonderful example of the gracious buildings of

Melbourne's pre-boom period. Behind the mansion's well proportioned façade are a series of furnished rooms evoking the comfortable and very sociable life lived here in the 19th century; the adjacent outbuildings contain the original laundry. Como's unselfconscious elegance was not imitated by the nouveau-riche owners of the next generation of villas to be built in the suburb of Toorak. Most of these pompous residences have not survived, but Como, thankfully, passed into the hands of the National Trust.

▶▶ Fitzroy Gardens   95E5

Just to the east of the city, and a popular place for lunchtime sandwiches and assignations, are the sweeping lawns and splendid trees of these 19th-century gardens, complementing the spires of St. Patrick's Cathedral in the background. Towards the southern end of the park is **Cooks' Cottage▶▶**. A modest stone building of the mid-18th century with a characteristic Yorkshire pantiled roof, this was the home of the great navigator's parents. It was dismantled and brought here in 1934 to mark the centenary of the founding of Melbourne. It is open to the public.

▶▶ Kings Domain   95B5

A splendid tract of parkland sweeps southeast along the Yarra from the city to the Kings Domain and the Royal Botanic Gardens (see page 103). Alexandra Gardens has a fine riverside view of the city. Altogether more functional is the **Sidney Myer Music Bowl**, whose soaring canopy shelters all kinds of open-air musical events. Crowning the higher ground is the great white **Government House**, the fourth to be built on this site (see panel). In contrast to this magnificence is the very first Government House, **La Trobe's Cottage**, a prefabricated, two-floored cottage brought from England.

▶▶ Melbourne Aquarium   94B2

Corner Queenswharf Road and King Street (tel: 03-9620 0999)
Open: Jan, daily 9.30–9; Feb–Dec 9.30–6. Admission: expensive
The Melbourne Aquarium is appropriately set on the north bank of the Yarra. Highlights include the Coral Atoll, an enormous tank containing a floor-to-ceiling coral reef, and the spectacular Deep Sea Oceanarium. The latter is home to sea creatures of many kinds—including turtles, rays and sharks—which are hand fed by divers throughout the day. Visitors can also take a thrilling simulated 'deep-sea shark dive' ride.

▶ Melbourne Cricket Ground (MCG)   95C6

Yarra Park, Jolimont (tel: 03-9657 8864 for tours)
Open: daily 9.30–4.30, regular tours from 10–3 on non-event days. Admission: museums moderate, tour/museums expensive
To the southeast of the city are sports grounds of all kinds, many of them laid out for the 1956 Olympics. The central site for the games was the great MCG—a vast stadium with a capacity up to 100,000, just as much associated with football ('Aussie Rules') as with cricket. Here, too, are the Australian Cricket Hall of Fame, Australian Gallery of Sport and Olympic Museum, recalling the triumphs and disappointments of the modern games since their revival in 1896. A guided tour of this large complex is a very worthwhile experience.

GOVERNMENT HOUSE
Built by government architect William Wardell in the 1870s, the present Government House was based on Queen Victoria's Osborne House on England's Isle of Wight. That monarch is supposed to have been rather miffed that Government House's ballroom was twice as big as the one in Buckingham Palace.

FEDERATION SQUARE
Melbourne's most controversial architecture can be found at the Federation Square precinct, opposite Flinders Street Station. The futuristic buildings here house the Ian Potter Centre (a branch of the National Gallery of Victoria; see page 100) and the Australian Centre for the Moving Image, as well as the Melbourne Visitor Centre, bars, restaurants and shops.

One of the world's greatest stadiums, the Melbourne Cricket Ground at Jolimont creates an incredible atmosphere

Victoria

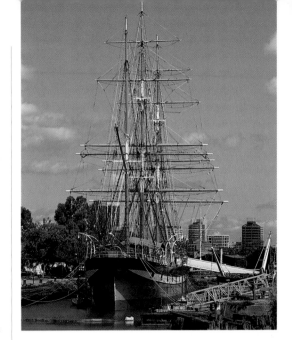

100

The carefully restored barque Polly Woodside *at the Maritime Museum*

The National Gallery of Victoria is also the site for international touring exhibitions

▶▶▶ **Melbourne Museum**   *off 94E3*
Carlton Gardens, Rathdowne Street, Carlton (tel: 13 1102)
Open: daily 10–5. Admission: moderate
This ultramodern establishment is Australia's largest museum. The vast building contains several themed galleries—the Australia Gallery has icons such as the famous 1930s racehorse, Phar Lap; Australian fauna is presented imaginatively in the Science and Life Gallery; and the Aboriginal section—Bunjilaka—is particularly good. The complex also includes an IMAX theatre, a digital interactive cinema and the Children's Museum.

▶▶ **Melbourne Observation Deck**   94C2
525 Collins Street (tel: 03-9629 8222). Open: daily 10AM–9PM. Admission: moderate
From this viewing area on the 55th floor of Melbourne's highest building the views of the city, Port Phillip Bay and many of the city's outlying regions are stupendous.

▶▶ **Melbourne Zoo**   *off 94E2*
Elliott Avenue, Parkville (tel: 03-9285 9300)
Open: daily 9–5. Admission: expensive
This vast zoo, with its progressive approach, is in Royal Park, the city's largest tract of open space. Visitors move easily through large enclosures that simulate the native habitat of the creatures within, including an African rain forest, an elephant village and a butterfly house. A wide range of Australian fauna is also on show.

▶▶▶ **National Gallery of Victoria**   94B3/94C3
Ian Potter Centre, Federation Square (tel: 03-8662 1553)
Open: Mon–Thu 10–5, Fri 10–9, Sat–Sun 10–6. Admission free (charge for special exhibitions)
NGV International, 180 St. Kilda Road (tel: 03-8620 2222)
Open: daily 10–5. Admission free (charge for special exhibitions)

Victoria's premier art gallery owns some of the finest artwork in Australia. The extensive collection of Australian art, in the new **Ian Potter Centre: NGV Australia**, Federation Square, includes Aboriginal, Colonial and contemporary works in 20 galleries on four levels

The international collection is in the original but redeveloped and expanded premises at St. Kilda Road, now known as the **NGV International**. Exhibits here range from European Old Masters to photography, and Asian and pre-Columbian to contemporary art.

▶▶ Old Melbourne Gaol   94E3

Russell Street (tel: 03-9663 7228)
Open: daily 9.30–5. Admission: moderate
Of all the countless jails that are such a feature of Australian townscapes, this grim bluestone building with its chilling interior seems to sum up the harshness of 19th-century concepts of justice and punishment. Here you can see the death mask of Ned Kelly, made in 1880. The most notorious and defiant of Australia's bushrangers looks peaceful enough, his wayward spirit expressed perhaps more strongly by the homemade suit of armour that is displayed alongside.

▶ Parliament House   95E4

Spring Street (tel: 03-9651 8568). Open: Mon–Fri, tours depart from 10–3.45 when Parliament is not sitting. Admission free
Begun in 1856, this great neo-Grecian building was planned on such an ambitious scale that it has never been completed. The state government was moved from its home here in 1901 to make way for the newly established Federal Parliament, which sat in Melbourne until finally persuaded to make the move to Canberra in 1927.

There are guided tours of the splendid interior when parliament is not in session; the Legislative Council Chamber was described by poet and connoisseur of Victorian architecture John Betjeman (1906–84), as 'the best Corinthian room in the world'.

▶ Polly Woodside Melbourne Maritime Museum   94A1

Lorimer Street East, Southbank (tel: 03-9699 9760)
Open: daily 10–4. Closed Good Friday, 25 Dec. Admission: moderate
Built in Belfast, Northern Ireland in 1885, the sailing barque *Polly Woodside* ended her working days as a rusty, dilapidated coal hulk in the Port of Melbourne. Fortunately she was immaculately restored and is now moored in an old dock basin at Southbank, as the proud focus of this maritime museum, whose numerous exhibits evoke the age of sail.

▶▶ Queen Victoria Market   94E1

Corner of Queen and Therry streets (tel: 03-9320 5822)
Open: Tue and Thu 6–2, Fri 6–6, Sat 6–3, Sun 9–4. Closed 1st Tue in Nov. Admission free
Melbourne's sole surviving 19th-century market, exuberantly multicultural, is an exciting place to shop or just wander. Trading has been carried on here since 1859, and more than a thousand stalls sell everything imaginable at affordable prices.

DREAM ON ELM STREET
Some of the prestige of the top end of Collins Street in early days was due to the fact that it was one of the few places to have any street trees. Early photographs of Melbourne show the young city, once the bush had been cleared to build it, was a virtually treeless town. Today the city enjoys the benefit of the countless trees, now fully mature, that were planted towards the end of the 19th century. Scorning the rich array of native trees, city fathers planted to remind themselves of 'home', and as a result, streets and parks are graced with wonderful specimens of oaks, elms and poplars.

101

The Botanic Gardens: a fine example of 19th-century English landscaping

Early European Australia was not distinguished by its architecture. No architect sailed with the First Fleet, and the very first structures were primitive affairs of sticks, mud, thatch, bark or any materials that came quickly and easily to hand. Some prefabricated structures were shipped out from England and reassembled on site, sometimes by guesswork.

The first proper edifice in Sydney was Government House, a two-floor brick dwelling that amazed the Aborigines when they found people walking around above their heads. A sense of restraint and emphasis on good proportion contributed towards simple but effective structures like Elizabeth Farm at Parramatta, built in 1793. Its veranda, destined to become a persistent motif in Australian building, was derived from British practice in India. But architecture capable of making some kind of civic statement had to await the rule of Governor Macquarie and his forger-turned-architect, Francis Greenway. Thanks to buildings like **Hyde Park Barracks** and **St. James' Church**, Sydney began to take on the airs of a real city for the first time.

The development of the terrace Gold was the making of Melbourne, and of many architects, too. Melbourne is still one of the world's great 19th-century cities in terms of building, with grand self-confident edifices in a variety of revived styles—Gothic for churches, Romanesque and Venetian for offices and banks, and Classical for public buildings. This was the period when terraced houses reached a high point of development, their elegance and cast-iron decoration helping to make the inner suburbs of both Melbourne and Sydney some of the most liveable of their kind in the world.

An Aussie style The terraced house was replaced after the turn of the 20th century by the detached villa, built for a decade or so in a wealth of varied forms and with features like terracotta kangaroos on the roof line and eucalyptus leaves in the barge boards.

The 20th-century suburbs are undistinguished. The interwar California bungalow has given way to brick veneer dwellings and bizarre neo-Grecian palaces. Similarly, the redeveloped cities do not seem to have embraced Australian style either.

AUSTRALIA'S OWN
What has been described as the most original local contribution to Australian architecture is the tropical house of Queensland. Raised above ground for ventilation, it is liberally provided with verandas and with a roof of corrugated iron—handsome, cheap and durable.

Right: Renovated Victorian building in downtown Melbourne

▶▶ Rippon Lea Estate off 95A4

192 Hotham Street, Elsternwick (tel: 03-9523 6095)
Open: daily 10–5. Admission: moderate
Begun in 1868 by the London-born Frederick Thomas Sargood, this two-tone brick house is perhaps the most splendid surviving late-Victorian mansion in Melbourne's suburbs. The gardens are both opulent and extensive.

▶▶▶ Royal Botanic Gardens Melbourne 95A6

Birdwood Avenue, South Yarra (tel: 03-9252 2300)
Open: Nov–Mar daily, 7.30–8.30; Apr–Oct 7.30–5.30. Guided walks Sun–Fri 11, 2. Admission free, walks inexpensive
These superb, lush and beautifully landscaped gardens rank among the finest in the world. The site was chosen as early as 1845, and the gardens were laid out and stocked with an incredible range of plants by successive directors. Ferdinand von Mueller (director, 1852–73) preferred a formal layout, while his successor, William Guilfoyle, re-designed the gardens in a more romantic, English style with sweeping lawns, informal lakes and curving paths.

Plants from all over the world thrive in Melbourne's climate. There are more than 6,000 tree species, ranging from cool temperate regions through to subtropical areas. English elms and oaks contrast with grass trees and river red gums. The Australian Lawn is planted with eucalypts from all over the country, and there is also the Australian Rainforest Walk, a rose garden, herb and succulent gardens and a fern gully. There are a number of buildings in the garden, which complement the plantings, including the classical Temple of the Winds and the restored Old Melbourne Observatory. A good way to familiarize yourself with these wonderful gardens is to take one of the guided walks from the modern visitor centre.

▶ St. Patrick's Cathedral 95E4

Cathedral Place, East Melbourne
Less hemmed in by modern buildings than the Anglican Cathedral (see page 104), the 103m (338-ft) central spire of this great Roman Catholic cathedral (see panel) features in many city views. It was designed by William Wardell, who also built the ANZ Bank.

One of the inhabitants of the highly acclaimed Melbourne Zoo (page 100)

THE SEPARATION TREE
This is the name given to one of the fine river red gums in the Royal Botanic Gardens, since it was beneath its branches that the grand public celebration took place in 1851 to mark the independence of Victoria from New South Wales.

INSIDE ST. PATRICK'S
St. Patrick's has a splendidly soaring interior, with magnificent stained-glass windows. Long regarded as an Irish stronghold, it also has a statue of Daniel O'Connell—the great 19th-century Irish patriot known as 'the Liberator'—in the churchyard.

On guard at the impressive Shrine of Remembrance

ARTS TOUR
The Arts Centre complex is adorned inside and out with numerous works of art, many of them specially commissioned. The Centre's guided tours are an excellent way of getting to grips with them all.

MELBOURNE'S MIGRANTS
Melbourne's fascinating Immigration Museum is well worth a visit. Housed in the beautifully renovated 1876 Old Customs House at 400 Flinders Street, the exhibits portray the departures, arrivals and impacts of Victoria's settlers during the last two centuries. Particularly interesting are the personal and often very moving stories of refugees and other migrants from many cultural backgrounds.

▶ **St. Paul's Cathedral**   94C3
Corner of Swanston and Flinders streets
No longer the dominant element in the cityscape, this fine Gothic Revival-style church still has a commanding presence. Standing on the site where the first official church service in Melbourne took place in 1836, the cathedral was built between 1880–1891 to a design by the British architect William Butterfield, also responsible for the Chapter House and Diocesan Offices in the cathedral complex.

▶▶ **Shrine of Remembrance**   95A5
St. Kilda Road (tel: 03-9654 8415)
Open: daily 10–5. Admission: donation
Based on the Parthenon, this shrine to the Victorian war dead sits massively on top of a rise in the ground in Kings Domain. It was completed in 1934 in memory of the 114,000 Victorians who served in World War I, of whom 19,000 died. The Stone of Remembrance in the central chamber is illuminated by a shaft of light at 11AM every 11 November. Below is the crypt, displaying regimental flags, and above is a gallery with fine views over the city and environs. The grounds have been laid out to commemorate those who fell in other wars.

▶▶▶ **The Arts Centre**   94B3
100 St. Kilda Road (tel: 03-9281 8000). Open: daily, tours Mon–Sat noon, 2.30, Sun 12.15 (backstage tour). Admission: Museum free, tours moderate Mon–Sat, expensive Sun
Not a cultural ghetto, but a vibrant part of city life, the modern arts centre, completed in 1984, comprises a complex of exciting buildings on the south bank of the Yarra.
  Next to the National Gallery is the **Theatres** building, topped by a 115m (377-ft) high spire, one of Melbourne's cultural landmarks. The three theatres themselves are below ground: the State Theatre is the home of the Australian Ballet; the Melbourne Theatre Company performs in the Playhouse; and the third is a highly adaptable studio space. The spectacular interior of the **Concert Hall** is done in mineral shades that reflect the geology of the Australian continent. The centre also embraces two restaurants, the Arts Centre shop, a Sunday market, the entertaining Performing Arts Museum and, in Kings Domain, the Sidney Myer Music Bowl.

Walk

Melbourne's city streets

See map on pages 94–95.

From the traditional meeting place of Melburnians—'under the clocks' at Flinders Street station—to grandiose Parliament House, this walk (about 2km/1.2 miles) covers civic and commercial aspects of Melbourne.

The station steps open on to the bustling heart of the city. Across the road is the new **Federation Square** development, where you'll find the Ian Potter Centre (see page 101), then Swanson Street and the Gothic grandeur of **St. Paul's Cathedral**. Modern City Square marks the junction with Collins Street, dominated by the splendid Town Hall. Commercial dynamism has taken many shapes along this prestigious artery, from American deco of the 1930s to Victorian Gothic.

In Queen Street, the elaborate Safe Deposit Building (No. 90) is dwarfed by the soaring **ANZ Tower**. Trams and shoppers throng Bourke Street Mall, off which runs the city's oldest shopping gallery, Royal Arcade. Traditional archways signal the entry to Chinatown. The grid of city streets ends where Little Bourke Street emerges into Spring Street, overlooked by the imposing colonnade of Victoria's **Parliament House**, and the Windsor Hotel of 1883. Nearby stands the **Old Treasury Building**, completed in 1862, which contains the Gold Treasury Museum, dealing with Melbourne's history, architecture and comtemporary life.

Return to Flinders Street station via the eastern end of Collins Street.

Walk

Along the Yarra

See map on pages 94–95.

A 5km (3-mile) walk along Melbourne's River Yarra into Kings Domain and the Botanic Gardens.

Downstream from Princes Bridge, the Yarra is crossed by a footbridge. Avoiding the tempting riverside cafés of the Southgate Precinct, you are rewarded with a stunning view of the city skyline from Southbank Promenade on the far side of Princes Bridge.

Negotiate the crossing of Alexandra Avenue with care and enjoy the calm of **Kings Domain**, with its various focal points like the Sidney Myer Music Bowl and the Pioneer Women's Memorial Garden. The far bank of the lake in the **Royal Botanic Gardens** marks the outermost point of the walk, excuse enough for a pause at the lakeside café.

Beyond the Herbarium and Visitor Centre is the **Shrine of Remembrance**, whose outside gallery gives a wonderful vista back towards the centre of Melbourne.

The return to Flinders Street station can be made on foot or by tram along St. Kilda Road.

At leisure on the Yarra River

Victoria

THE BIRDS OF WYPERFELD
Much of this national park is alive with great flocks of birds: white and pink cockatoos, galahs and regent parrots. The most curious bird, though, is the mallee-fowl, builder of underground nests in which its young are hatched in meticulously controlled incubation conditions.

PEAKS AND BEACHES
Although Victoria cannot lay claim to any of Australia's World Heritage regions, this small state encompasses an extraordinary variety of national parks and wilderness areas. Apart from the alpine regions, Victoria's most popular park is probably the superb coastal region of Wilsons Promontory (see page 121).

At Point Nepean on the Mornington Peninsula—the entrance to Port Phillip Bay

National parks

From high alps to rolling downlands, from luxuriant rain forests to desert scrub, and from the spreading floodplains of the Murray River in the north to some of the country's most dramatic coastline in the south, Victoria's landscape is as varied as its climate. A high rainfall over much of the state contributes to the luxuriance of the forest cover as well as to the productivity of grasslands and other farmed areas; by contrast, the far northwest is extremely arid.

Victorian Alps The dominating physical feature of the state is its mountain backbone, a southern stretch of Australia's Great Dividing Range. Majestic alpine summits rise to almost 2,000m (6,560ft), while foothills and lower ranges stretch southward and westward to form a hilly backdrop to the metropolitan area of Melbourne. Many of the highest and most spectacular parts of the Victorian Alps are protected as national parks; they include **Mount Buffalo** (1,720m/5,643ft), whose characteristic hump-backed shape was first seen by the explorers Hume and Hovell in 1824. Beneath the summit, stretches a vast upland plateau bounded by cliffs falling abruptly to the plains below. Used for skiing in winter, the plateau is embroidered with wildflowers in spring.

The vegetation cover varies with altitude, the dense wet forest of the valleys becoming more open farther up the slope, with peppermint gums giving way to alpine ash and finally to snow gums. In the early days of white settlement, cattlemen drove their beasts high into the uplands to feed off the summer pastures, building stone huts for shelter. Many of the huts remain, but grazing has been forbidden because of erosion. A number of physically separate national parks—Bogong, Cobberas-Tingaringy and Wonnangatta-Moroka parks—have since been grouped together to form the exhilarating **Alpine National Park**, Victoria's largest at 646,000ha (1,596,000 acres).

Southeastern Victoria Along the border with New South Wales lies some of the most unspoiled scenery in the state. Inland are a number of national parks. **Errinundra National Park** encompasses a large tract of cool, temperate woodland, and there are other pockets of rain forest at **Lind** and **Alfred national parks**. The splendid gorges along the course of the **Snowy River** offer exciting whitewater canoeing; this park is also the habitat of the rare brushtailed rock wallaby. Running from Sydenham Inlet to the NSW boundary is one of the country's finest coastal reserves, the **Croajingolong National Park**, with savage cliffs and headlands protecting pristine beaches and tranquil inlets. In complete contrast is **The Lakes National Park** to the west, where the seemingly infinite Ninety Mile Beach is backed by lagoons and waterways.

As well as the Dandenongs (see page 114), day-trips from Melbourne can take in Point Nepean at the tip of **Mornington Peninsula National Park**, the **Brisbane Ranges**, the forests and fern gullies of **Kinglake National Park** to the northeast and the basalt columns of **Organ Pipes National Park** to the northwest. The **Grampians (Gariwerd) National Park** in the west is one of Victoria's highlights. With its Aboriginal sites, stunning scenery and abundant wildlife—more than 900 wildflower species, 40 species of native mammals and 200 species of birds—the reserve is reachable in a day, but merits a longer stay.

Victoria's southwestern coastline The best can be seen in two contrasting parks: Between Lorne and Cape Otway, the high ranges of the **Otway National Park**, still covered in glorious rain forest, rise steeply from the sea; farther west, the breakers are constantly resculpting the cliffs of the **Port Campbell National Park**, creating some truly spectacular coastal scenery. Inland, at **Mount Eccles**, volcanic activity has given rise to fertile farmland interspersed with crater lakes and worn-down volcanic cones. Far from the coast and wooded uplands is **Wyperfeld National Park**, a complex system of normally dry lakes and lagoons, with mallee (see panel) stretching to the horizon.

The basalt columns of the aptly named Organ Pipes National Park

107

MASTERING THE MALLEE
Much of northwestern Victoria was once covered in mallee, 'a blue and level sea stretching to the horizon'. Mallee is an Aboriginal word describing the fire-resistant scrub composed of 20 or so species of low-growing eucalyptus. The mallee burns fiercely, but quickly regenerates from the surviving roots, making it difficult for farmers to clear. Its demise came about with the invention of mullenization; a heavy roller was dragged through the scrub by oxen, followed by an ingenious 'stump-jump' plough. Years of burning and cropping finally eradicated the troublesome mallee, except in areas like Wyperfeld, itself threatened with clearance as late as the 1960s.

Getting around Melbourne is easy using the city's trams

THE GREAT OCEAN ROAD
One of Australia's most famous drives, the Great Ocean Road stretches 300km (186 miles) from south of Geelong towards the South Australian border, and takes in beaches, charming ports and villages, forested hillsides and, around the town of Port Campbell, dramatically eroded coastline (see page 119).

THE UNPREDICTABLE STATE
The weather in Victoria can be very changeable; desert influences may be felt one moment, with searing dry winds and high temperatures, giving way suddenly to cold and wet air from the ocean to the south. If you don't like our weather, say Melburnians, just wait a minute—it's bound to change!

How to travel

By air Melbourne Airport is 22km (13.5 miles) northwest of the city and is connected to many overseas destinations as well as to all major cities in Australia. Domestic and international flights share the same terminal. Frequent Skybus services link the airport to Spencer Street station downtown, from where a shuttle transports passengers to the city's hotels.

By bus Express buses travel to major destinations in Australia and within Victoria. Because of the (relatively!) small size of the state, public transport is a reasonable proposition for most journeys. Many places in Victoria are accessible in a day's outing from Melbourne. There is the usual excellent range of organized bus tours; shop around for the one that suits your requirements.

By train Greater Melbourne's comprehensive public transportation network is marketed under the name of **The Met**. Electric suburban railways that travel as far afield as the Dandenong Ranges and Mornington Peninsula are supplemented by systems of tramways and by urban buses. Through-ticketing is based on a zoning system, and there are a number of special deals like day tickets or weekly passes that are worth considering. The principal station is Flinders Street, and most trains travel around the underground loop that circles the city, with useful stops at Spencer Street, Flagstaff Gardens, Melbourne Central and Parliament. There is also a free City Circle Tram, which runs every ten minutes.

Quite a number of towns in Victoria can be reached by **V-Line train** (sometimes supplemented by a V-Line bus). There are interstate services to Adelaide and Sydney as well as to Perth (changing at Adelaide or Port Pirie), and Alice Springs and Darwin on the famous *Ghan* (see pages 134 and 189).

By car Road conditions in Victoria are generally good. Melbourne has an excellent freeway system and the traffic flows much more freely than in Sydney. To visit the more inaccessible national parks renting a car is recommended.

▶▶ Apollo Bay 90A2

This little fishing port about 185km (115 miles) to the west of Port Phillip Bay has magnificent beaches and makes an excellent base for exploring the superb forests of the **Otway Ranges▶▶**. The hills reach the sea at Cape Otway, the 'fearful coastline' described by the explorer Matthew Flinders, with a lighthouse rising from high cliffs.

▶ Ararat 90B2

This town (200km/125 miles northwest of Melbourne) owes its foundation to the gold strike of 1857, when 85,000g (3,000 ounces) of alluvial gold were found in the space of three weeks. Then Ararat's population was more than double its present total; now sheep outnumber people by about 150 to one. To the north is the world-famous **Seppelt Great Western Winery▶**, where the sparkling wine is stored in underground galleries originally dug out by the gold miners.

▶ Avoca 90B2

On the Pyrenees Highway between Ararat and Castlemaine, Avoca was once a gold town and is now the hub of an agricultural area. Since the 1960s, vineyards have been replanted on the north-facing slopes of the foothills, making this one of the state's newer wine districts. The solid Court House complex with bluestone jail, powder magazine and police residence dates from the mid-19th century.

▶▶▶ Ballarat 90B2

No bigger since its gold-rush heyday, Ballarat has preserved much of its 19th-century townscape and the atmosphere of those heady times. Gold was first found in 1851, and within a few months thousands of ill-assorted diggers were frantically prospecting in spite of mud, cold and frequent bitter disappointment. Surface deposits were soon exhausted, and individual miners were succeeded by companies with sufficient clout to dig deep mines and buy the machinery to run them. Gold may have made Melbourne, but it made Ballarat too; profits were not gambled or drunk away, but invested in bricks and mortar, giving the town as splendid an array of fine 19th-century building as can be seen anywhere in the country. Banks, churches, a synagogue, clubs, a mining exchange, a splendid town hall and an art gallery all demonstrate how quickly the raw life of the diggings was transmuted into civic respectability.

BALLARAT'S BOTANICS
By the side of beautiful Lake Wendouree, the Botanic Gardens in Ballarat are a perfect example of High Victorian taste, with white marble statuary among the pretty pavilions and bedding plants. On plinths beneath the trees stand the busts of former prime ministers, some, like notorious protagonists Gough Whitlam and Malcolm Fraser, none too comfortable at seeing each other in such close proximity again.

The gold-rush town of Ballarat contains many grand buildings that date from the 19th century

*A statue of Queen
Victoria presides over
formal gardens in
Bendigo*

Sovereign Hill▶▶▶ is a superb re-creation of life and work on the goldfields in the 1850s. Visitors can pan for gold, ride Cobb & Co.'s stagecoach, shop in the emporiums of Main Street, enjoy the unique world of the Chinese Village or even spend the night in 1850s-style accommodation at the Sovereign Hill Lodge. Other highlights include the Quartz Mine, with 600m (1,970ft) of underground workings, and the Gold Museum, which has displays showing the history of the precious metal.

▶▶ Beechworth   91B4
This exceptionally well-preserved gold town in the foothills of the Australian Alps, 268km (167 miles) northeast of Melbourne, has a fine array of old buildings, many of warm, honey-tinged stone. Over 30 of these structures are National Trust-listed and, outside town, **Beechworth Historic Park**▶ preserves a collection of significant gold-mining sites. As well as the post office, with its imposing tower, there is also the **Burke Museum**▶▶. Named after the ill-fated explorer, the museum is packed with memorabilia, including mementoes of Ned Kelly who spent a night in the cell beneath the town hall.

▶▶ Bellarine Peninsula   90A3
Stretching eastward into Port Phillip Bay, this broad peninsula, with its fine surf beaches and popular resorts like Ocean Grove and Barwon Heads, has become a popular summer desination with the inhabitants of Geelong. One of the peninsula's greatest attractions is the charming resort town of Queenscliff (see page 119), known for its fort, lighthouse and grand old hotels.

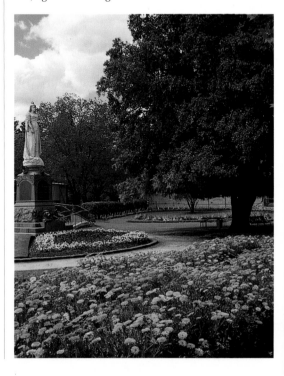

▶▶ Bendigo 90B2

Like Ballarat, Bendigo began as a gold-rush town, expanding rapidly from 1851 onwards to become one of the state's largest inland towns. Many of its fine late 19th-century buildings, erected with the wealth won from the ground, remain in peak condition. These include the vast Shamrock Hotel, a number of imposing churches and a fine group of public buildings. The work that paid for all this architectural glory is celebrated in the completely preserved **Central Deborah Goldmine▶▶**, with its impressive underground galleries, while the special contribution of Chinese miners is recalled in the delightful **Joss House▶▶** at Emu Point. The best way to get acquainted with this fascinating town is to take the 'Talking Tram', which runs along an 8km (5-mile) route and gives a full commentary on all the sights.

▶ Brisbane Ranges National Park 90A2

This extensive block of slate and sandstone has been eroded in places to form deep defiles like Anakie Gorge, a popular spot for not-too-demanding bush walks. Gold was once mined in quantity at the ghost town of Steiglitz, now a historic park.

▶ Camperdown 90A2

This township is on the sweeping plains formed from lava and ash that ran from the South Australian border to Port Phillip Bay and have long been the basis of a prosperous grazing industry. Now silent, the volcanic cones responsible for all this fertility are scattered over the area. Mount Leura and Mount Sugarloaf are to the southeast of town, while to the west there are two examples of crater lakes—Lake Bullen Merri (brackish water) and Lake Gnotuk (salt water).

▶▶ Castlemaine 90B2

Once gold had been discovered here in Specimen Gully by a shepherd, 25,000 diggers joined the rush, although Castlemaine declined fairly quickly because of the lack of reef gold. Today it is an attractive township, popular with Melbourne folk and full of interesting old buildings. Most striking is the classical market hall, an almost exact reproduction of a Greek temple which now contains the local visitor centre. Castlemaine is also home to an excellent art gallery and historical museum, some fine botanic gardens and the mansion known as Buda, begun in 1857.

The **Castlemaine and Maldon Railway▶▶** is a steam train ride that is very popular with children. It is based at Maldon station, 17.5km (11 miles) northwest along Highway 122 (see also page 117).

▶▶ Coal Creek Heritage Village, Korumburra 90A3

The railways of Victoria used to run on Korumburra coal, and after the last mine had been closed down in the late 1950s it was decided that the days of coal and steam should be re-created at Coal Creek Mine just outside town (about 120km/75 miles southeast of Melbourne). As well as the gallery of the mine, the popular site has a railway station and tramway rides, tradesmen plying their crafts, old stores and settlers' cottages.

THE GIPPSLAND WHOPPER
Of the 100 or so species of Australian worms, *Megascolides australis* is easily the biggest, measuring up to 3.5m (11.5ft) long and 2.5cm (1in) thick. This extraordinary creature has its own worm-shaped museum at Wildlife Wonderland at Bass, near the turn-off for Phillip Island on the Bass Highway.

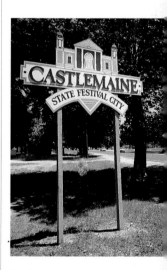

Castlemaine is a former mining town about 40km (25 miles) north of Daylesford

For much of its length, the Murray forms the boundary between Victoria and New South Wales. The longest river in Australia rises in the Great Dividing Range near Mount Kosciuszko, flowing past red gums and irrigating the land around Mildura before entering the sea at Encounter Bay in South Australia.

For thousands of years, the rich wildlife of the Murray and its tributaries gave sustenance to the Aborigines who lived along its banks. It was discovered by Hume and Hovell in 1824, and explored more thoroughly by Charles Sturt in the course of his expedition of 1829–30. As settlers arrived, in the beginning strongly opposed by the Aborigines, the river took on great importance as a transport route. A spirited contest took place in 1853 between the *Mary Ann* and the *Lady Augusta*, to see which would be the first steamboat to make it up the Murray as far as Swan Hill. With the prize money of £4,000, the master of the winning steamboat founded the Murray River Navigation Co., whose sternwheelers dominated river traffic for many years until the coming of the railway rendered them obsolete.

The greatest handicap to navigation was the irregularity of the Murray's flow; for many months of the year there would not be enough water to float a boat of any size, and the risk of running aground was constant. Today, a number of proud vessels survive to carry cargoes of nostalgic tourists rather than the bales of wool that filled the holds in their 19th-century heyday.

Attractions Upstream from the twin towns of Albury (NSW) and Wodonga (Victoria) is **Lake Hume**, several times the size of Sydney Harbour. Built to regulate river flow, it is now an ideal place for watersports. Downstream are the wineries around **Rutherglen**, while **Yarrawonga**, thanks to Lake Mulwala, has become a major inland water recreation area. Around **Cobram** are dozens of fine sandy beaches.

Echuca was once Australia's busiest inland port, with a truly magnificent wharf more than 1.5km (1 mile) long built from the timber of red gums. The people of the town are very proud of its heritage, and have taken pains to preserve it for the pleasure of visitors. The **Port of Echuca** has been fully restored and has a whole series of visitor attractions, including the Cargo Shed with life-like dioramas. The Bridge Hotel is full of

BARMAH FOREST
Spreading for 30,000ha (74,130 acres) over the floodplain of the Murray upstream from Echuca is this magnificent forest of river red gum trees, some of them 500 years old. Australia was largely built on the timber milled from these majestic trees, which was used for railway construction, bridges, mines, fences and wharves. When the river spills over its banks during exceptionally rainy spells, the forest comes alive with the calls of more than 200 species of migrating birds.

A journey to the past aboard a paddle steamer...

...stopping at Echuca, Swan Hill, Mildura and other places along the Murray

113

period furniture, and the old Customs House has been put to use as the information centre. It is rare to see so many steamboats, either under restoration or in action.

To the northwest of the Kerang Lakes is another river port, **Swan Hill**, named by explorer Thomas Mitchell who was kept awake at night by the swans on a nearby lagoon. In addition to paddle-steamer cruises, the town's outstanding attraction is the **Swan Hill Pioneer Settlement**, a painstaking riverside re-creation, put together using original buildings as well as accurate replicas, and brought alive by the presence of craftspeople practicing traditional trades. The Pioneer Settlement also has a sound and light show, which concentrates on the early pioneers. A strong sense of the past can also be experienced in two fine old properties, the **Tyntyndyer Homestead** to the north, and **Murray Downs** to the east, the latter designed to repel attack by Aborigines.

Red to green At the heart of the irrigated area, **Mildura** was originally laid out on the American pattern, with streets given numbers rather than names. In the language of the Kulkyne Aborigines, Mildura meant 'dry red earth', but here red has turned to green—the Chaffey brothers, who arrived in 1885 from Canada, brought advanced irrigation techniques (see panel). Avocados, melons, oranges and grapes, both for the table and for wine-making, are all grown here, as is a whole range of fruit for drying. A number of establishments are happy to share their production secrets with you, among them **Orange World** and the **Lindemans Karadoc** and **Stanley wineries**. Alternatively, you could take a trip upriver aboard one of the paddle steamers that operate from here.

THE CHAFFEYS
Canadians George and William Chaffey pioneered artificially irrigated settlements in California before being invited to bring their expertise to the Murray. They both succeeded and failed; from the 1880s on, thousands of new settlers flocked to the newly irrigated areas around Mildura, and the town itself prospered, but there were floods, problems with leaching and salinity, and the great slump of the 1890s. By 1896 George had had enough and borrowed his fare home, but William stayed on, helping to put the area's economy on a firmer footing once the railway arrived in 1903. The water pumps that George had designed continued to work into the 1950s.

The lovely National Rhododendron Gardens at Olinda in the Dandenong Ranges

A FEATHERED PHILANDERER
The forests and gullies of the Dandenongs provide a habitat for *Menura novae-hollandiae*, the superb lyrebird, a wonderful singer and mimic of the calls of other birds. The rather ordinary-looking male of the species comes into his own in winter, when he senses that female lyrebirds are ready to respond to his advances. Having built a series of mounds through-out his territory, the male mounts one and undergoes an extra-ordinary transformation, fanning out his lyre-shaped tail-feathers so that his body disappears in a froth of plumage, at the same time pouring forth a cascade of song. The more impressive the display, the greater the bird's chances of winning his way with a succession of females.

▶ **Colac**   *90A2*

Colac is the market town for the agricultural wealth of the surrounding basalt plains. This southwestern area incorporates a lake district of some 50 to 60 water bodies. Those that have formed in deep craters contain fresh water, while the shallower lakes contain salty water because the rate of evaporation from them exceeds the rate of replenishment; Lake Corangamite is a saline lake, and is also Victoria's largest. There are superb views of the lake and surrounding plains from Red Rock Lookout.

▶▶ **The Dandenong Ranges**   *90A3*

Melbourne is fortunate to have these magnificently wooded hills, part of a national park, on the eastern edge of the metropolitan area; a wonderful destination for a day's outing. The highest point is **Mount Dandenong**▶▶ (633m/2,077ft), with fantastic views over the sprawling city to the west and the hills farther to the east.

Because of their accessibility, the Dandenongs have long been a popular residential area, and there are pretty townships and many fine mansions, some converted into hotels and restaurants. There are lush gardens, too, like the **National Rhododendron Gardens**▶ at Olinda, whose exotic shrubs contrast with the native vegetation of towering mountain ash trees, massive tree ferns and rampant creepers. At Belgrave is the terminus of **'Puffing Billy'**▶▶, the vintage narrow-gauge steam locomotive that pulls trainloads of tourists on a scenic trip through the forest.

▶▶ **Daylesford**   *90B2*

Between them, Daylesford (109km/67 miles northwest of Melbourne) and Hepburn Springs contain half of Australia's mineral springs. The supposedly therapeutic waters were discovered in the course of gold mining in the 1850s and 1860s, and by the turn of the 20th century the place had taken on the character of the spa resorts so common in Europe, perhaps because many of the early inhabitants were originally immigrants from the Swiss canton of Ticino. At the **Hepburn Spa Resort**▶▶, the old spa building is still intact; you can buy bottled water, take various treatments and enjoy relaxing walks. The excellent **Daylesford Historical Society Museum**▶ is housed in the old School of Mines, and there are attractive botanical gardens. To the north is the old volcanic cone of Mount Franklin with a fine view from its summit.

▶ Dunolly 90B2
The area around Dunolly, 173km (107 miles) northwest of Melbourne, yielded more nuggets than any other Australian goldfield, including the Welcome Stranger, weighing 71kg (2,505 ounces). Reproductions of this and other mega-nuggets are in the town's **Gold Museum**▶.

▶ Geelong 90A2
This industrial port city, Victoria's second largest, once saw itself as a rival to Melbourne, but has long since given up the struggle, though its harbour still exports the rich produce of its agricultural hinterland. In spite of much redevelopment, including a lively waterfront dining strip, there is plenty of evidence of 19th-century grandeur; imposing public buildings adorn the city and prosperity is reflected in the many elegant properties, such as Barwon Grange overlooking the Barwon River. Corio Villa above Eastern Beach was prefabricated in Scotland and re-assembled here by guesswork after the plans and instructions had been destroyed. One of the fine old bluestone woolstores has been splendidly restored to house the **National Wool Museum**▶▶. This is the place to come if you want to understand how Australia 'rode to prosperity on the sheep's back'.

▶▶ Gippsland 91A4
Named in the 1840s by Polish explorer Count Strzelecki after the Governor of NSW, Gippsland is the loosely defined region comprising most of southeastern Victoria between the highlands of the Great Dividing Range and the coastline of Bass Strait. The superb temperate rain forest that once blanketed the area has mostly been cut down to yield rich dairying and fruit-growing land, though fine tracts of woodland remain in the state forests and national parks along the NSW border in the far east. This is one of the areas where protest action by conservationists has focused public attention on the fact that the glories of Australia's natural heritage are not inexhaustible. The La Trobe Valley in the heart of Gippsland has one of the world's biggest deposits of brown coal, burned here in power stations to provide something like 90 per cent of the state's electric power, while oil and gas is extracted in quantity from offshore wells in Bass Strait.

The scale of contemporary opencast mining can be appreciated in the course of tours of the **PowerWorks**▶ visitor centre and lookouts, while more traditional activities can be contemplated in the **Gippsland Heritage Park**▶ at Moe, with its collection of old buildings from many parts of Gippsland. Inland is some of Victoria's most attractive countryside, running up into the alpine foothills of the Great Dividing Range, while the Gippsland Lakes (see panel) lie landward of Ninety Mile Beach.

GIPPSLAND LAKES
Sometimes described as 'the best example of a coastal lagoon in the world', and with a near-Mediterranean climate, this area has unrivalled opportunites for sailing, cruising, fishing or just taking it easy. Both beach and lakes are protected as national parks.

115

Rich dairy lands make for fine Gippsland cheeses

Victoria

OUR PEOPLE
Following the 1988 Bicentenary, Australia's indigenous people decided to try to replace the overall term 'Aborigine' with names from their own languages. 'Koori', meaning 'our people', is now widely in use in southeastern Australia. The Grampians are an outdoor gallery of Koori art, to be seen in the Billimina, Larngibunja and Ngamadjidj shelters, and at Flat Rock.

YARRA VALLEY
An hour away from Melbourne, Australia's fastest-growing wine region is among the rolling hills and rich soils of the Yarra Valley. There are over 40 wineries to visit, particularly around the town of Yarra Glen. The valley is becoming famous both for its fine dining and its excellent range of rustic bed-and-breakfast accommodation.

► **Goulburn Valley** *90B3*

The Goulburn River runs northwest from artificial Lake Eildon in the foothills of the Victorian Alps through a rich fruit- and vine-growing area to join the Murray River near Echuca. With an indented shoreline more than 480km (300 miles) long, Lake Eildon is an immensely popular place for watersports of all kinds. There is also some good walking in this area. The lake is fringed by **Lake Eildon National Park►**, a forested environment that is also rich in wildlife. To the west of the river, Rushworth is a fine example of a gold-rush town of the 1850s.

►► **Grampians (Gariwerd) National Park** *90B1*

The Aborigines, who left many traces of their rock art here, knew the Grampians as Gariwerd. Forming one of the largest national parks in Victoria, the region consists of a succession of sandstone ridges sloping gently to the west, ending in sheer cliffs and jagged rock formations to the east. The area is rich in wildlife and is carpeted with wildflowers in summer.

The park has an excellent network of trails and paths, and can also be appreciated by car, thanks to a series of scenic roads. There are any number of spectacular viewpoints; **Boroka Lookout►►** gives a fine panorama over the town of Halls Gap, where there is a visitor centre and the **Brambuk National Park and Cultural Centre►**, which brings the history and culture of local Aborigines to life. To the west are two of the most spectacular sights of the ranges; the rock formation known as the **Balconies** and the grandiose water staircase of the **Mackenzie Falls**.

► **Hamilton** *90A1*

Focal point of much of the prosperous agricultural plains of central western Victoria, Hamilton likes to style itself the 'Wool Capital of the World'. Its outstanding attraction is the **Hamilton Art Gallery►**, with a large and varied collection including wonderful examples of the applied arts

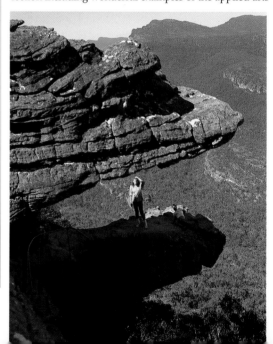

The huge overhanging rocks in the Grampians National Park known as the Balconies

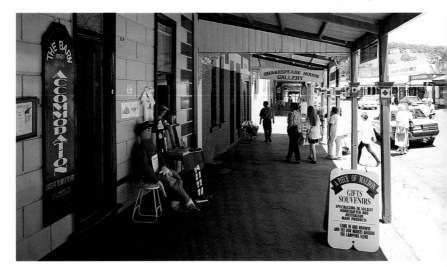

of many countries, plus a splendid array of the water-colours and etchings by the British topographical artist Paul Sandby.

Maldon's wide main street, sloping gently downhill has some typically Australian country architecture

▶▶ Healesville 90B3

Nestling among its green hills in the Yarra Valley, this attractive township is a good place for walks and picnics, but it is mostly visited now for the **Healesville Sanctuary▶▶**. A visit to this wildlife park is an excellent way to appreciate the strange and wonderful fauna of the Antipodes, in a range of cleverly re-created habitats and walk-through enclosures. Other local attractions include an Aboriginal cultural centre, galleries, antique shops and the wineries of the Yarra Valley (see panel opposite).

▶▶ Lorne 90A2

Protected from the north by the steep forested slopes of the Otways, this charming little village, facing on to the curving beach of Loutit Bay, has enjoyed a high reputation as a Great Ocean Road beach resort for over a century. There are also delightful walks in the forest park.

▶▶ Maldon 90B2

Among the many old gold-rush townships of central Victoria, Maldon is outstanding, 'the best preserved town in Australia of the gold-mining era' according to the National Trust. It is certainly full of charm; the scale of the place is modest and the tone is set by delightful cottages, many of them with pretty gardens.

▶ Marysville 90B3

In the foothills of the Victorian Alps, the township of Marysville has long been popular with weekending Melburnians. In summer, there is wonderful bushwalking to the Steavenson Falls, some of the highest in Victoria, or to the Cumberland Valley where the state's tallest trees grow, while in winter there is good cross-country skiing, particularly on the popular snowfields of Lake Mountain.

DUCKBILLED DENIZEN
The normally bashful platypus can be observed going about its daily life at the Healesville Sanctuary. The sanctuary has the distinction of being the first place to successfully breed this reclusive egg-laying mammal in captivity.

The endearing little fairy penguins that live along the coasts of southern Australia are the smallest of the species in the world, being only about 35–40cm (less than a foot) in length. At Phillip Island they spend their days feeding at sea, then as evening falls they gather in groups to waddle to their burrows at the back of Summerland Beach. They maintain this routine with apparent indifference to the flood-lighting and to the countless tourists huddled in the stands watching them.

The dramatic Twelve Apostles coastline near Port Campbell, on the Great Ocean Road

▶▶ Mornington Peninsula   90A3

Melbourne's best-loved weekend and holiday area embraces Port Phillip Bay in a great curve of sheltered beaches before ending at Point Nepean, overlooking the dangerous currents of the narrow entrance to the bay known as The Rip. Much of the peninsula is suburban in character, with dwellings crowding along the main road and spreading out from the residential and resort towns like Frankston and Mornington, but there are over 100 wineries to visit. In the season, the foreshore is crowded with campers and motor-homes.

Towards the tip, refined Sorrento and exclusive Portsea have retained the feeling of early days, when paddle steamers plied across the bay from Melbourne. Once off limits as a naval base, Point Nepean is now part of the **Mornington Peninsula National Park**, reached from the visitor centre by shuttle. The 'front' beaches facing the bay tend to be calm but busy, while the 'back' beaches looking out on to the Bass Strait are rough—no place for inexperienced swimmers. Former Australian Prime Minister Harold Holt disappeared here in 1967, and was presumed drowned.

The peninsula's importance in Victoria's history is recalled by the graves of the 'early settlers' at **Sorrento▶**, and by the 1844 **McCrae Homestead▶**, the home of the first permanent settler family. The best overall view is from 305m (1,000-ft) high **Arthur's Seat▶▶**.

▶▶ Phillip Island   90A3

Bounded to the west by the Mornington Peninsula, the great tidal estuary of Westernport Bay is broken up by a number of islands. French Island and little Churchill Island—the latter is part of the Phillip Island Nature Park—

are rich in wildlife, but the most famous is Phillip Island, whose irresistible **Fairy Penguin Parade**▶▶▶ (see panel opposite) pulls in hundreds of thousands of onlookers. Reached by bridge and about 130km (80 miles) from Melbourne, Phillip Island has a varied coastline that includes rugged cliffs and long surf beaches. Muttonbirds nest on **Cape Woolamai**, the island's highest point; the **Koala Conservation Centre**▶▶ has a large koala colony; and Seal Rocks is home to the world's largest Australian fur seal colony. **Cowes** is the main resort, with restaurants, shops, a good range of accommodation and boat trips to see the seals and French Island.

▶▶▶ Port Campbell National Park   90A2
Backed by the Great Ocean Road running west from Geelong, this park comprises 30km (19 miles) of some of the world's most spectacular coastal scenery, a succession of high cliffs, headlands and strange rock formations standing out to sea. Biscuit-like beds of limestone, sand, mud and seashells formed beneath the sea and then uplifted 25 million years ago are now being eaten away by the breakers rolling in from the Southern Ocean. Because the rock varies in strength and texture, the sea advances more rapidly in some places than others, leaving behind isolated features that have been given evocative names like the **Twelve Apostles** (at Port Campbell). In a dramatic demonstration of the rate of erosion, the arch of 'London Bridge' collapsed into the surf in 1990, stranding the walkers who had ventured on to it. Quickly rescued, they were luckier than the many passengers and crewmen who perished along what was named the 'Shipwreck Coast' in the days of sail (see pages 242–243).

▶▶ Port Fairy   90A1
This delightful little Great Ocean Road fishing port and beach resort at the mouth of the Moyne River is one of the oldest settlements in Victoria, having been home to sealers and whalers in the early years of the 19th century. There are 50 buildings classified as historic by the National Trust, including Mott's Cottage and a wooden house erected by a whaling skipper in the 1830s.

▶ Portland   90A1
Founded in 1834, this busy deep-water port is the oldest permanent settlement in Victoria. To the southwest are the spectacular seascapes of Cape Nelson and the blowholes and petrified forest of Cape Bridgewater.

▶▶ Queenscliff   90A3
Separated from Point Nepean on the Mornington Peninsula by the treacherous waters of The Rip, Queenscliff is an old-fashioned place, with a harbour, a fort (1882), grand hotels and the Black Lighthouse, prefabricated in Scotland and shipped here in 1863.

▶▶ Strzelecki Ranges   91A3
The best way to see these forested ridges is to follow the Grand Ridge Road from Nyora, southeast of Melbourne, to Carrajung (about 128km/80 miles), passing through some of Victoria's finest upland scenery and numerous pretty towns and villages.

Queenscliff on the Bellarine Peninsula— where Melburnians come to get away from it all

119

COUNT THE CONSONANTS
The Polish explorer Paul Edmund de Strzelecki styled himself 'Count', a claim with little apparent substance. Although it was Angus McMillan who had first blazed a trail through the almost impenetrable rain forest jungle of southeast Victoria, it was not his name for the area ('New South Caledonia') that was adopted, but Strzelecki's 'Gippsland'. Strzelecki's own venture into Gippsland was only saved from disaster by the skill of his Aboriginal guide, Tarra, after whom the Tarra-Bulga National Park has been named.

Gum trees or, to give them their more correct name, eucalypts, are the trees most closely identified with Australia. They comprise more than 500 different species, and grow in most parts of the country; some three-quarters of all Australian trees are eucalypts, many of them with wonderfully descriptive names like peppermint, iron-bark, bloodwood or blackbutt.

EUCALYPTUS LEAVES
All eucalyptus leaves contain a fragrant oil that is used for various medicinal purposes. Their indigestible look doesn't deter the koala either, which in fact depends entirely on a single eucalyptus species for its food source.

120

WORLD-BEATER
The confusingly named mountain ash (*Eucalyptus regnans*) is the tallest flowering plant in the world, reaching an extraordinary height of up to 100m (328ft) in the forests of Victoria and Tasmania.

Early settlers didn't much like the look of the unfamiliar eucalypts, with their pale greyish-green or peeling, untidy bark hanging in strips and tatters and the unseasonal failure of their dull grey leaves to fall at the proper time of year. Many farmers and sheep graziers brought cuttings of other trees from home, and trees such as elm, oak, willow and poplar are now considered environmentally inappropriate in their Australian context. The same was true of townsfolk, who preferred the more orderly European trees for their parks.

Forests and felling But eucalypts have their own distinct allure, individually or in mass, forming magnificent forests or growing with other trees, shrubs and grasses to form the surprisingly park-like landscapes of many parts of the interior. Over the millennia, eucalypts have also learned to live with fire, regenerating almost miraculously after the all-too-common bushfires from buds concealed within their bark. Many species, like jarrah and messmate, yield first-rate wood, and in consequence were felled ruthlessly until quite recently. Others are logged, somewhat demeaningly, to be turned into woodchip for foreign pulp mills.

Varieties There are many types of eucalypts, from the Tasmanian blue gum that provided the wood for railway ties, to the river red gum of semi-arid areas, the ghost gum of deserts and the hardy, cold-resistant snow gum, symbol of the Australian Alps.

The great river red gum forest at Yarrawonga

▶ Walhalla 91A4

Tucked away in the deep wooded valleys north of Moe, isolated Walhalla boomed in the late 19th century when more gold was extracted here than from any other area in Victoria. By the time the railway reached here in 1910, via a series of spectacular tunnels and trestle bridges, the gold had more or less run out. A stroll along the crooked main street recalls some of the atmosphere of former days, and you can visit the **Long Tunnel Extended Gold Mine▶**. You can also ride on the restored **Walhalla Goldfields Railway▶** through this magnificent upland scenery.

▶ Wangaratta 90B3

The Hume Highway is the main route north between Melbourne and Sydney. About 240km (150 miles) from Melbourne is Wangaratta, a service hub for the surrounding agricultural area. The body of the notorious bushranger Daniel 'Mad Dog' Morgan is buried here minus his head, the latter having been sent to Melbourne in order to establish whether he really was mad, or just plain bad. The town's major attraction is the annual Festival of Jazz (November).

▶ Warrnambool 90A1

The biggest town on Victoria's southwest coast, Warrnambool has superb beaches. Founded by whalers in the 1840s, it is still frequented by southern right whales, which come here in winter to calve (see panel). **Flagstaff Hill Maritime Museum▶▶** is a conscientiously re-created port village with several historic vessels, a sound and light show and other fascinating displays.

▶▶ Wilsons Promontory National Park 91A4

The southernmost point of mainland Australia, this wild and mountainous granite peninsula protruding into Bass Strait is perhaps Victoria's best-loved national park. Many of its rocky headlands, splendid beaches and dense forests are only accessible on foot, and in spite of its popularity it is always possible to find whatever degree of isolation you want (except for kangaroos, of course). The only settlement is at Tidal River, where the road ends and a network of wonderful hiking trails begins.

Southern right whales playing off Warrnambool

THE WARRNAMBOOL WHALES
Between May and August, southern right whales gather off Logan's Beach to bear their young. A special viewing platform has been built from which you can observe these magnificent creatures, once hunted to near-extinction, as they dive and play, making spectacular fountains from their blowholes or leaping bodily from the waves.

'THE PROM'
Discovered by maritime explorer George Bass in 1798 and named after a friend of Bass's colleague Matthew Flinders, Wilsons Promontory attracts all kinds of nature-lovers. In summer, the area is great for scuba diving and snorkelling; there are wonderful walks; and the hundreds of species of plants make the park a botanist's dream.

Drive

The Dandenong Ranges

Less than an hour from Melbourne, the 'Blue Dandenongs' are a popular recreation area and summer retreat for the inhabitants of the city.

Canterbury Road (Route 32) leads to Montrose at the northern end of the Dandenong Tourist Road. If you have time, continue 30km (19 miles) to **Healesville Sanctuary** in the Yarra Valley, one of the best places to see Australian wildlife at close quarters.

Mount Dandenong, at 633m (2,077ft) the highest point of the range, and the sculptures of the **William Ricketts Sanctuary** are accessible from the Tourist Road. The route to the village of Kallista passes the Nicholas Memorial Gardens and the Sherbrooke Forest section of the **Dandenong Ranges National Park**, where you can see the tree ferns and the magnificent mountain ash trees for which the area is famous.

Belgrave is the terminus for the irresistible *Puffing Billy*, a restored steam train that hauls delighted passengers through the forest along its narrow-gauge track.

Drive

Mornington Peninsula

The 100km (62-mile) drive to Point Nepean at the tip of the Mornington Peninsula passes through resorts and residential areas with access to the beaches of Port Phillip Bay. Frankston

marks the end of the commuter railway line from Melbourne. Beyond **Dromana** with its excellent Tourist Information Centre the coast is lined with holiday homes and campsites, while above the town **Arthur's Seat** rises 305m (1,000ft) to give a fine panorama over bay and ocean. On its northern slope is the little **McCrae Homestead**, built in 1844 and still evocative of pioneer days despite its proximity to nearby suburbia.

With its broad main street, **Sorrento** has a charm all of its own, while posh **Portsea** does its best to maintain its exclusivity. On the outer rim of the peninsula, the 'back beaches' face the ocean surf of Bass Strait. For a long time off limits as defence land, the **Point Nepean** section of the **Mornington Peninsula National Park** can now be visited. With 40km (25 miles) of rugged coastline, this park and its adjacent marine reserve encompass excellent surfing beaches, diving spots and wildlife, including dolphins from November to March.

Other attractions on the Mornington Peninsula include wineries, golf courses and a reputation for boutique guest houses and dining. From Frankston, the Mornington Peninsula Freeway and South Eastern Freeway can be used to speed your return to Melbourne.

Right: Port Phillip Bay begins at the tip of the Mornington Peninsula

123

WESTERN HIGHWAY

Melbourne International Airport

31

8

Melbourne Zoo

Yarra Valley

Healesville Sanctuary & Yarra Valley

Schwerkolt Cottage

MELBOURNE

Yarra

Nunawading

Montrose

Mt Dandenong ▲633m

Silvan Reservoir

William Ricketts

Nicholas Memorial Gardens

CANTERBURY ROAD

Como House

Waverley

Ferntree Gully Nat Park

Williamstown

Point Gellibrand

Luna Park

Rippon Lea

SOUTH EASTERN FREEWAY

Kallista

Knox

Belgrave

Werribee

PRINCES

Altona Bay

Brighton

Oakleigh

Puffing Billy Railway

Werribee Park

Point Cook

Churchill Nat Park

Werribee South

NEPEAN

Air Museum

PRINCES

Dandenong

Cardinia Reservoir

Ricketts Point

Mordialloc

HIGHWAY

HIGHWAY

Berwick

1

Chelsea

Cardinia Creek

Port Phillip Bay

Cranbourne

Clyde

Portarlington

Point George

Royal Botanic Gardens

Bellarine Peninsula

Indented Head

St Leonards

Frankston

Davey Point

Langwarrin Baxter

Pearcedale

Tooradin

Warneet

Adams Point

Schnapper Point

Edwards Point

Swan Bay

Swan Island

Mornington

HIGHWAY

Moorooduc

Westernport Bay

Balcombe Bay

Tyabb

Scrub Point

Queenscliff

Mud Islands

Mt Martha

Martha Point

Devilbend Reservoir

Point Lonsdale

The Rip

Point Nepean

Dromana Bay

Hastings

Portsea

London Bridge

Sorrento

Settlers Graves

McCrae Homestead

Dromana

Red Hill

Hastings Bight

French Island

Bittern

Crib Point

Sorrento Back Beach

Rosebud

Arthurs Seat Chairlift

HMAS Cerberus

NEPEAN

Merricks

Balnarring

Mornington Peninsula

Point Leo

Sandy Point

Long Point

Mornington Peninsula National Park

Shoreham

Westernport Bay

Cowes

Rhyll

Phillip Island

Flinders

West Head

Phillip Island Wildlife Park

Koala Conservation Centre

Cape Schanck

Seal Rocks Sea Life Centre

Seal Rocks

Penguin Parade

San Remo

Cape Woolamai

Bass Strait

0 5 10 15 km

0 5 10 miles

Dandenong Ranges

Mornington Peninsula

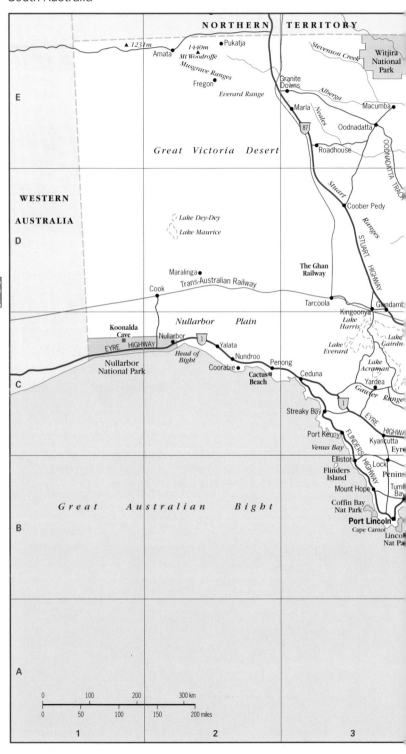

NORTHERN TERRITORY

Witjira National Park

▲ 1231m

Amata
▲ 1440m
Mt Woodroffe
Musgrave Ranges
Fregon
• Pukatja

Stevenson Creek

Granite Downs
Alberga
Macumba

Everard Range

Marla
Neales
Oodnadatta

87

Roadhouse

Great Victoria Desert

Stuart

E

WESTERN

AUSTRALIA

Coober Pedy

D

Lake Dey-Dey
Lake Maurice

Ranges
STUART HIGHWAY

The Ghan Railway

124

Maralinga •
Trans-Australian Railway

Cook

Tarcoola
Glendamb

Nullarbor Plain

Kingoonya
Lake Harris
Lake Gairdn

Koonalda Cave
Nullarbor

1

Yalata

Lake Everard

Lake Acraman

EYRE HIGHWAY

Head of Bight
Nundroo
Coorabie •
Perlong
Ceduna

Yardea

Gawler Range

Nullarbor National Park

Cactus Beach

C

Streaky Bay

1
EYRE HIGHWA

Port Kenny
Venus Bay

Kyancutta
Eyre

FLINDERS HIGHWAY

Elliston
Flinders Island

Lock
Penins

Great Australian Bight

Mount Hope

Tum Bay

Coffin Bay Nat Park

B

Port Lincoln
Cape Carnot
Linco
Nat Pa

A

0   100   200   300 km

0   50   100   150   200 miles

1   2   3

South Australia

QUEENSLAND

Simpson Desert

Goyder Lagoon

Cordillo Downs

Ephemeral Lakes

Clifton Hills

Macumba

Warburton Creek

Sturt Stony Desert

Innamincka

Lake Eyre North

Tirari Desert

Moomba

Lake Eyre Nat Park

Strzelecki Desert

Lake Gregory

Lake Blanche

Lake Eyre South

Howard Springs

Marree

STRZELECKI TRACK

BIRDSVILLE TRACK

COOPER Creek

Lake Callabonna

Roxby Downs

Lyndhurst

Arkaroola

Andamooka

Leigh Creek

Gammon Ranges Nat Park

Balcanoona

Bosworth Lake

Beltana

Lake Frome

Woomera

Lake Torrens

Blinman

Pimba

Flinders Ranges Nat Park

Island Lagoon

Bookaloo

Wilpena 1165m

Curnamona

Lake Macfarlane

Hawker

Cradock

Flinders Ranges

NEW SOUTH WALES

Port Augusta

Quorn

Waukaringa

Cockburn

Lake Gilles

Iron Knob

Mt Remarkable Nat Park

BARRIER HIGHWAY

Yunta

Simba

Whyalla

Port Pirie

Peterborough

Cleve

Cowell

Crystal Brook

Jamestown

32

Wallaroo

Kadina

Clare

Burra

Riverland

Moonta

Balaklava

Morgan

Spencer Gulf

Maitland

Kapunda

Murray

Renmark

Yorke Peninsula

Gawler

Barossa Valley

STURT Hwy

Berri

Yorketown

Port Adelaide

Adelaide Hills

Birdwood

Loxton

Innes NP

ADELAIDE

St Vincent

Hahndorf

Murray Bridge

Inneston

Cape Jervis

Strathalbyn

Investigator Strait

Kingscote

Goolwa

Pinnaroo

Penneshaw

Fleurieu

Victor Harbor

DUKES HIGHWAY

12

Kelly Hill Caves

Coorong Nat Park

VICTORIA

Flinders Chase Nat Park

Kangaroo Island

Keith

8

Bordertown

PRINCES HIGHWAY

Kingston SE

Robe

Bool Lagoon

Naracoorte

Coonawarra

Beachport

Millicent

Mount Gambier

Canunda Nat Park

Cape Northumberland

4   5

South Australia

WOWSERS NO MORE
A wowser originally meant someone who didn't know how to enjoy himself. The epithet was maliciously applied to the good citizens of Adelaide because of their supposed piety and apparent aversion to letting their hair down. The visitor to South Australia is unlikely to see much trace of this today, least of all in Adelaide. It may still be a city of churches, but it is now also a city of restaurants, watered by the products of its wineries. And it was in South Australia that the country's first nudist beach, Maslin, was opened, on the coast south of Adelaide.

SOUTH AUSTRALIA Virtually all the inhabitants of Australia's third largest state live along the fertile coasts of its gulf lands and southeastern plains, three-quarters of them in Greater Adelaide. Northward from this tamed littoral with its almost Mediterranean climate stretches an immense and arid area of Outback and desert, some of it bearing the traces of failed European settlement, and huge tracts of it returned to the Aborigines. This is a land of sharp differences, with a capital that is the most elegant and obviously cultured of all Australian cities.

IN THE BEGINNING South Australia was not a prison colony but a 'province', settled by free people (mostly from the south of England, but also many from Germany) under the auspices of the South Australia Company. The first group landed from the *Buffalo* in 1836, but the true founding father was Colonel William Light, a brilliant and unorthodox character whose visionary plan for Adelaide has shaped the city to the present day. The development of the colony was erratic. Within a few years of its foundation it was only saved from economic collapse by the discovery of copper at Kapunda and Burra. Attempts to push the frontier of agriculture north were defeated by long years of drought, although the peninsula's corn lands flourished.

For many years Adelaide remained simply the middle of a vast agricultural and mining area, its affairs conducted by merchants who lived sober lives ('wowsers' to other Australians, see panel). Much of the tone of South Australian life was indeed set by the seriousness with which its Nonconformist (British) or Lutheran (German) citizens took their religion; not for nothing was Adelaide known as the city of churches.

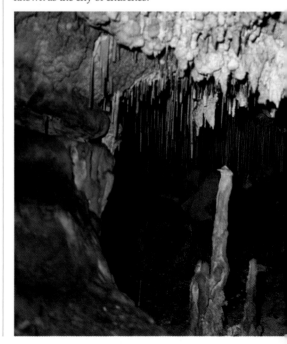

The vulnerability of what was an almost entirely rural economy became apparent in the years of the great Depression, and following World War II the state underwent an industrial transformation, with shipyards at Whyalla and car factories at Adelaide's satellite town of Elizabeth. In the 1970s, these activities showed themselves to be vulnerable in their turn, and South Australia, along with much of the rest of the country, has had its share of economic and financial troubles.

Given the state's range of landscapes, it is not surprising that tourism is of increasing importance. Adelaide attracts visitors with its biennial Festival of Arts (even-numbered years), as well as with the elegance of its townscape and its reputation for good living. A relatively new attraction is the Womadelaide Festival—a biennial celebration of world music (odd-numbered years). An immensely long coastline offers endless opportunites for water-based activities of all kinds at unspoiled towns such as **Robe**, south of the spectacular Coorong National Park. Coastal landscapes vary from the wild isolation of rugged headlands to delightful little fishing ports and resorts. Offshore islands invite those with a taste for escapism; the biggest of them, **Kangaroo Island**, offers sea lions, koalas, kangaroos, pelicans, sea eagles and fairy penguins in their native environment. The state is also becoming increasingly famous for its excellent wines, gourmet foods and fine dining opportunities.

South Australia is the starting point for many of the country's great tourist itineraries. Outback Tarcoola is the junction for two trains of almost legendary reputation—the *Ghan*, on its way north to Alice Springs and Darwin, and the *Indian Pacific*, pausing here on its transcontinental run westwards across the Nullarbor.

Bethany's Lutheran church and hall in the Barossa Valley

DASHING DON'S DERRING-DO
South Australia's Premier from 1967 to 1968 and again from 1970 to 1979, Don Dunstan not only cultivated a progressive and dynamic image, but was also instrumental in dragging his state into the late 20th century. Under his leadership, South Australia passed legislation outlawing racial and sexual discrimination. Pastor Sir Douglas Nicholls, a distinguished Aborigine, became Governor, while a police chief who refused to reveal who had instructed him to keep secret files on MPs and other potential subversives was dismissed. Sadly, the popular ex-premier died in 1999.

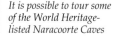

It is possible to tour some of the World Heritage-listed Naracoorte Caves

The map shows the central Adelaide area with the following labels:

City of Adelaide Golf Links

St Peter's Cathedral

Lights Vision

Adelaide Zoo

Pennington Gdns

Peace Park

ALBERT BRIDGE

ADELAIDE ROAD

Montefiore Park

Adelaide Oval

Creswell Gardens

FROME ROAD

"Par 3" Golf Course

MONTEFIORE ROAD

Memorial Drive Tennis Courts

ADELAIDE BRIDGE

Old Adelaide Gaol

Weir

Lake

Pinky Flat

Popeye Wharf

Elder Park

Migration Museum

Port Adelaide

Torrens

WILLIAM ROAD

University of Adelaide

PORT ROAD

Light and Fisher Memorial

Convention Centre

Adelaide Festival Centre

Government House

Royal South Australian Society of Arts

Museum of Classical Archaeology

FROME ROAD

Adelaide Station

Casino

Parliament House

State Library

GLOVER AVENUE

NORTH TERRACE

Lion Arts Centre & JamFactory Contemporary Craft and Design

HINDLEY

Holy Trinity Church

Old Parliament House

South Australian Museum

Art Gallery of South Australia

Ayers House

NORTH

RUNDLE MALL

RUN

Edmund Wright House

CURRIE STREET

WEST TERRACE

LIGHT SQUARE

PLACE

GRENFELL STREET

WAYMOUTH STREET

CITY

Town Hall

GAWLER PLACE

PIRIE STREET

PULTENEY STREET

Ellis Park

FRANKLIN STREET

GRAY

MORPHETT STREET

GPO

Treasury Building

Town Hall

FLINDERS STREET

Telecommunications Museum

Adelaide Airport

BURBRIDGE ROAD

GROTE STREET

VICTORIA SQUARE

KING WILLIAM STREET

WAKEFIELD STREET

Kingston Gardens

GOUGER STREET

Chinatown

Central Market

ANGAS STREET

WRIGHT STREET

WHITMORE SQUARE

Supreme Law Courts

CARRINGTON STREET

STURT STREET

Glenelg Tramway

HALIFAX STREET

PULTENEY STREET

West Terrace Cemetery

GILBERT STREET

MORPHETT SQUARE

GILLES STREET

Glenelg

SOUTH TERRACE

Lundie Gardens

Veale Gardens

SOUTH TERRACE

Park Lands

128

THE WINE EXPERIENCE

Opened in 2001 and located in Adelaide's delightful Botanic Garden, the National Wine Centre of Australia showcases the produce of Australia's 50 wine regions. With a state-of-the-art exhibition gallery, wine industry objects, a tasting area, a wine tourism information and travel booking counter, and its own vineyard, the centre aims to offer 'the complete Australian wine experience'.

Adelaide

Australia's fifth largest city, with a population of 1.1 million, likes to be known for its biennial Festival of Arts and its generally high cultural tone. Many of its early citizens were religious dissenters escaping from persecution in their home countries; they pursued both work and recreation with what seemed a kind of earnest dullness, in rationally planned surroundings of dignified elegance.

These surroundings were the vision of one man, Colonel William Light, who, as South Australia's Surveyor-General, drew up a brilliant plan in 1836, to which the city has adhered ever since. Having found a suitable site on the banks of the little River Torrens, he set out a square-mile grid of streets on the south bank. The central thoroughfare was impressively wide, and the whole was

129

SON OF A GUN!
Most Australian cities developed in a totally chaotic way. It was left to an army officer, illegitimate offspring of the English founder of Penang in Malaysia and a Eurasian woman, to conceive and implement the ambitious plan for Adelaide. William Light had served as an intelligence officer with the Duke of Wellington, gaining his rank of colonel on a temporary posting in Spain; he revelled in the commission to survey and plan not only the site of Adelaide but much of the rest of the new province. Married to the daughter (also illegitimate) of the Duke of Richmond, he left his wife at home in England, and when he died (probably from overwork) in 1839, was refused the last rites because he had been 'living in sin' with another lady.

enlivened with a series of squares. A green belt around the city was to remain parkland in perpetuity, a fit setting for public buildings such as Government House; on the far bank of the river was the fine suburb of North Adelaide. In spite of opposition at the time, in spite of the building boom of the 1970s and 1980s, and in spite of the automobile, all these elements are in place today, helping make Adelaide a delightful city.

It is rare in a metropolis to be able to live in a Victorian villa looking on to splendid parkland, walk or cycle to work in the city, spend the evening at the theatre, then walk home again, but here the residents can do exactly that. The majority of people, however, live in the pleasant, uncrowded suburbs that have spread across the coastal plain between the magnificent beaches along the gulf and the Adelaide Hills to the east.

Sailing is a popular pursuit at Port Adelaide, the city's harbour town

FESTIVE SEASON
They say in Adelaide that the Adelaide Festival Centre cost less to build than it did to carpet Sydney's Opera House. The centre is busy all year round, with three theatres and two outdoor performance areas. Its plaza, designed by the German environmental sculptor Otto Hajek, has been described as Australia's biggest outdoor art work.
   The Adelaide Festival is held in even-numbered years for three weeks in February/March. Warm days and mild nights help create the right atmosphere for a wonderful choice of events—opera, ballet, concerts, theatre, exhibitions, children's activities, the Fringe Festival and a literary festival—all of which are within walking distance of each other.

▶▶ **Adelaide Botanic Garden**   129C4
North Terrace (tel: 08-8222 9311). Gardens: Mon–Fri 8–dusk, Sat–Sun 9–dusk; Bicentennial Conservatory: daily 10–4 (5 in summer). Admission: Gardens free, Conservatory inexpensive
Founded in 1855, these 20ha (49 acres) of trees, shrubs, lawns and lakes glitter with an array of heritage buildings. As well as the Museum of Economic Botany, there is the 1868 Victoria House with its giant waterlily, and the wonderful Palm House, brought from Germany in the 1870s. But most extraordinary is the 1988 **Bicentennial Conservatory▶▶**, a soaring environmental capsule, within whose high-tech skin flourishes a profusion of plants from the tropical rain forests of North Australia and its neighbours.

▶▶▶ **Art Gallery of South Australia**   128C3
North Terrace (tel: 08-8207 7000). Open: daily 10–5
Admission free (varying charges for special exhibitions)
Behind this classical portico is one of the country's most important collections of Australian, European and Asian art. Some of the paintings by Australian artists are familiar, seeming to encapsulate key aspects of the country's character, like the stampeding sheep in Tom Roberts' *The Breakaway* of 1891 or the subtle beach flirtation depicted in Charles Conder's *Holiday at Mentone* (1888). The Aboriginal section is particularly good, and the gallery also has a large collection of Rodin's works.

▶ **Glenelg**   *off 128A1*
Once Adelaide's most popular seaside district, with splendid sandy beaches stretching far in either direction, suburban Glenelg still has plenty of charm, epitomized by the 1920s trams that link it to the city's Victoria Square (a 30-minute trip). It was here that Governor Hindmarsh and the first band of settlers landed in 1836.

▶▶ **Migration Museum**   128C3
82 Kintore Avenue (tel: 08-8207 7580 or 08-8207 7570)
Open: Mon–Fri 10–5, Sat–Sun 1–5. Admission: donation
Housed in the city's old Destitute Asylum, this innovative institution presents the story of the immigrant groups who have populated South Australia. The museum tells stories of the successful adaptation to life in a new country, as well as those of disappointment and difficulty.

▶▶ North Adelaide off 128D3

Adelaide's classiest and oldest suburb has many fine houses. Melbourne Street has shops, restaurants and boutiques, while O'Connell Street is famous for its restaurants. St. Peter's Cathedral boasts the heaviest bells in the southern hemisphere, and at Light's Vision lookout, overlooking the historic Adelaide Oval, a statue of the good colonel surveys the city he created.

▶▶ Port Adelaide off 128C1

Some 14km (8.5 miles) northwest of the landlocked city, Adelaide's harbour town has been deserted by most of its maritime traffic, leaving it free to concentrate on its fascinating past; it has South Australia's largest collection of distinguished 19th-century buildings. Among the long quayside sheds is the bright red 1869 lighthouse; river and ocean cruises are available from the nearby wharf. A short distance inland on Lipson Street are a couple of first-rate museums, each well worth the bus or train trip out from the city. The main building of the fascinating **South Australian Maritime Museum▶▶** is an old bond store, while the **National Railway Museum▶▶**, with steam train rides and many locomotives, is the biggest of its kind in the country.

▶▶▶ South Australian Museum 128C3

North Terrace (tel: 08-8207 7500)
Open: daily 10–5. Admission free
The state's museum of natural history has geological and zoological displays on five floors, but its main attraction is its outstanding Australian Aboriginal Cultures Gallery. All its exhibits are presented in an imaginative and accessible fashion, making the museum perhaps the best place to study the past of the original Australians.

▶▶ Tandanya National Aboriginal Cultural Institute 129B4

253 Grenfell Street (tel: 08-8224 3200)
Open: daily 10–5. Admission: inexpensive
This exciting addition to Adelaide's vibrant East End offers the opportunity to learn about contemporary Aboriginal culture. There are dance and theatre performances, meetings, talks, celebrations, constantly changing exhibitions, and demonstrations and sales of arts and crafts.

OTHER ADELAIDE SIGHTS
The 19th-century Ayers House with its curving bays is perhaps the most elegant structure in North Terrace. Seven times premier of South Australia, Sir Henry Ayers (after whom Ayers Rock was named) used his home for state functions; the hub of city life, its ballroom was washed down with milk to give it a smooth and fast surface.

The Adelaide Zoo, next to the Botanic Garden, is worth a visit, and a cruise on the tranquil Torrens offers a different perspective of the city.

NGURUNDERI'S DREAMING
An extensive display in the South Australian Museum tells the story of Ngurunderi, one of the great ancestral dreaming figures of the Ngarrindjeri people. His travels from high up the Murray River to Kangaroo Island in pursuit of his miscreant wives are said to explain many of the features of the river and coastal landscape. The bends of the Murray were made by the giant cod Ponde sweeping his tail, while Long Island near Murray Bridge is Ngurunderi's spear, which missed its target. Another spear thrust created the islands off Victor Harbor, while his abandoned club became The Bluff. As his wives fled west along the causeway that then connected Kangaroo Island to the mainland, Ngurunderi caused the waters to rise and drown them. They turned into the rocky Pages Islands, while Ngurunderi rose to become a star in the Milky Way.

Impressive Ayers House is open to the public

The Tandanya National Aboriginal Cultural Institute in Adelaide's East End

Walk

Green spaces and old buildings

See map on pages 128–129.

Linking some of Adelaide's splendid green spaces with North Terrace, the city's boulevard, this walk passes through the central shopping mall before ending in Victoria Square, the geographical heart of the city.

A walkway leads to North Terrace from the **Adelaide Festival Centre** complex overlooking parkland along the River Torrens. Stay on the north side of North Terrace to admire the sequence of historic buildings and monuments revealed as you walk eastwards. The postmodern forecourt of the Hyatt Regency hotel contrasts with the grandiose railway station building now housing the city's casino. The **Old Parliament House** of 1855 seems modest compared with the ultra-conservative design of its successor,

completed in 1939. **Government House** behind its garden wall gives way to the State Library (1884), the **South Australian Museum** (1898) and the **Art Gallery of South Australia** (opened in 1881). The south side of the Terrace has both imposing edifices and modern buildings, ending with the fine colonial mansion of **Ayers House** and the Botanic Hotel with tiers of verandas.

A detour to **Adelaide Botanic Garden** should take in the remarkable Bicentennial Conservatory and National Wine Centre (see page 128). Rundle Street is the heart of Adelaide's lively East End region. Here you will find the IMAX theatre, plenty of shops, historic pubs and dozens of great cafés and restaurants. Take a short detour to the excellent **Tandanya National Aboriginal Cultural Institute** in Grenfell Street just to the south.

Rundle Mall is a cheerful pedestrian precinct, the main focus of city shopping. It leads into King William Street, Adelaide's main north–south route. The General Post Office and Town Hall stand at the northern end of Victoria Square, where the city's last surviving original tramway waits to take its passengers down to the sea at **Glenelg**.

National parks

Dry as dust The interminable flatness of the interior is broken only by two mountain ranges. Part of the vast Pitjantjatjara Aboriginal Lands, the Musgrave Ranges in the far northwest parallel the other ridges of the Red Centre just over the boundary with the Northern Territory. The ancient Flinders Ranges run some 480km (300 miles) from near the head of Spencer Gulf toward Lake Eyre, their most spectacular single feature being the magnificent natural fortress of **Wilpena Pound**, a 77sq km (30-sq-mile) natural amphitheatre. Northwards are the interminable sand ridges of the **Simpson Desert**, laid down by winds that ceased to blow in prehistoric times. In the rare bouts of rain, its sparse cover of spinifex is supplemented by a sudden tapestry of wildflowers, while its inhabitants include unique creatures like hopping mice and marsupial moles. The Sturt Stony Desert is a virtually impassable plain of wind-polished stones known as gibbers, while, much farther south, **Mount Remarkable** has deep gorges.

The wildlife-rich south Towards the sea, the near-total aridity of South Australia's interior gives way to a Mediterranean-type climate, whose hot summers are relieved by relatively cool and moist winters. More than a century and a half of settlement has converted much of the area into productive farmland. There is still plenty of wilderness left, along the coast from **Coffin Bay** and **Lincoln national parks** at the tip of the Eyre Peninsula in the west to **Coorong National Park** in the far southeast. In between are the dunes and cliffs of **Innes National Park** on the toe of Yorke Peninsula and the scenic and wildlife wonders of **Kangaroo Island**. The extraordinary Coorong begins at the mouth of the Murray where the great river reaches the sea. A 144km (90-mile) beach stretches southeastwards, backed by sand dunes and a long, shallow lagoon. This is one of the best places for observing the pelican.

AUSTRALIA'S DEAD SEA
Much of the huge expanse of Lake Eyre is below sea level. When filled with water, an event that has only occurred four times in living memory, the lake becomes alive with birds. On the map it appears to be fed by rivers over 960km (600 miles) long, but their waters usually run dry long before they reach the lake. Its salty surface, flat and featureless, made it ideal for Donald Campbell's successful attempt on the world land-speed record in 1964.

133

The Remarkable Rocks on Kangaroo Island are famous for their strangely weathered granite shapes

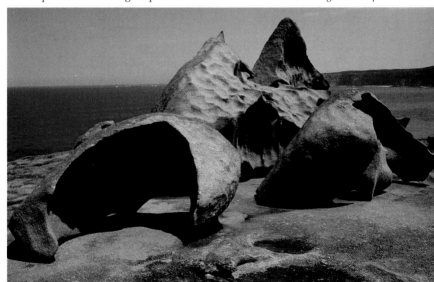

South Australia

One of Australia's most famous railway lines runs from Adelaide to Alice Springs and Darwin in the Northern Territory. The route is named after the Afghan (and other) camel drivers that the railway superseded in the late 19th century. (See also page 189.)

BY CAR
Roads in the relatively densely populated coastal area are good and the main interstate highways are all paved, including the Stuart Highway north to Alice Springs. In the Outback, roads are of variable quality and you must check conditions first and take adequate provisions (see page 143).

134

BY WATER
You can take the car or passenger ferry to Kangaroo Island from Cape Jervis at the tip of the Fleurieu Peninsula.

A diesel commuter bus on Adelaide's 'O-Bahn' line

How to travel

By air Only 6km (4 miles) from the city, Adelaide's airport is served by both international and domestic flights, linking it to all important destinations in Australia and many overseas. The size of South Australia makes flights within the state an attractive proposition. There are frequent flights between Adelaide and places on the Eyre Peninsula such as Port Lincoln, or to Kangaroo Island and Mount Gambier. Other flights serve Port Augusta and Broken Hill in NSW, though many tourists heading into the Outback get there by road.

By bus Adelaide has a comprehensive metropolitan transport system with integrated ticketing, mostly based on buses, but also including suburban trains. The free City Loop and Bee Line buses run frequently between the main railway station and the Glenelg tram terminus in Victoria Square. The Passenger Transport InfoCentre in King William Street is helpful in planning tours around Greater Adelaide. The Glenelg Tram (a vintage 1929 model) and the replica Adelaide Explorer tram, which tours the principal attractions on a 2.75-hour circuit, are an excellent introduction to the sights.

Long-distance buses operate express services to all major destinations, and even quite remote places in the Outback may have a bus service of some kind, albeit an infrequent one. If you have a little time to spare, a fun way to travel between Adelaide and Melbourne or Alice Springs and take in many of the good things en route is by the very reasonably priced **Wayward Bus** (three days to Melbourne and three to eight to Alice).

By train Long-distance trains leave Keswick terminus in the city for Perth, Alice Springs, Darwin, Melbourne, Broken Hill and Sydney. There are also services to the Barossa Valley, Port Pirie and Mount Gambier. Adelaide's suburban network based at the main station on North Terrace is quite extensive, with services to places of interest like Port Adelaide.

Visitors and cuddly residents at Cleland Wildlife Park

▶▶ Adelaide Hills 125B4

Sprawling over the coastal plain, Greater Adelaide is defined to the east by the gorges and steep slopes of these beautiful hills. With scenic drives and hiking trails through wild bushland, this is an area of richly varied landscapes— vineyards, avenues of tall conifers, towns of rough-hewn stone, with some of the oldest settlements in South Australia. The forest has regrown since 'Black Sunday' (2 January 1955), when an uncontrollable bush fire raged for days. As well as vineyards, orchards and gardens there are many other attractions. These include the **Toy Factory▶**, its emblem the biggest rocking horse in the world; the **Cleland Wildlife Park▶▶** on the slopes of Mount Lofty, 20km (12.5 miles) southeast of Adelaide; and the **Warrawong Earth Sanctuary▶▶** at Mylor.

▶▶ Arkaroola 125D4

Formerly a vast sheep station, the Outback resort and wildlife sanctuary of Arkaroola is now a great base for exploring the northern parts of the spectacular Flinders Ranges. The rugged ridges of the **Gammon Ranges National Park▶▶** glint and glitter with quartz, fluorspar and other minerals. There are hot springs, a vast salt lake, an observatory and an abundance of wildlife.

▶▶▶ Barossa Valley

See page 144.

▶ Birdwood 125B4

The **National Motor Museum** is a good excuse for a leisurely drive through the Adelaide Hills. Australia's biggest collection of vintage, veteran and classic cars is grouped around the stone-built Birdwood Mill of 1852.

▶▶ Burra 125B4

In the 1840s, the discovery of rich copper deposits in Kapunda and Burra rescued the ailing South Australian economy. Miners flocked to Burra, 154km (96 miles) north of Adelaide, and within 10 years had created the Monster Mine, 13km (8 miles) long and 6km (3.75 miles) across. Today, an 11km (7-mile) heritage trail includes a museum, a mine captain's cottage and the extraordinary riverbed dugouts in which as many as 2,000 miners once lived.

DEUTSCHLAND DOWN UNDER
Germans sailed into Sydney Harbour with the First Fleet, and many thousands have come since. South Australia was the destination in the 1830s and 1840s for whole communities from Brandenburg and Silesia suffering religious intolerance at the hands of the Prussian authorities. The first settlements were Klemzig, now overwhelmed by Adelaide's suburbia, Hahndorf and Lobethal in the Adelaide Hills, then in the Barossa Valley, originally called Neuschlesien (New Silesia).

HOLDEN'S HEROES
Australia became one of the world's major car-owning nations from early on; by the beginning of the 1960s there was one car per family. Sir Edward Holden's car body firm merged with General Motors in 1931, initially assembling British and American vehicles. 'Australia's Own Car' rolled off the Holden production line in 1948, the millionth in 1962. With the advent of the inexpensive and reliable Japanese cars Holden faltered, but in recent years has made something of a comeback.

The lives of the first 'opal gougers' on display at Coober Pedy's Old Timer's opal mine

136

THE AUSSIE WAVE

When you're watching an Australian game of cricket on TV, why do the spectators always seem to be waving casual greetings to unseen friends? It's not friends, but the persistent flies—as noted by Dutch Commander Pelsaert in 1629: 'Such a host of flies came to sit in the mouth and eyes that they could not be beaten off.' This early observation would seem to disprove the theory that the plague is due to the dung dropped in quantity by all those cattle in the Outback. Australians protect themselves from this nuisance with door and window screens at home and, outside, with insect repellent and as nonchalant a wave as possible, since frantic swatting seems only to encourage the fly. No one (except in jest) wears a hat with dangling corks to keep the flies away.

▶▶ **Coober Pedy**   *124D3*

The search for opals has created a landscape of mounds and holes in the ground that greets you on the Stuart Highway, some 858km (535 miles) northwest of Adelaide. The name Coober Pedy comes from the Aboriginal *kupa piti* meaning something like 'white fellow's burrow'. Ever since opals were first discovered here in 1915, enterprising folk from all over the world have been hacking away in the hope of making their fortune, living underground in order to escape the sweltering conditions on the surface. As well as comfortable troglodyte homes, there are underground shops, restaurants, hotels and even a couple of churches. Several old, non-working mines in the area can be visited.

▶ **Eyre Peninsula**   *124B3*

This vast triangle faces the breakers of the Great Australian Bight to the west and the sheltered waters of the Spencer Gulf to the east. The northern base of the triangle is formed by the uninhabited Gawler Ranges, while its southern apex is near the deep-water harbour of Port Lincoln. The sandy soils of the peninsula support wheat and sheep, while the subsoil yields iron ore, converted into steel at Whyalla, South Australia's second city.

The Eyre Highway runs from Port Augusta at the head of the Gulf toward the Western Australian border. The journey south on the Lincoln Highway reveals a magnificent coastline of cliffs and white sandy beaches, dotted with fishing towns and holiday resorts. There are seals and dolphins around **Tumby Bay▶**, while **Port Lincoln▶** is home to Dangerous Reef, sea lions and white pointer sharks. To the south, **Lincoln National Park▶** is famous for its beaches and scenic drives. Beyond here the unspoiled coastline stretches northwestwards to remote **Ceduna▶**, from where migrating whales can be seen between June and October.

▶▶ **Fleurieu Peninsula**   *125B4*

Rolling countryside, vineyards and a superb coastline of wild cliffs and fine beaches provide a wonderful holiday region right on Adelaide's doorstep. Within half an hour's drive south of the city is the **McLaren Vale wine district▶▶**, focused on the township of McLaren Vale amid delightful hills. Farther south, around Willunga, the crop changes to almonds, with a froth of blossom in July. Studded with sandy beaches, including the country's first official nudist one, Maslin, the coast runs southwestwards along the gulf to terminate in rugged terrain around Cape Jervis. The far shore of Backstairs Passage belongs to Kangaroo Island, reached from here by ferry.

Around the corner of the Cape the scenery is no less spectacular, particularly at **Deep Creek Conservation Park▶** where the land falls sheer into the ocean. **Victor Harbor▶ ▶** (see page 142) is a pleasant resort, guarded by the massive lump of rock known as Rosetta Head. From here the vintage Cockle Train chuffs eastwards past the breakers crashing on the beaches of Port Elliot to the charming town of **Goolwa▶** near the mouth of the Murray River (see page 138). The story of the Murray, including its current problems, is told at the impressive interpreattive centre at Signal Point (see page 138).

►►► Flinders Ranges 125C4

These ranges are made up of some of the world's most ancient rocks, marking the landscape northeast of Port Augusta with steep ridges and rugged gorges. These peaks have been cracked, folded and sculpted by millions of years of rain and sun. Of no great height, the ranges owe their popularity to their vivid mineral tones, dramatic landforms and fascinating plant and animal life.

One of the gateways to the main part of the ranges is the township of Quorn, once an important railway junction, but now a small town of 1,500 or so people; here is the terminus of the **Pichi Richi Steam Railway►**, part of the old *Ghan* line. Beyond Quorn, the road to Hawker passes close to the ruins of the old **Kanyaka Homestead►**, which was constructed in the 1850s but has long since been abandoned, as well as the **Yourambulla Caves►►** with their Aboriginal rock-paintings.

The road to one of the country's great geological curiosities, the mighty natural stronghold of **Wilpena Pound►►►**, turns off at Hawker. The Pound is a great oval, 20km (12.5 miles) long by about 8km (5 miles) wide, protected from the outside world by sheer 1,000m (3,280-foot) high walls, sloping steeply to a park-like interior where the flat floor is rich in sugar gums and, in spring, wildflowers. Like any great fortress, the Pound has only one way in, a narrow gorge cut by the Wilpena Creek, sometimes a torrent but usually just a trickle. A number of marked trails of varying difficulty lead from the visitor centre near this entrance; anyone capable of walking 20km (12.5 miles) lengthwise and 500m (1,640 feet) vertically should consider the trek across the Pound and up to its highest point, St. Marys Peak. The stunning panorama includes the dazzling white surface of salty Lake Torrens.

Beyond Wilpena on unpaved roads is the main part of the Flinders Ranges National Park. Its wildlife includes hosts of birds and two types of kangaroo, as well as the rare yellow-footed rock wallaby.

REPTILIAN RAMPARTS
Like so many features of the Aboriginal landscape, the walls of Wilpena Pound are perceived to be the petrified forms of the animal ancestors who assisted at their creation. Two giant serpents were lying in wait here for those who gathered to celebrate the very first ceremony of initiation of a young man into adulthood by circumcision. The serpents devoured them all, save for Wala the wild turkey, Yulu the kingfisher and the young man himself, who all escaped and founded new tribes. The serpents expired, their bodies curling round to enclose the Pound for ever.

137

Typically dry, rugged scenery in the Flinders Ranges

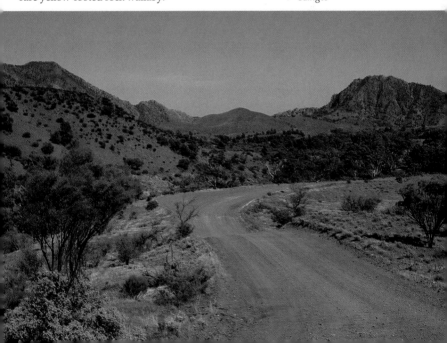

South Australia

The Germanic town of Hahndorf was home to Sir Hans Heysen

SIR HANS HEYSEN
Young Hans came to South Australia from Germany in 1884 at the age of seven. He is one of the best-loved painters of the Australian landscape, whose natural features, particularly its trees and the play of light on them, he studied with great meticulousness. His charming works grace many an Australian gallery, and can also be seen at his Hahndorf home, The Cedars (and its adjacent studio), where he lived from 1912 until his death in 1968. Sir Hans is remembered by having the long-distance walking trail from the Fleurieu Peninsula to the Flinders Ranges, as well as part of the ranges themselves, named after him.

▶ Goolwa 125B4

This little riverport on the lower reaches of the mighty Murray River is the terminus for two enjoyable trips: the old-timer Cockle Train that runs along the coast, and cruises to the mouth of the Murray. The **Signal Point River Murray Interpretive Centre▶** has comprehensive displays on the theme of the Murray River yesterday and today.

▶▶ Hahndorf 125B4

South Australia's second-oldest German settlement (dating from 1839) can be found in a pretty spot in the Adelaide Hills. Conveniently close to the South Eastern Freeway, Hahndorf is full of Teutonic tradition, with German-style architecture and cafés serving traditional foods. Other attractions are the fine artworks of the Hahndorf Academy and **The Cedars▶▶** (see panel). You can still see how the first settlers laid out their homes in orderly fashion along the main street.

▶▶▶ Kangaroo Island 125B4

Separated from the Fleurieu Peninsula by the deep straits known as Backstairs Passage, this is Australia's third largest island, a paradise for lovers of nature, with wild coastal landscapes and a particularly rich animal life. The island was named by the redoubtable Matthew Flinders; when the *Investigator* called here in 1802, his crew shot a few of the locals, members of the subspecies of grey kangaroo still present in large numbers.

Most visitors arrive by ferry from the mainland at the little fishing port of Penneshaw on the Dudley Peninsula at the eastern end of the island. Fairy penguins frequent Christmas Cove just to the west of the harbour. On Nepean Bay, Kingscote preserves some traces of its past in its oldest building, Hope Cottage of 1859. A paved main road heads past the airport into the interior, but the island's unique sights lie on the south coast.

Seal Bay Conservation Park▶▶ is home to Australia's largest colony of sea lions, seemingly indifferent to their many human visitors. Farther west is the spectacular underground world of **Kelly Hill Caves▶**, discovered by a horse of that name that disappeared forever into their still unexplored depths (Kelly's rider was saved).

AUSTRALIAN SEALS
Of the three species of seal that inhabit Australian waters, two live around Kangaroo Island: the New Zealand fur seal and the Australian sea lion. The former were almost hunted to extinction in the 19th century; now protected, their numbers are recovering. Sea lions had an easier time, largely because they lack the warm coat of the fur seal.

The surging waters around Cape du Couedic at the southwestern tip of the island are often visited by another marine mammal, the New Zealand fur seal. At the cape itself is awesome **Admirals Arch▶**, a natural bridge hollowed out in the limestone cliffs, while to the east are the aptly named **Remarkable Rocks▶▶**. Crowning a smoothly planed promontory, great blocks of granite have been eroded into strange shapes as if by the chisel of an abstract sculptor at his most imaginative.

These dramatic natural features are part of **Flinders Chase National Park▶▶**, much of which is a wilderness of low-growing eucalyptus and shrubs. The headquarters of the park is at Rocky River, where friendly kangaroos, wallabies and emus are likely to pester you for your sandwiches. Koalas can be seen in the trees nearby, and platypuses sometimes reveal themselves to the patient observer. The northwestern tip of the island is marked by the isolated lighthouse at Cape Borda. To the east, accessible by a rough road, stretches a spectacular coastline of cliffs, some rising to over 200m (650ft), and sandy bays.

▶ Mount Gambier 125A5

The most important town in the southeast of South Australia had a turbulent volcanic past that only came to an end in relatively recent times. This has left a legacy of cones and craters, with one water-filled hole right in the middle of town. Blue Lake, just outside town, mysteriously changes its hue according to the season.

▶ Murray River 125B5

The sluggish Murray (see pages 112–113) meanders into South Australia near Renmark. From here to where it meets the sea at Lake Alexandrina, the river is popular with holidaymakers. A great way to experience the river is to stay on a houseboat—they can be rented at Renmark, Berri, Loxton, Murray Bridge and several other towns.

ALONG THE MIGHTY MURRAY
Massive irrigation projects have transformed the area into a vast orchard and vineyard, producing oranges, apples, pears and some 40 per cent of the state's grape harvest. Loxton Historical Village re-creates life as it was in the difficult early days of settlement. Many of the places along the river have a poignant feel about them, now that the great days of river trade have gone. There is another evocation of bygone times at the Old Tailem Town Pioneer Village, and the old paddle steamer *Marion* moored at Mannum has been fully restored as a working boat that cruises the river.

A trip up the broad Murray River is a wonderfully relaxing way to travel and view the striking scenery

Vine cuttings were among the plants imported with the First Fleet, though the very first attempts to produce an Australian wine met with failure. However, persistence has paid off, and today Australian wines enjoy a high reputation at home and abroad.

140

AMBER FLUID IN ICE-COLD TUBES

Despite the rise in wine consumption, Australians remain some of the most committed beer drinkers in the world. A century ago, most beers tended to be top-fermented on the model of British ales and stouts, but these have steadily been displaced by bottom-fermented, lager types. These were first brewed by Melbourne Germans as well as by the Foster brothers, originally from New York, who gave their name to Foster's Lager. Visitors used to six-packs may be surprised at the standard-sized 'slab' (a 24-pack).

A winery at Nuriootpa in the Barossa Valley

In the early days, the colonists preferred rum; later it was the country's beer that was rated highly, in contrast to its wines, which foreigners wrote off as crude imitations utterly failing to fulfil the promise of their labels.

Since the 1960s things have changed as a result of increased prosperity and greater sophistication. A visit to a well-stocked wine merchant reveals a whole world of home-grown wine; like other great wine countries, Australia has no real need to import. In fact exports of wine are now reaching AU$2 billion.

New South Wales This state has the most venerable vineyards, in the highly reputed Hunter Valley only a short journey north of Sydney. Wine has been produced in this area since the 1830s, and the valley's 100 or so wineries include some of Australia's best. Quality is the keynote here, whereas far to the southwest, in the irrigated valley of the Murrumbidgee River, producers concentrate on making as great a quantity as possible for the inexpensive wine casks that are Australia's '*vin ordinaire*'.

Victoria Here there were once as many vineyards as NSW and SA had put together, but most were wiped out by *phylloxera* in the 19th century and later replaced by *phylloxera*-resistant American root stock. Victorian wines could now be described as up and coming; there are many 'boutique' wines, some of the best from the **Yarra Valley** near Melbourne. The Great Western area is famous for sparkling wine.

Western Australia This state has its old vineyards too, planted along the Swan Valley in the early days of settlement. Exciting (and expensive) wines come from the **Margaret River** area.

Tasmania Lying closer to the South Pole, Tasmania is benefiting from a fashion for growing vines over a long ripening period in a cool climate, and there is an increasing number of vineyards (mostly around Hobart and Launceston) producing wines of fine quality.

South Australia This is the heartland of Australian wine, contributing over half of the country's total production. Most of the original vineyards of the Adelaide Plains have disappeared, and the huge quantities of grapes grown along the Murray are the basis of Australia's bulk wine trade, but other districts make wines of the highest reputation. Far-off **Coonawarra** in the southeast produces wonderful reds on a tiny band of volcanic soil, while **Adelaide Hills** is the most successful of the newer, cool climate regions. The boutique wines made among the rolling hills of the **McLaren Vale wine district** are much in vogue and the **Clare Valley's** cool-climate vintages are excellent, but perhaps the best of all wine districts is the **Barossa Valley**, north of Adelaide. The combination of suitable soils, summer sun and reliable winter rain makes for an excellent product, grown amid a delightful landscape of old-established towns and well-ordered countryside.

Tastings Vintners welcome visitors to their wineries. Tastings have become a popular pastime, though choosing can be difficult. The name of a reputable vineyard is generally considered a good starting point.

A RUM CORPS
Historical records show that in the early days of NSW coinage was short; in its absence Bengal rum took over many of the functions of currency. Its sale was controlled by the officers of the New South Wales Corps, perhaps the least prestigious of the British regiments of the time. With little to occupy them in the way of genuine military activity, these gentlemen devoted their time to enriching themselves by all possible means, only stirring into martial action when their monopoly on rum was threatened by Governor Bligh. Their march on Government House on 26 January 1808, and arrest of the governor has become known disparagingly as the 'Rum Rebellion'.

Mount Pleasant in the Hunter Valley, New South Wales

Petrel Cove at Victor Harbor

STRANGE MEETING
Two centuries ago, Britain
and France competed in
the race for colonization
of the Pacific, and
Australia was one of the
prizes. In the early 19th
century, an expedition
under the command of
Nicolas Baudin made an
extensive exploration of
the southern coast and of
Tasmania, leaving a sprin-
kling of Gallic names, like
Tasmania's Freycinet
Peninsula. On 8 April
1802, Baudin's ship the
Geographe was sighted
coming westwards along
the South Australian
coast by Matthew
Flinders, in the course of
his circumnavigation of
the whole continent.
Eventually convinced of
her peaceful intentions,
Flinders went aboard the
French ship. This meeting
of two great navigators is
marked by the name given
to the broad body of water
where they met off Victor
Harbor—Encounter Bay.

▶ Naracoorte   *125A5*

This southeastern town celebrates the prosperity of its pastoral surroundings in the excellent Sheep's Back wool museum. But most visitors come to marvel at the beauty of the World Heritage-listed **Naracoorte Caves▶**. Only a few of the 25 or so known caves are accessible; there are guided tours into Blanche Cave and Alexandra Cave. In 1969, the bones of hitherto unknown marsupials, giant kangaroos and wombats were found in Victoria Cave. To the south, Bool Lagoon forms an important wetland region that attracts thousands of waterbirds and other wildlife.

▶ Strathalbyn   *125B4*

Strathalbyn, at the neck of the Fleurieu Peninsula, has something of Scotland in its dignified public buildings and neat public gardens on the banks of the Angas River. The town's past has been tidily gathered up and is pre-sented by the National Trust in two buildings, the 1858 police station and the 1867 court house.

▶▶ Victor Harbor   *125B4*

Victor Harbor's setting on Encounter Bay is superb, protected as it is from the ocean by both Rosetta Head ('The Bluff') and Granite Island, the latter reached across a causeway by horse-drawn tram. The island's colony of fairy penguins generally puts in an appearance in the evening, and whale watching is a popular winter activity.

▶ Yorke Peninsula   *125B4*

This boot-shaped peninsula projects southwards, bounded by Spencer Gulf on the west and Gulf St. Vincent to the east. South Australians come here for quiet vaca-tions, fishing, boating and all kinds of water activities. Towards the tip of the peninsula, around **Innes National Park▶**, the coastline becomes more rugged, though there are still splendid beaches. Copper was once mined around Moonta in the north, and this area, known as 'Little Cornwall', offers evidence of this rich mining history, par-ticularly in the **Moonta Mines State Heritage Area▶▶**.

Strangely compelling, South Australia's Outback includes some of the least hospitable parts of the earth's surface. Distances are vast, water is sparse and summer temperatures are almost unbearable. Human life is spread thinly over cattle stations the size of small European states and 'towns' no bigger than hamlets. But the Outback has its own fascination; its arid beauty is liable to sudden and miraculous change when rain falls, as salt lakes fill with water and wildflowers carpet the land.

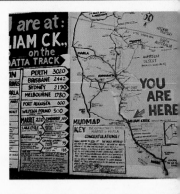

The great vastness of the South Australian Outback is penetrated by a small number of roads, tying together the isolated stations and settlements. Some are paved throughout, while others are still rightly referred to as 'tracks' and set a challenge for the more adventurous.

The Oodnadatta Track This track is part of a route north from Adelaide to Alice Springs, an alternative to the Stuart Highway. Beginning at Marree near the southern end of Lake Eyre, it follows the route taken by the explorer John McDouall Stuart and subsequently by the Overland Telegraph and the original *Ghan* railway line. Before the line was completed to The Alice, Oodnadatta was the railhead, goods being carried on from here on the backs of camels. The old station, now a museum, still stands.

The Strzelecki Track Named for the Polish explorer Count Paul Strzelecki, this track runs northeast from Lyndhurst towards the Queensland border, following the trail used by the notorious Captain Starlight to drive stolen cattle down to southern markets in 1871. The track fringes the northern Flinders Ranges before crossing the interminable sandhills of the Strzelecki Desert and ending at Innamincka where the unfortunate explorers Burke and Wills finally expired.

The Birdsville Track Also a cattle-driving route, this track was traced out by stockmen possibly more law-abiding than Captain Starlight but equally tough. Like the Oodnadatta Track it begins at Marree, but this track ends up in Queensland's Birdsville some 512km (320 miles) later.

Above: William Creek, on the Oodnadatta Track

BIRDSVILLE TRACK SIGHTS
Along the track's course are hot springs, deserted homesteads, 10m (30-ft) high sandhills and the wind-polished pebbles of the Sturt Stony Desert stretching to the horizon. The old frontier post of Birdsville, with its famous pub, comes alive when its annual horse races are held—an event that can yield up to 50,000 empty beer cans!

Drive

Barossa Valley

The world-famous wine-growing district of the Barossa Valley can be reached by this indirect but rewarding route through the varied countryside of the northern Adelaide Hills.

Adelaide's Payneham Road, then Gorge Road lead to the rocky defile followed by the River Torrens, and so into the orchard and vineyard country around **Gumeracha**. Among the many dams built to take advantage of the relatively high rainfall of these uplands, the **Barossa Reservoir** is a popular stopping point because of the curious sound effects produced by its

'Whispering Wall'. The little town of Lyndoch is the gateway to the Barossa Valley, while **Tanunda**, with its informative Barossa Wine & Visitor Centre and charming main street, is the cultural hub of what was Australia's major German-settled area. All around are inviting wineries. **Bethany**, founded in 1842, the valley's oldest village, sits beneath Mengler's Hill Lookout, with its splendid panorama over the neatly ordered countryside. It is worth taking a detour to Angaston's 1850s **Collingrove Homestead**, now managed by the National Trust but once the heart of the huge estate belonging to the Angas family, early pioneers of South Australia.

The route back to Adelaide passes through **Nuriootpa**, the commercial heart of the Barossa, the prosperous agricultural centre of **Gawler** and the satellite town of **Elizabeth**, home to many British immigrants in the post-war years.

Bird-attracting banksias

Drive

McLaren Vale wine region and Fleurieu Peninsula

This drive leads through the attractive vine-growing countryside of the McLaren Vale wine region, across the rolling farmland of the Fleurieu Peninsula to the mouth of the Murray River and the dramatic ocean setting of Victor Harbor.

From Adelaide, Unley Road soon reaches the surrounding hills and climbs to the **Windy Point Lookout**, from where there is a fine panorama of city and suburbs sprawling over the coastal plain. The uplands are a popular residential area for the city's more affluent commuters, but the suburban housing soon gives way to farmland and forest, and to the vineyards and welcoming wineries around **McLaren Flat** and **McLaren Vale.**

A beautifully engineered highway speeds you towards the coast through the broad 'waist' of the **Fleurieu Peninsula** to the small town of Goolwa. Here the excellent **Signal Point River Murray Interpretive Centre** tells all you could want to know about the longest river in Australia, the Murray, which flows through the bird-thronged barrage to the east of the town. You can take cruises from here to the mouth of the Murray and the Coorong rivers.

A short drive along the shore of Encounter Bay leads to **Victor Harbor** with its causeway linking the resort to Granite Island. The view of town and ocean is worth the 100m (330-ft) climb up **The Bluff**, to the west of town. Return to Adelaide by the direct route to complete a 200km (125-mile) drive.

146

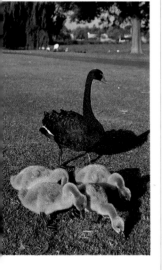

Perth's Swan River was named after the black swans that live here

Cape Londonderry

Cape Bougainville
Admiralty Gulf
Port Warrender
Kalumburu
Joseph Bonaparte Gulf
Drysdale River Nat Park
Ord
Mirima (Hidden Valley) National Park
Wyndham
Kununurra
Kuri Bay
Collier Bay
Kimberley
Lake Argyle
Cape Leveque
Gibb River
King Sound
Beagle Bay
Windjana Gorge Nat Park 937m
Purnululu Nat Park (The Bungle Bungles)
Derby
Mt Ord
Geikie Gorge Nat Park
Halls Creek
Broome
Tunnel Creek Nat Park
Fitzroy Crossing
Roebuck Bay
Camballin
Fitzroy
Wolfe Creek Crater Nat Park
GREAT NORTHERN HIGHWAY

Tanami Desert
Balgo

Great Sandy Desert.

N O R T H E R N   T E R R I T O R Y

Percival Lakes
Paterson Range
Telfer
Minjoo
CANNING STOCK ROUTE
Lake Mackay

Rudall River Nat Park

Jigalong
Lake Disappointment

Gibson Desert

Little Sandy Desert

Giles

arnarvon Ranges
Lake Carnegie
Warburton
1085m▲ *Mt Aloysius*

Wiluna
Lake Wells
Ida Range

Cosmo Newbery
Great Victoria Desert

Leinster
Laverton

gnew
Leonora
Malcolm
Lake Carey

Menzies
Goongarrie Nat Park
Lake Rebecca

Great Victoria Desert Nature Reserve

S O U T H   A U S T R A L I A

Trans-Australian Railway

Kalgoorlie
Kanowna
Coolgardie
Boulder
Kambalda
Lake Lefroy

Eucla Nat Park

Nullarbor Plain
Madura
Eucla
Mundrabilla
Boorabin Nat Park
Lake Cowan
Cocklebiddy

Norseman
Balladonia
Caiguna
EYRE HIGHWAY
rank Hann Nat Park
Lake Dundas

Peak Charles Nat Park
Cape Arid Nat Park
Great Australian Bight

Ravensthorpe
Esperance
Hopetoun
Cape Le Grand Nat Park
zgerald River Nat Park
Archipelago of the Recherche

3   4

Virgin karri forests at Warren National Park, southwest of Pemberton

ON TOP OF THE STATE
The Stirling Range is the highest mountain range in southwestern Australia, and is carpeted by wild-flowers during the spring (September to October). The area has numerous hiking trails, but don't forget your rain gear, because sudden storms are common.

TROPICAL NORTH
Parts of the Kimberley are subject to monsoonal rain-fall; rivers that may have been reduced to a few pools in the Dry quickly fill and spill over the sur-rounding plains. In the far north are habitats of such biological value that their national park status, far from opening them up to the public, has led to the banning of all access.

WESTERN AUSTRALIA Devotees of this state, Australia's largest, are fond of producing maps showing how much of Europe or the USA might be fitted into its 2,500,000sq km (965,000sq miles). Western Australia is undoubtedly *big*—larger than Alaska and Texas combined. With a population of just under 2 million it is also very empty, much of it consisting of variations on the theme of desert—voids of various kinds extend from the desert beaches of the Indian Ocean in the far northwest to the cliffs of the Nullarbor being eaten away by the Southern Ocean. A further factor is its isolation. Perth is generally reckoned to be the most remote city on earth; its nearest large neighbour, Adelaide, is over 2,700km (1,678 miles) away and Sydney is 4,176km (2,595 miles) away. For all this, the West has some of Australia's great holiday destinations.

Friendly, sunny **Perth** is every Australian's second best-loved city, next to Sydney; until recently, this was the place other Australians migrated to in search of the good life at an affordable price. It certainly ranks high in the hierarchy of Australian cities, not least because of its stunning site on the beautiful Swan River, just inland from its port of **Fremantle**, one of the country's most atmospheric historic towns.

Perth and its metropolitan region dominate the coastal plain spreading westwards from the **Darling Range**, Western Australia's modest equivalent of the Great Dividing Range. With a Mediterranean climate, an often spectacularly rugged coastline, fine forests and the lion's share of fertile farmland, this is the most densely inhabited part of the state. Inland stretches the Wheat Belt, its yields of grain dependent on a variable rainfall, gradually merging into the scrublands that herald the desert itself. Straggling along the desert rim is a line of gold-rush towns, some defunct, some, like **Kalgoorlie–Boulder**, still with plenty of kick in them.

In the rest of the state, people are thinly spread. Towns, none of them of any size, are widely spaced along the immensely long coast. The old pearling base of **Broome** is enjoying a revival as a tourist attraction, while **Port Hedland** deals efficiently with the iron ore being extracted in huge quantities from its Pilbara hinterland. Here are strange new settlements of prefabricated buildings, erected quickly to create air-conditioned shelter from the fierce temperatures for miners and prospectors.

The grandeur of Western Australia's natural landscapes is more attractive to its visitors than the urban amenities. The paving of the highways to the north and the north-west of the state has encouraged visitors to explore areas previously considered to be well off the beaten track. Even more than the harsh, vast **Hamersley Range** in the Pilbara, the far-off tropical **Kimberley** is attracting tourists to its wealth of natural wonders, sometimes as part of a trip to the adjoining Northern Territory.

HISTORY New Holland was the unlikely name bestowed in the early 1600s on the western rim of the unknown continent by Dutch seamen on their way to their country's possessions in the East Indies. They would race eastwards across the Indian Ocean, then sail along the Australian coast towards Java. Sometimes they were sailing too fast, and Western Australia's earliest European history is studded with the names of famous ships such as the *Zeewijk* and *Batavia* wrecked on the reefs and shoals of its treacherous coastline.

The first British impressions were not good either; William Dampier's reports in 1688–89 on the barren northwest were distinctly discouraging. It was a (largely imaginary) French threat in the 1820s that impelled the British to add the west of the continent to the Empire; the port of Albany was founded on the south coast in 1826, and in 1829 Lieutenant-Governor Stirling and his band of free settlers established the Swan River colony where Perth now stands. Progress was fitful, and the colony was only saved by a massive infusion of convict workers in the 1850s and 1860s, then in the 1880s and 1890s by the opening up of the Eastern Goldfields, where the combined city of Kalgoorlie–Boulder still thrives on mining today.

In the early 20th century, Western Australia's adherence to the Federation was only secured by a promise to link it to the rest of the country by the construction of the Transcontinental Railway. Even as late as the 1930s, a referendum revealed a majority wanted secession. Today, in spite of extraordinary financial mismanagement on the part of politicians and unscrupulous entrepreneurs, the west's position seems to be secure, based on massive postwar immigration and seemingly unlimited mineral wealth.

A LAND APART
Despite modern transportation and communications facilities, Western Australia is still very much a land apart. Anything east of the South Australian border—be it Adelaide, Melbourne or Sydney—is often referred to under the blanket term 'Eastern States', and West Australians are more likely to vacation in Bali than on the Great Barrier Reef.

The Stirling Range National Park near Albany in the southwest

149

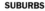

150

Perth

Perth, like Sydney, is an inspired fusion of fine buildings in a splendid natural setting. The view eastwards from **Kings Park** reveals one of the world's great urban panoramas—to the left are the office towers of the city, glittering in the constant bright sunlight; to the right lies the glorious stretch of Perth Water alive with pleasure craft.

The city seems to offer its citizens most of the ingredients of the good life: a Californian-style climate unspoiled by smog; attractive homes in every price category in suburbs that range from the merely pleasant to the opulent; and every kind of outdoor playground, from the sweeps of the Swan River and superb ocean beaches, to lavish parklands that bring the bush almost into the heart of the city.

SUBURBS

The plush succession of waterside suburbs you pass if you take the ferry to South Perth (see panel opposite) may tempt you to sell up and move here without further ado. This is where the millionaires of the 'Golden West' choose to live, with easy access to their yachts at the marina or yacht club.

Covering a large area of bushland and parks, Kings Park in the middle of Perth is an ideal place to relax

RIVERSIDE PERTH
True Perth is a synthesis of city and river, and you should make sure that you enjoy this not only from Kings Park but from the river itself. At the very least, take the ferry across to South Perth (and back again!), but better still travel by ferry to Rottnest Island or Fremantle. For much of the latter part of the journey, your eye will return again and again to the unforgettable image of the city's clustering towers rising over the functionally elegant Narrows Bridge.

CITY OF PLENTY Perth used to be known for its dullness. True or false at one time, this is no longer the case. Contrasting with the historic and lavishly restored **His Majesty's Theatre**, the home of Western Australian opera and dance, the **Perth Concert Hall** is a major addition to the city's cultural life. Another modern landmark is the white tower of the **Burswood Casino**, one of the biggest in the southern hemisphere.

Other buildings of high cultural significance (the Art Gallery and State Library) have been grouped together to form an urban focal point. The city is compact. A network of futuristic walkways straddles streets and tunnels through buildings, linking transportation terminals, shopping arcades, pedestrian precincts and civic plazas. Spectacular sights may be few, but there are a host of urban pleasures.

Perth, viewed from the Kings Park area—a most attractive city

SUN, SAND AND SURF
Perth's suburban beaches are the finest in Australia. The white sands and clear blue Indian Ocean waters of Cottesloe, Scarborough, Swanbourne and many other beaches are far superior to those of more famous Bondi, Sydney's most popular strip of sand.

SIGHTSEE BY WATER
Ferries connect the jetty at Barrack Square in Perth with South Perth, Fremantle and Rottnest Island, and there are trips upstream, too, visiting the early colonial landscapes and wineries of the upper reaches of the Swan River. Cruise ships still occasionally call at Fremantle.

►► Art Gallery of Western Australia   *150C3*
Perth Cultural Centre, James Street Mall (tel: 08-9492 6600 or 08-9492 6622 – recorded information). Open: daily 10–5 Admission free (varying charges for special exhibitions)
This gallery, housed in a spacious modern building, has a fine collection of mostly Australian artworks, including an acclaimed array of Aboriginal art. There are also collections of traditional and contemporary crafts, ceramics, textiles, jewellery, woodwork and glass. The museum extends its influence beyond its doors with sculpture gracing the plaza linking the city to Northbridge.

►► Kings Park   *150C1*
Few cities in the world enjoy anything like this great swath of natural landscape on the very edge of the city. From the founding of the colony in 1829, it was always intended that this area, known as Mount Eliza, should be kept as an open space. About two-thirds of the park is bushland, glorious with wildflowers in the spring, and accessible by scenic drive as well as on foot. Fraser Avenue, with its monuments, memorials and lines of lemon gums, gives an unequalled panorama of Perth in its Swan River setting, while the **Botanic Garden** encapsulates the incomparable floral wealth of Western Australia in a series of richly planted gardens.

►► Perth Mint   *151C4*
310 Hay Street, East Perth (tel: 08-9421 7223). Open: Mon–Fri 9–4, Sat–Sun 9–1 (except 25 Apr). Admission: moderate
Established as a branch of London's Royal Mint in 1899, the Perth Mint still operates as a gold refining and coining facility. This is one of the city's most popular attractions, where visitors can see molten gold being poured, view a collection of nuggets and mint their own medallion.

► Perth Zoo   *150A2*
20 Labouchere Road, South Perth (tel: 08-9474 0444 or 08-9474 3551—recorded information)
Open: daily 9–5. Admission: moderate

An excellent reason for taking the ferry to South Perth, the city's zoo has a fine collection of exotic animals as well as Australian creatures such as emus, koalas and kangaroos, all of which you can meet in the Australian Walkabout. The zoo is famous for its research and breeding of endangered species, and one resident of Western Australia now on the endangered list, the little termite-eating numbat, a small marsupial, is provided with its own quarters.

The zoo is constantly developing innovative features such as the Alinta Reptile Encounter, a Nocturnal House and the African Savannah, a complete reconstruction of an African ecosystem.

▶▶▶ Western Australian Museum   150C3

Perth Cultural Centre, James Street Mall (tel: 08-9427 2700)
Open: daily 9.30–5. Admission: donation
This museum complex comprises a cluster of buildings of many different dates and styles contributing in their various ways to the attractive ambience of Perth's Cultural Centre. Half a day spent here is no substitute for a month spent exploring the natural wonders and human heritage of Western Australia, but it will go a long way towards it.

The highlight of the complex is the modern Francis Street building, which has a **Marine Gallery**, dominated by the awesome 24m (79-ft) skeleton of a blue whale, as well as an **Aboriginal Gallery**, a magnificent attempt to review in a comprehensive and sympathetic way the art, religion and culture of the first Australians. Displays of mammals and fossils are in the old Beaufort Street building, while the history of white settlement of the west is evoked in the cool spaces of the stone-built **Old Gaol**, Perth's original prison complex, which dates from the 1850s.

ALL THAT GLITTERS
Perth is home to several shops that sell precious and semiprecious stones. You can buy pearls from Broome, opals from Coober Pedy and, not least, pink diamonds from the state's own Argyle Diamond Mine.

SUBURBAN ATTRACTIONS
In the southern suburb of Canning Vale you can tour the famous Swan Brewery, while the northern coast offers the AQWA (Aquarium of Western Australia), at Sorrento and Hillary's Boat Harbour at Hillarys. The historic port of Fremantle lies downstream, and a cruise to the Swan Valley wineries is highly recommended.

153

The mock-Tudor London Court, built in 1937, runs between the Hay Street Mall and St. George's Terrace

Walk

Through the heart of Perth

See map on page 150.

This walk of about 4km (2.5 miles) takes in many of the contrasts of old and new that make Perth such a stimulating capital city.

North of Perth's City Railway Station are the buildings and plazas of the **Cultural Centre** including the Western Australian Museum and Art Gallery of Western Australia. The pedestrian mall south of the station is dominated by the sandstone **General Post Office** (1925). The junction of Hay Street Mall with Barrack Street is overlooked by the tower of the **Town Hall**, behind which is **St. George's Cathedral** and the cottage-style **Deanery** (1859) facing on to **St. George's Terrace**.

Government House was built in the mid-19th century and enclosed in luxuriant gardens. Towards the Swan River are **Stirling Gardens** and **Supreme Court Gardens**. Next to the Supreme Court itself is the city's oldest surviving building, the **Old Court House** (1837). Beyond here is Barrack Square and the dramatic Swan Bell Tower, containing the bells of St. Martin-in-the-Fields, one of London's most famous churches.

The mock-Tudor arcade known as **London Court** links St. George's Terrace with Hay Street Mall. Despite its ecclesiastical Gothic appearance, 139 St. George's Terrace is not a church but the National Trust-listed **Old Perth Boy's School**. Farther west is **The Cloisters**, founded in 1858 as Perth's first secondary school and now tastefully converted to offices.

You can complete your walk here, or continue on foot or by free Central Area Transit (CAT) bus past **Barracks Archway** to the viewpoints in **Kings Park**. If you're walking, be sure to have a look at impressive **Parliament House** (which can be toured on weekdays) beyond the archway.

Drive

The southwest

This day's outing from Perth follows the coastline south of Fremantle toward the state's southwestern tip, an area rich in forests and vineyards.

Beyond the resort of **Mandurah**, the old coast road passes close to the lakes, swamps and woodland of **Yalgorup National Park**. **Bunbury** has fine beaches; between here and **Busselton** on Geographe Bay the highway runs through fine stands of tuart trees, some of the few remaining after the uncontrolled felling that took place in colonial days. The coastline of the **Leeuwin-Naturaliste National Park** stretches for about 120km (75 miles) between Cape Naturaliste in the north and Augusta in the south. The back-

bone of the area is formed by a granite ridge capped by limestone; erosion by water has given rise to hundreds of caves, some of which are open.

There are 70 or so wineries in the region—mostly around the little township of **Margaret River**. To the south are the karri trees of the **Boranup Forest**, best seen from the forest drive and the **Boranup Lookout**. There are fine coastal views at Prevelly Park at the mouth of the Margaret River.

If time permits, the tour can be extended to **Augusta** and to **Cape Leeuwin**. The return to Perth is faster via the South Western Highway beyond Bunbury.

Drive

Mundaring Weir

This short excursion enters the heavily wooded Darling Range.

The Great Eastern Highway leaves the city behind as it winds up the Darling scarp. The **John Forrest National Park** is a recreation area, with streams, waterfalls and a pool, while the dam and reservoir of **Mundaring Weir** have an attractive bushland setting. Make your return journey via Lesmurdie Falls and Kalamunda.

155

156

The eerie landscape of The Pinnacles, 243km (151 miles) north of Perth, within Nambung National Park

GRASS-TREES
Among the oddest of Australian plants are the grass-trees. They used to be known as blackboys, from their supposed resemblance to an Aborigine brandishing a spear, but this term has been discarded, at least officially. Resin exudes from the blackened, stubby trunk above which flares a skirt of grass-like leaves and a spectacular flower spike (the 'spear'). Grass-trees depend on fire for their growth, reaching a maximum height of about 5m (16ft).

National parks

The immense spaces of Western Australia include great swaths of unvarying country of little obvious interest, but there are also any number of landscapes well deserving of their national-park or special-interest designation. The state contains one of Australia's 12 World Heritage-registered sites—spectacular Shark Bay on the mid-north coast.

The southwest Facing the meeting point of the Southern and Indian oceans, the southwest of the state enjoys a reasonably high rainfall that encourages the growth of magnificent forests, notably of the karri tree. Its numbers much reduced by the 19th century's insatiable appetite for wood, this forest giant nevertheless survives in substantial patches in a number of national parks. In the southwest, these include the Stirling and Porongurup Ranges, the Boranup Forest in the Margaret River area, and the **Walpole-Nornalup National Park**, a coastal park beautifully sited around the Nornalup Inlet, where deep rivers wind seaward through heath-covered dunes.

Battered by breakers, these southwestern coasts have a rugged quality, well exemplified in the wild cliffs and rocky shoreline of the **Leeuwin-Naturaliste National Park**. On the shoreline farther north, resorts mix with wildlife-rich lagoons and lakes, as at **Yalgorup National Park**. The backdrop to the coastal plain is formed by the escarpment of the Darling Range, covered with jarrah woods and bushland. The jarrah (a eucalyptus) is one of the characteristic trees of the southwest, much logged in the past and sawed up for railway ties. The range is accessible at any number of points along its length, from the **John Forrest National Park** east of Perth, or **Lane-Poole Reserve** on the Murray River, to Marrinup and Pinjarra.

One of the privileges of life in Perth is easy access to unspoiled nature. Only 40km (25 miles) out of the city to the northeast is **Walyunga National Park**, an area of wild bushland where the Swan and Avon rivers have cut through the Darling Range. Equally near the city, but due north, is **Yanchep National Park** where the bush is home to honey possums, kangaroos and bandicoots; a lake and limestone caves can be explored. Few sights are as compelling as the countless limestone pillars known as **The Pinnacles** in the Nambung National Park.

The northwest A great contrast of natural landscapes is found in the vast northwest. Some of the most stunning scenery is on the coast. Among the inlets and peninsulas of the World Heritage-listed **Shark Bay** is unique and dazzlingly white Shell Beach, 60km (37 miles) long and built up to a 10m (33-ft) depth of crushed and compacted shells. The North West Cape has twin parks of outstanding interest. To the east are the parched plateau and deep rocky gorges of the **Cape Range National Park**, descending to the west through fossil reefs and sand dunes to Australia's 'other' barrier reef, the **Ningaloo Marine Park**, 260km (160 miles) of coral reef, sheltering a shallow lagoon. Running inland from the tidal flats and mangrove swamps of the coast is the **Pilbara**, a spectacular upland deeply incised by river valleys and culminating in the vivid gorges of the **Karijini (Hamersley Range) National Park**.

Between the Pilbara and the Kimberley, the Great Sandy Desert claims part of the coastline. Where it merges with the Little Sandy Desert, far inland, are the salt lakes of the **Rudall River National Park**, an extremely remote area which offers no facilities whatsoever.

The Kimberley Beyond the desert, dramatic landforms include **Geikie Gorge**, **Windjana Gorge**, the world's second largest meteorite crater at **Wolfe Creek**, and the strange beehive rock formations of the **Bungle Bungles** (see page 160). Plant life ranges from sparse spinifex to scenes of great luxuriance in spots with a guaranteed water supply.

A possum—part of the myriad wildlife of the state

A RARE BIRD
In 1894 Windjana Gorge in the Kimberley was the scene of a gun battle between heavily armed police and a band of Aborigines led by Jundumurra, known to his adversaries as Pigeon. A skilful horseman and tracker, Pigeon had been compelled to work for the police against his own people. Eventually turning against his masters, he shot a constable, set prisoners free, and for years waged a minor guerilla war. He was finally hunted down and killed at Tunnel Creek on 1 April 1897.

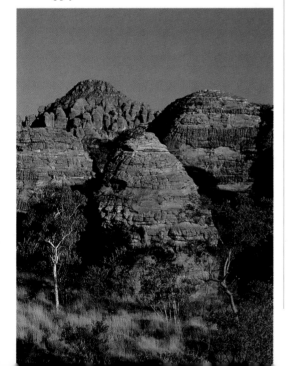

The fragile silica and sandstone forms of the Bungle Bungles are best seen between April and October

The rugged wilderness of Kalbarri National Park can be appreciated by helicopter

EYRE TRAVEL
The 1,195km (742 miles) of the Eyre Highway between Ceduna (SA) and Norseman are less of an obstacle than might be supposed. Plenty of Australians refuse to be deterred by such distances and plan their driving accordingly, settling down to a steady pace and accepting the discipline of distance. At holiday periods it's wise to reserve ahead if you plan to stay in any of the motels along the route. Your vehicle should be absolutely roadworthy before setting out, since repair facilities are limited. Two hazards to remember: The sign 'Road Train' identifies a truck with up to three trailers—make sure the road is clear before attempting to overtake a road train; and when journeying west, you will have the setting sun to reckon with for long and disagreeable periods. One solution (reserve well in advance!) is to put the car on the train for the westward journey and drive back to the east.

How to travel

By air The remoteness and sheer size of Western Australia mean that air travel is often used for journeying between major cities, to reach faraway places of interest and for day and half-day trips. Perth has direct connections to numerous overseas destinations, as well as daily flights to all state capitals and a number of other Australian cities.

By bus Express buses link Perth to the rest of the state, and to other Australian cities (given time!). The metropolitan area of Perth has a comprehensive network of buses, some of them operating out of the futuristic terminal near The Narrows. The capital also enjoys free services in the central area: Central Area Transit (CAT) buses circle the city each day at regular intervals, a great boon once you've got the hang of their routes.

By train Perth has a four-pronged suburban rail service, connecting City Station with Midland, Armadale, Joondalup and Fremantle. Fares are reasonable, and the service is efficient. Most of the state's long-distance railways now carry freight only, though there are passenger trains from Perth to Bunbury in the south (the *Australind*) and west to Kalgoorlie (the *Prospector*). One of the world's great trains runs from Perth Terminal Station, the twice-weekly *Indian Pacific* to Sydney via Adelaide. Linking west and east across the Nullarbor Plain, this train is the railway experience of a lifetime—the journey to Adelaide takes 38 hours, and it is a three-night trip to Sydney.

By car The alternative routes north from Perth to Port Hedland, the **North West Coastal Highway** and the **Great Northern Highway**, are both paved, as is their continuation onwards to the Kimberley and the Northern Territory. It's a long way, though. The road network around Perth and much of the southwest is well developed, but many places can only be reached on unpaved roads, in varying states of upkeep. Some popular routes, like the rough but very scenic **Gibb River Road** through the Kimberley, can definitely only be negotiated by 4WD, and this road is often closed during the December–April wet season.

▶▶ Albany 146A2

Albany was the first European settlement in Western Australia, founded in 1826 by Major Edmund Lockyer to preempt any possible French interest in this quarter of the continent. It became an important base for whalers, then a coaling station for ships on the India–Sydney run; it is now a popular holiday town. The 19th-century buildings include the **Old Gaol;** the **Patrick Taylor Cottage▶** of 1832, constructed from wattle and daub and now a folk museum; the **Old Post Office▶**, now a telecommunications museum and restaurant; and the excellent **Albany Residency Museum▶**. Nearby is the **Amity Replica**, a full-size reproduction of Major Lockyer's brig, which was built from local timber in 1975.

The town nestles between Mount Clarence and Mount Melville, the summits of which give terrific views over coast and countryside. Farther inland are the granite domes and karri forests of Porongurup National Park, and farther still the high Stirling Range. To east and west lies one of Australia's finest stretches of coastline, and protecting the sound to the south is the rugged peninsula of **Torndirrup National Park▶▶**, with spectacular features like the **Blowholes▶**, **The Gap▶**, and **Natural Bridge▶**, a huge granite bridge-like suspension. The old whaling station on Frenchman Bay is now **Whaleworld▶**, which claims to be the world's largest whaling museum.

▶ Augusta 146A2

Augusta is one of Western Australia's oldest settlements, founded in 1830. This popular holiday resort overlooks the mouth of the Blackwood River and has some delightful beaches, plenty of good fishing spots and offers river cruises. This region is perhaps best known for its remarkable series of caves, particularly the spectacular **Jewel Cave▶**, with its strange rock formations that include an enormous straw stalactite and an underground river. In town, the Augusta Historical Museum is worth a visit, and there are panoramic views from lighthouse-capped **Cape Leeuwin▶**, 8km (5 miles) to the south.

DIGGERS ON HORSEBACK
Australia's Desert Mounted Corps distinguished itself in the Middle East in the course of World War I. Albany was the port of embarkation for many of its troops, and they and their mounts are commemorated by the dramatic statue on top of Mount Clarence. This is a recast of the bronze erected on the banks of the Suez Canal in 1932, which came to a sorry end during the Suez crisis of 1956. The original of the horse's head was recovered, and is on view in the Residency Museum.

A LADY LION
The map of Australia reveals a number of names of Dutch origin. Perhaps the most famous of these is Cape Leeuwin, with its lighthouse overlooking the meeting point of the Indian and Southern oceans. Its name recalls the Dutch vessel that first put it on the map, the *Leeuwin*, or lioness, which passed this way in 1622.

The town of Albany viewed from the water

BROOME'S ZERO HOUR
It was not only Darwin that suffered Japanese air raids in World War II. On 3 March 1942, a squadron of Japanese Zero fighter planes spent a leisurely hour attacking a number of Allied flying boats moored off Mangrove Point. At very low tides, the remains of some of these machines can be seen in the bay.

A STAIRWAY TO THE SKY
Another effect of Broome's exceptional tidal range is the optical illusion known as 'The Staircase to the Moon', visible only at certain times of the year when the rays of the moon are reflected off the exposed bed of the ocean.

The pleasant town of Bunbury is a major seaport and the heart of the southwest

▶▶ Broome   147D3

The tourist's southwestern gateway to the Kimberley, Broome makes the most of its lively past, when divers from all over Asia braved the bends and fierce rivalry to harvest precious mother-of-pearl from the sea bed (see page 161). Although only a few luggers still sail today, cultured pearls are farmed in the vicinity.

The past can best be enjoyed in the **Broome Historical Society Museum▶**, at the facinating **Pearl Luggers▶** displays or in the **cemetery**, its graves a grim record of the dangers of life as a diver. The Japanese section is particularly impressive. The town overlooks the mud flats and mangroves of Roebuck Bay, a rich haven for birdlife.

The tidal range at Broome is exceptional, up to 10m (33ft), and at very low tide the footprints of dinosaurs can be seen at **Gantheaume Point▶▶** to the south of the town. From here the splendid white sands of **Cable Beach▶▶** stretch north for 22km (14 miles).

▶ Bunbury   146A2

Bunbury's population of over 50,000 inhabitants makes it one of Western Australia's largest settlements. The viewpoint known as Boulter's Heights provides a panorama over the town and its surroundings. As well as a port, Bunbury is a popular resort, with good fishing, a fine string of beaches along Ocean Drive and, a relatively recent phenomenon, a friendly school of dolphins that enjoy the company of visitors to Koombana Beach.

▶▶ Purnululu National Park (The Bungle Bungles)   147E4

The soft sandstone of this part of the East Kimberley has been eroded into strange rock formations resembling domes, turrets and beehives. Access to the national park, World Heritage listed in 2003, is by 4WD only and there are no facilities: the region is closed from January to March during the wet season. Most visitors prefer to see the park by plane or helicopter; the aerial perspective reveals nature's weird beauty and striking hues. The park also has numerous examples of the art of the indigenous people who lived here, plus a number of burial sites.

Pearl oysters thrive in the tropical seas from Cape York in northern Queensland right round to Shark Bay in the west of Western Australia, a distance of some 3,000km (1,865 miles). There is a particularly large concentration of them between Derby and Cossack in the northwest. From early on, the pearls themselves were a bonus, the mainstay of the industry being mother-of-pearl shell, used for jewellery and, above all, for humble buttons.

Commercial exploitation This began in the 1880s, when Aborigines were more or less forced by pearling masters into diving for the shell on the sea bed, an often lethal task; even if they could avoid the danger of drowning, there were shark attacks, and many boats and their crews were lost in the frequent cyclones. With the expansion of the trade and the introduction of diving suits later in the century, there was an influx of Chinese, Filipinos, Malays, Koepangers from Timor and the most expert of all pearlers, the Japanese. In the 1920s Broome, one of the world hubs of pearling, had a population of about 3,000, some 1,200 of Japanese descent. A typical pearling lugger might have had a European master, a pair of Japanese divers and a crew from Timor. The different races lived in sometimes uneasy proximity in Broome, with occasional outbreaks of violence. Each August during the famous Shinju Matsuri (Pearl Festival), Broome remembers its golden days.

Pearling today By the 1930s, the shell beds had been seriously depleted and, later, mother-of-pearl was displaced by plastic in the manufacture of buttons. Today, a few luggers still set off for the oyster beds some 6.5km (4 miles) off the coast, but most of Broome's current output comes from cultured pearls, raised in 'farms'. Pearling's history is explained in the **Broome Historical Society Museum**, while old pearling luggers can be seen at Broome's **Pearl Luggers** display and at the **Maritime Museum** in Fremantle. A real curiosity connected with the trade is the Catholic mission at Beagle Bay, 128km (80 miles) north of Broome, its altar shimmering with mother-of-pearl.

THE PEARL FARMER'S YEAR
From December to March there is little to do, for this is the region's wet season; from April to August the young oysters are seeded so that they produce pearls; during the remainder of the year the large oysters are removed and their shells used for mother-of-pearl.

Until recently, Broome relied on pearling for its livelihood

WESTERN ROCK

Mount Augustus, 450km (280 miles) inland from Carnarvon, may lack the unique beauty of Uluru but beats it hands-down for size. This is the world's largest monocline, created—according to the Aborigines—when a man called Burringurrah was speared by his enemies in the Dreamtime. From a viewpoint southeast of the rock, his form can still be made out, with the stump of the spear in his leg.

WATERING THE GOLDFIELDS

Extracting gold from the fields of Western Australia posed fewer difficulties than finding water in this utterly arid area. The Irish-born engineer Charles Yelverton O'Connor solved the problem. Already responsible for the construction of Fremantle Harbour and the building of much of the state's railway system, this late-Victorian genius built one of the wonders of the age, known as the Goldfields and Agricultural Water Supply Scheme. Beginning at the splendid dam at Mundaring Weir near Perth, O'Connor's great pipe sucked water 558km (347 miles) eastward in sufficient quantities to quench the miners' thirst and leave some over to irrigate the farms of the Wheat Belt. Attacked by landed interests and ridiculed by critics, O'Connor lost heart and committed suicide a year before completion of the project.

Coolgardie—model of Ned Kelly

▶ Busselton   146A2

Busselton is a pleasant family resort with good beaches, facing north across Geographe Bay and sheltered from the west. The 2km (1.2-mile) long Busselton Jetty is a major attraction, with an interpretative centre, train rides and the **Underwater Observatory▶**, which has viewing windows that look out on to coral and a profuse array of marine life.

The approach to the town from the north passes through a splendid forest of tuarts, a tree unique to Western Australia. Just off the highway is the long and low tin-roofed 1830s colonial mansion known as **Wonnerup House▶**, furnished in period style and open to the public.

▶ Carnarvon   146C1

Only about 144km (90 miles) south of the Tropic of Capricorn, Carnarvon wears a tropical air, with palm trees lining its fascine promenade, and hibiscus and bougainvillaea blooming in its elegantly broad main street. Famous for its fishing industries (you can visit the prawn (shrimp) and scallop processing plant), it is also the heart of a prosperous fruit and vegetable growing area, the Gascoyne district. The **Bibbawarra Bore▶**, 16km (10 miles) north of town, produces a constant gush of water at 65°C (149°F). At **The Blowholes▶**, 69km (43 miles) north, jets of water spout 20m (65ft) into the air.

▶ Coolgardie   147B3

A classic boom-and-bust town 557km (346 miles) east of Perth and 39km (24 miles) from Kalgoorlie–Boulder, Coolgardie was the focus of Australia's most frantic gold rush, with a peak population in the 1890s of 15,000. The then residents' needs were catered for by two stock exchanges, three breweries and a couple of dozen hotels. The population is now only a tenth of its former size.

Looking like an exceptionally grand railway terminus, the old Government Buildings are now the home of the **Goldfields Exhibition Museum▶**, with extensive displays including a model of the town at its height. Opposite is the weird **Ben Prior's Park**, its scrapped machinery and statues of Australian heroes standing out surrealistically in the implacable sun. More abandoned machinery, rolling stock and a locomotive have been preserved in Coolgardie's **Railway Station Museum**, which is in the 1896 railway terminal.

▶ Darling Range   146A2

The unbroken line of this wooded escarpment stretches far to the north and to the south of Perth, rising to a height of about 580m (1,902ft) and defining the boundary of the coastal plain. Not far from the city are several popular recreation areas, like the bushland and streams of the John Forrest National Park or Mundaring Weir. The reservoir here was built between 1898 and 1902 to supply the far-off Eastern Goldfields with water; attractively landscaped, it is a popular picnic spot. The **C. Y. O'Connor Museum►** at the reservoir is named after the engineer who oversaw this vast project and tells the story of its construction (see panel opposite).

► Denmark   *146A2*

Rugged coastal scenery contrasting with the tranquil Denmark River and attractive farmlands makes the small town of Denmark in the extreme southwest a popular place for family holidays. Wilson Inlet offers fine fishing, boating and other aquatic pleasures. To the west, **William Bay National Park►** has sand dunes and pristine beaches, as well as heathland and karri forest, while Walpole has the 600m (1,969-ft) long Tree Top Walk.

► Derby   *147E3*

On the shores of King Sound to the north of the mouth of the Fitzroy River, and within striking distance of the West Kimberley, Derby likes to describe itself as the 'Gateway to the Gorges'; indeed, Windjana Gorge is only about 139km (86 miles) east of the town. Nearer at hand (8km/5 miles away) is a famous boab tree, popularly supposed to have served as a lock-up for a small part of its 1,000-year life.

The fine port and city of Fremantle lies southwest of Perth, where the Swan River meets the Indian Ocean

► Esperance   *147A3*

This deep-water port on the south coast flourished and declined in parallel to the boom and bust in the goldfields to its north. Now tourism has discovered Esperance, not least because of the magnificent beaches and the islands of the Recherche Archipelago. A scenic drive takes in part of the fine coastline and leads to **Pink Lake►**, an extraordinary salt lake that is genuinely pink. Some of the best coastal scenery is some 48km (30 miles) to the east; here is the **Cape Le Grand National Park►**, with stunning bays of blue water and white sand set between rocky headlands.

►►► Fremantle   *146A2*

Now part of the built-up area of Greater Perth, the old harbour town of Fremantle continues to serve as Western Australia's principal port. Founded in 1829, Fremantle owes some of its attractive appearance to the convict craftsmen shipped in to save the colony's faltering fortunes in the gold-rush building boom of the 1890s. These were Fremantle's great days, when the harbour was improved by the great engineer O'Connor (see panel opposite).

The heart of town is compact, its venerable townscape best enjoyed on foot. A good place to get your bearings is the **Round House►**, erected in 1831 as the new colony's prison. The highlight here is the **Western Australian Maritime Museum►►**, housed in two buildings—the original museum that concentrates on shipwrecks, and a modern structure at Victoria Quay, with various galleries and a 1960s submarine, HMAS *Ovens*. Other museums include the **Fremantle Prison►**, with displays and a fascinating convict database, and the **Fremantle Motor Museum►**. There is also Fisherman's Wharf, a lively café strip and the famous **Fremantle Markets**.

HOW FREMANTLE GOT ITS NAME
Fremantle is named after the commander of the British naval force sent here to claim the west before anyone else. Captain Charles Howe Fremantle planted the Union Jack here on 2 May 1829, a month before the first settlers arrived to found the Swan River colony. An optimist, he believed that the colony would become 'in time, a place of consequence', in spite of 'its sandy and uncompromising appearance'.

UNWILLING IMMIGRANTS
It was on the shores of Kalbarri that Australia's first known European settlers made their landfall, albeit an involuntary one. Wouter Loos and Jan Pelgrom had been among the mutineers of the *Batavia* (see page 242). After their arrest by Commander Pelsaert, they were put ashore at the mouth of the Wittecarra Creek in late 1629, where they are commemorated by a cairn. Their further story is unknown; ordered to look for them in 1644, Abel Tasman could find no trace.

Crumbling sandstone has created rugged cliffs around the resort of Kalbarri

▶▶ Geikie Gorge National Park   *147D4*

The tiny settlement at **Fitzroy Crossing** has grown up around the point where the Northern Highway traverses the 640km (400-mile) long Fitzroy River that drains much of the Kimberley. Reduced to a series of pools in the Dry, the Fitzroy rises 16m (52ft) in the Wet (between December and March, when the park is generally closed), flooding vast areas. The effects of this phenomenal difference in water level can be observed by taking a boat trip up nearby Geikie Gorge, where the lower parts of the sheer cliffs have been dramatically scoured by the annual floodwaters. The gorge is home to tropical aquatic life forms, including stingrays and freshwater crocodiles, and is fringed by reeds and dense forest supporting a rich range of birdlife.

▶ Geraldton   *146B2*

This prosperous harbour town to the north of Perth, noted for its export of locally caught lobsters, is popular with visitors year round but particularly in winter because of its excellent sunshine record. Some 60km (37 miles) off shore is the archipelago named the Houtman Abrolhos (derived from the Portuguese for 'Keep your eyes open!') Islands, notorious as a death trap for ships. Relics from famous wrecks are the mainstay of the **Western Australian Museum Geraldton▶**, while the **HMAS *Sydney* Memorial▶** commemorates the 645 men who lost their lives in 1941 while engaged in battle with the German ship *Kormoran*.

▶ Halls Creek   *147D4*

Halfway through the Kimberley on the Great Northern Highway, Halls Creek seems the archetypal Outback town, the middle of a vast area thinly populated by cattlemen and mineral prospectors. A short distance away is Old Halls Creek, with its evocative remains of an 1880s gold rush. Between the two settlements is a natural curiosity, a vein of white quartz standing clear of its surroundings and named the **China Wall▶**. A 130km (80-mile) drive south brings you to the **Wolfe Creek Meteorite Crater▶**.

▶ **Kalbarri** *146B1*

The gorges in the **Kalbarri National Park**▶▶ are up to 80km (50 miles) long and 170m (558ft) deep, cut into the vivid red tumblagooda sandstone. A number of easily accessible viewpoints, like Hawk's Head Lookout, overlook this landscape in its setting of sandy plains. The coastal scenery has its drama, too, with high red cliffs dropping sheer into the ocean. The national park is also famous for its spring wildflowers, which bloom in a great diversity of species.

▶▶▶ **Kalgoorlie–Boulder** *147B3*

The classic gold-rush towns of Kalgoorlie and Boulder were amalgamated in 1989. Gold was first found at nearby Coolgardie; not long after, on 10 June 1893, Patrick (Paddy) Hannan and two mates made the greatest find of all—known for ever after as Hannan's Reward—and within a year, tens of thousands of eager prospectors had swarmed to the 'Golden Mile'. In under a decade, both places had been transformed from ragged settlements to solid-seeming municipalities.

Hannan's slightly bemused statue sits outside the massive 1908 Town Hall on the pavement of the street named after him. This gently sloping roadway is of boulevard dimensions, wide enough to turn a camel train. On either side are monuments to the town's great days: grand public buildings, canopied shopfronts and several elaborate 19th-century hotels. Other attractions include the Royal Flying Doctor Service base and a range of mining-related museums (see panel page 167).

▶▶▶ **The Kimberley** *147E4*

See page 173.

▶ **Kununurra** *147E4*

This town in the East Kimberley was created in the 1960s to act as an urban focus for the Ord River Irrigation Scheme (see panel). A solitary relic of the past, the **Argyle Downs Homestead** was rescued when the land on which it stood was flooded, and is now a pioneer museum. Outside town at **Mirima (Hidden Valley) National Park**▶, 300 million years of erosion have created spectacular patterns in the red sandstone.

THE WILD WEST
Kalgoorlie always was a rip-roaring kind of place, and even today takes a perverse pride in being known as the most crime-ridden of Australia's smaller towns. In 1926, gold thieves hacked to death the detectives sent after them, and ten years later anti-immigrant riots raged for two days before a train-load of police could be brought up from Perth. Many of today's misdeeds seem to be the result of enthusiastic weekend drinking getting out of hand rather than anything more serious.

165

OUT OF ORDER
Frustrated at seeing the floodwaters of the Ord River in the Kimberley running uselessly into the sea while for the rest of the year the land lay scorched and thirsty, the goverment spent huge sums on the Ord River Irrigation Scheme. Completed in 1972, its dams held back the muddy tide and distributed it among thousands of acres of irrigated cropland. But the desert, on the whole, failed to bloom. The cotton crop was killed by caterpillars, and other crops have been only partially successful, while DDT-resistant insects seem to enjoy life in the 984sq km (380sq miles) of the project's main water body, Lake Argyle.

'We can make this country a quarry to serve the whole world,' enthused Henry Bolte, the Premier of Victoria (1955–72). The prosperity of Australia's states and territories rests largely with the abundant mineral resources locked up in their ancient rocks.

Visitors can pan for real gold at the Sovereign Hill historical park in Victoria

IRONING OUT THE LANDSCAPE

Long suspected, the existence of unbelievably rich deposits of iron ore in the Pilbara were confirmed almost by accident in the 1950s. Forced by poor weather to fly low over one of the area's many gorges, Lang Hancock noticed that its walls gave off a metallic sheen. Subsequent investigation revealed what proved to be the world's greatest concentration of iron ore. The topography of whole tracts of land has been transformed by its removal, for example at the BHP Billiton Mount Whaleback Mine near Newman, the biggest opencast iron ore pit in the world, which can be toured.

A wealth of minerals Western Australia really came alive with the discovery of gold in unprecedented abundance in the Eastern Goldfields at the end of the 19th century, but the state also has (or had) reserves of antimony, bismuth, asbestos, coal, tin, copper, iron and nickel, as well as such rarities as tungsten, tantalite and beryl. Exploration and prospecting are very much a matter of the present as well as of history. The world's biggest iron mountain was discovered by accident in the Pilbara in the 1950s (see panel); while the incredibly productive Argyle Diamond Mine near Kununurra, which produces exquisite white, champagne and pink stones, and is the world's largest producing diamond mine, only came on stream in the 1980s.

The first rush But it is the lure of gold that still catches the imagination most. Gold rushes, here as everywhere, were epic events, with their extraordinary mixture of greed, determination and endurance amounting to heroism. The first rush in Western Australia was to Halls Creek in the Kimberley, in 1885, when Charlie Hall's Christmas present to himself was a 800g (28-ounce) nugget. Conditions in this utterly remote and harsh area were perhaps the worst anywhere; one devoted mate, Russian Jack, carted a sick friend 320km (200 miles) in a wheelbarrow in search of a doctor.

Halls Creek failed to live up to its promise, and the prospectors soon abandoned the Kimberley for the greater pickings to be found in the Eastern Goldfields. In 1892 Arthur Bayley rode into Southern Cross with the gold that he and his partner, Bill Ford, had found at Fly Flat, 200km (125 miles) to the east; bars emptied as the news got around, and within hours the greatest rush in the colony's history had begun. Fly Flat was renamed

Coolgardie; within six months thousands were living in a city of tents, having trekked through the waterless waste on foot or horseback, while supplies were brought up by dray or camel train. A year later, the biggest find of all was made at Boulder. The rush greatly increased Western Australia's population and was an immense stimulus to the colony's development. Terrible conditions endured for a while, with plagues of flies, outbreaks of typhoid and water that sometimes cost as much as champagne. Before the completion of O'Connor's pipeline from Perth in 1903 (see panel on page 162), traders in water often became richer than prospectors.

Companies move in Within the space of a few years, individual prospectors had scarred most of the Eastern Goldfields area with their shallow diggings ('specking') and extracted most of the alluvial gold. From now on it became necessary to mine more deeply, requiring the use of sophisticated machinery and the outlay of capital. Companies took over from rugged individuals.

Contemporary opencast methods of gold extraction and the extraordinary landscape they are creating can be observed from the viewing platform overlooking Kalgoorlie's **Super Pit**, which stretches for 3km (2 miles) and will eventually reach a depth of 600m (1,970ft).

KALGOORLIE–BOULDER
The Australian Prospectors & Miners Hall of Fame tells the story of the past, present and future of the region's, and Australia's mining history. Based at the Hannans North Mine complex, the hall of fame—a faithful reconstruction of a mine and its surroundings in its heyday—has displays dedicated to prospecting and minerals. The site also offers underground mine tours and gold panning.

Other Kalgoorlie–Boulder mining-related attractions include the WA Museum Kalgoorlie–Boulder, with exhibits, hands-on activities and outdoor displays, and the School of Mines Rocks and Minerals Museum.

Pilbara: Giant trucks transport the iron ore

The golden sandy beaches around the resort of Mandurah are always popular

RAILS THROUGH THE FOREST
In the early part of the 20th century, the jarrah forests inland from Mandurah echoed to the hiss of steam and the toot of whistles as narrow-gauge locomotives hauled timber to the mills. One of these forestry railways, the Hotham Valley Tourist Railway, running between Pinjarra and Dwellingup, has been kept alive by enthusiasts, and historic steam and diesel trains meet passengers off the modern *Australind* train from Perth. The enthusiasm is such that an additional line, the Etmilyn Forest Tramway, was opened in 1986, leading deep into the heart of the atmospheric jarrah woodlands.

▶ **Mandurah**   *146A2*

Less than an hour's drive south of Perth, Mandurah is deservedly popular with city weekenders. Vast areas of sheltered water along the Murray and Serpentine rivers and the Peel Inlet, 40km (25 miles) of beaches, and shady picnic spots help distribute the crowds and keep at least some of the town's tranquil atmosphere.

▶▶ **Margaret River**   *146A2*

The township of Margaret River is at the heart of the attractive district named after it, where the manicured landscape of prestige wineries contrasts with the savagery of surf pounding a rugged coastline and with a mysterious underground world of limestone caves. Arts, crafts and gourmet foodstuffs abound in the town, while once a year music of the highest calibre is performed in the delightful grounds of the Leeuwin Estate winery.

Among the more sheltered places along the coast, most of which forms part of the Leeuwin-Naturaliste National Park, is **Prevelly Park**▶. This is one of Australia's premier surfing spots, and the Margaret River Classic surf competition is held in the area each November. Only a few of the hundreds of caves are accessible, among them **Mammoth Cave**▶ (named for its size) and **Lake Cave**▶. The **Boranup Forest**▶ in Leeuwin-Naturaliste National Park is a good place to see the massed ranks of karri trees.

▶▶ **Monkey Mia**   *146C1*

Some of the several hundred bottlenose dolphins living in Shark Bay mix with humans and accept fresh fish. To stand in the water of Monkey Mia beach and be nuzzled by a dolphin is an experience that few can resist, but the rangers at the Dolphin Information Centre ask that you check with them first. (See also page 174.)

▶ **New Norcia**   *146B2*

The Benedictines came to Western Australia as early as 1846, leaving the unmistakable imprint of Mediterranean Catholicism here in the bush 128km (80 miles) north of Perth, where they established a mission for the Aborigines. As well as the Abbey Church and Monastery, there is a fine museum and art gallery.

The 'strangeness' of Australian plants, including eucalypts, wattles and banksias, fascinates visitors from abroad. Australia's native vegetation provides a constant reminder that you're not in the northern hemisphere anymore.

Early settlers tackled the isolation of this unfamiliar land by manipulating its appearance to recall the landscapes left behind. Planted in uncountable numbers, oaks, elms, willow and poplars transformed whole tracts of countryside—particularly in Tasmania – into a version of lowland England; the occasional eucalyptus looked like an intruder.

A great variety One of the joys of springtime is the abundance of wildflowers, particularly in Western Australia. Here a twofold isolation, not only from the rest of the world but from the rest of the continent, has resulted in flora of extraordinary variety. The state has some 8,000 named species, plus a further 2,000 that are still anonymous, three-quarters of them unique to the area though not necessarily unrelated to plants elsewhere in Australia. Some of Western Australia's most famous plants are the kangaroo paw, with its strangely shaped red or green flowers; a range of banksias, including the scarlet and acorn varieties; and the 60 species of tooth-leafed dryandras.

Springtime spectacular Wildflowers pattern the ground from north to south as springtime advances. At the **Kalbarri National Park**, 600km (370 miles) north of Perth, flowers begin to bloom in July. Some of the most spectacular displays occur in the heathlands of the southwest, where there are more species of plants than in the rain forest. In places like the **Stirling** and **Porongurup ranges** spring arrives much later, with November being the most rewarding month. **Kings Park** in Perth has extensive areas of natural bushland and a special section devoted to Australian trees, shrubs and wildflowers.

Below: Trailing orchid in bloom

169

Wildflowers in coastal Western Australia

The lesser-known rival of the Great Barrier Reef, Ningaloo Reef is home to over 500 varieties of fish

►► Ningaloo Marine Park and Exmouth area 146C1

A long detour leads off the North West Coastal Highway to far-off North West Cape, whose backbone is formed by the rugged **Cape Range►**. This national park is made up of a high limestone plateau cut into by gorges and ravines, some containing deep pools. To the west stretch rarely visited dunes and beaches, protected from the ocean rollers by a barrier reef, 260km (160 miles) long and extending some 16km (10 miles) from the coast. The reef of Ningaloo Marine Park, with its 220 species of coral, whale sharks (the world's biggest fish) and more, is as yet hardly exploited; there is fishing, camping, diving and swimming, and glass-bottomed boats operate from Coral Bay and **Exmouth**. The best place to begin your exploration of these natural wonders around Exmouth is at the innovative Milyering Visitor Centre in the Cape Range National Park.

► Northam 146A2

An important road and rail junction and depot for the Goldfields Water Scheme, this Wheat Belt town is the regional focus for much of the attractive Avon Valley. The railway from Perth, 96km (60 miles) away, used to terminate here, so Northam was the point at which prospectors would begin their thirsty trek to the Goldfields 450km (280 miles) east. Nowadays, visitors can catch the modern Avonlink rail service from Perth.

► Northcliffe 146A2

This tiny place, lost among the magnificent karri forests of the extreme southwest, began as one of the townships of the ill-fated Group Settlement Scheme of the 1920s, whose hopes and failures are documented in the excellent **Pioneer Museum►**. A good base for viewing the karris (some of the tallest of them grow in the nearby Forest Park), Northcliffe is also the starting point for a 27km (17-mile) road leading to Windy Harbour, the only readily accessible beach between Augusta and Walpole.

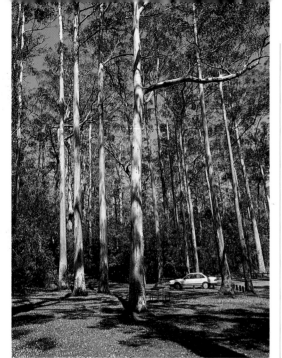

A forest of karris, the tallest of the eucalypts, which can reach a height of 85m (280ft) or more

171

THE GLOUCESTER TREE
It was difficult to build fire-watch towers of sufficient height to rise above the canopy of the giant karris. The answer was to wind a peg ladder around the trunk of a suitable tree and make a lookout cabin at the top. Planes perform the lookout function nowadays, but the Gloucester Tree in Gloucester National Park, near Pemberton, has been kept for fearless tourists to climb its 153 rungs and be rewarded with a stupendous view over the treetops. It's the loftiest fire lookout tree in the world, but at around 60m (195ft) it is by no means the tallest karri.

► Nullarbor Plain   147B4

Renowned for its utter desolation, the world's largest flat surface stretches interminably eastwards into South Australia, covering an area of more than 200,000sq km (77,000sq miles). Few plants (other than saltbush) and fewer animals flourish in this unyielding environment—the name Nullarbor means 'no trees'.

The explorer Edward John Eyre survived his terrible journey across the plain from east to west between 1840 and 1841 by keeping close to the coast, where brackish water could occasionally be found beneath patches of sand dunes. The highway named after him also follows a southern route, while the transcontinental railway strikes off boldly from the goldfields far inland. The landscape along the highway, which is coated entirely in asphalt, is not entirely without incident, since only a relatively short section traverses the Nullarbor proper, but the 144km (90-mile) continuous straight between Balladonia and Caiguna tests any driver's ability to stay alert.

►► Pemberton   146A2

Steeped in logging lore, the township of Pemberton in the southwest corner of the state is the best place to experience the magic of the magnificent karri forest. Its wonders can be appreciated in a variety of ways—by car, on foot or aboard a steam train or 1907 replica tramcar of the Pemberton Tramway, which travels through the forest. The **Gloucester Tree►** (see panel) can be climbed, and the area is renowned for its trout fishing. You can visit a restored 1865 sawpit, take a guided tour around a huge modern sawmill, or trace the area's history in the nearby **Manjimup Regional Timber Park►**. The beauty of the forest is enhanced by clear streams, pretty cascades and a wealth of wildflowers in the spring.

RAILS ACROSS THE DESERT
Passengers on the Trans Australia Railway have the dubious distinction of taking part in one of the world's few railway journeys where the view from your sleeping berth in the morning is identical to the one on which you closed the curtain the night before! Imposing-sounding stations turn out to be nothing more than a marker planted in the wilderness, or at the very most a huddle of railway paraphernalia with a section of loop allowing trains to pass. The 478km (297-mile) 'Long Straight' between Ooldea and Watson tests the patience of the most disciplined driver of the big diesel hauling its train of stainless steel cars.

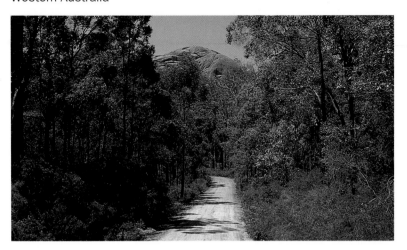

There are several high peaks in Porongurup National Park in the Albany hinterland

KARRIED TO EXTREMES
One of the tallest of all eucalypts is the karri (*Eucalyptus diversicolor*), a magnificent tree reaching a height of 85m (280ft), and with a life-span of up to 1,000 years. Growing together in the forest, the soaring stems of the karris create the stately atmosphere of a Gothic church. The finest tracts of karri forest are found in the well-watered south, inland from the coast between Augusta and Albany; much of it was cleared after both world wars to make small-holdings for returned soldiers. Most of these settlements failed, since the deep loamy soil preferred by the karris was good for trees but not for crops.

▶ **Pilbara** 147C2

Until the 1960s, a few cattlemen were the only inhabitants of this wasteland in the northwest. The accidental discovery in the 1950s of what proved to be the world's largest deposit of iron ore (see page 166) was the stimulus for the construction of mining cities like Tom Price and Newman and the growth of deep-water harbours like Dampier and Port Hedland. Trains 2,000m (6,560ft) long haul the ore from the huge opencast pits down hundreds of kilometres of track to the sea. Much of this exported raw material is later returned to Australia in the form of Japanese cars.

Tourists come this way for winter sun and for the stunning landscapes of the **Karijini (Hamersley Range) National Park▶ ▶**. The vivid rocks of this ancient plateau have been bitten into deeply by the action of rivers, forming splendid gorges where intensely cold water gathers in pools and where a surprisingly lush vegetation flourishes. Even more luxuriant plants are a feature of the **Millstream-Chichester National Park▶**, to the north, where there is a large colony of fruit bats and permanently flowing water, nourishing the palm trees of a relict rain forest.

▶▶ **The Pinnacles (Nambung National Park)** 146B2

The thousands of limestone monoliths scattered around the sandy plain south of the coastal township of Cervantes were mistaken by Dutch sailors for the remains of an ancient city. Varying in size from 6m (19-ft) giants to finger-thick pieces of piping, they may well be the fossilized roots of long-dead trees and shrubs. Whatever their origin, they remain compelling in their desert setting. The Cervantes area boasts several beautiful beaches, popular with sailboarders and boaters.

▶ **Porongurup National Park** 146A2

The ancient granites of this range of hills in the Albany hinterland have been eroded into domes and formations like Balancing Rock. Castle Rock (570m/1,870ft) gives stunning views over karri forest and the country beyond. In spring, the forest floor is brilliant with wildflowers.

This remote land in the far north of Western Australia was explored in 1879 by Alexander Forrest, who thought that it might sustain grazing animals. Huge stations still graze their stock on the sparse vegetation. There is diamond mining in the East Kimberley, and tourists pass through on around-Australia trips or make the Kimberley their prime destination, drawn by the lure of a 'last frontier'.

East Kimberley The modern township of Kununurra is the gateway to the East Kimberley, a region of ancient volcanic rocks and sandstone ranges. Tropical rainfall fills the rivers in the Wet, supporting a rich pattern of vegetation and wildlife, while mangrove swamps clothe the margins of estuaries. The Ord River Irrigation Scheme has attempted to harness the river's summer flow to irrigate vast areas of cropland, with only limited success; remote **Wyndham**, the state's northernmost harbour and a port town since the 1880s, exports cattle as well as whatever crops the project produces. Persistence will lead the determined visitor to natural wonders like the **Mitchell Falls**, or even (with a permit) along the Kalumburu Road to the far off Aboriginal Reserve and Mission near the mouth of the King Edward River. Some areas, like the Drysdale River National Park, of unresearched biological value, may not be visited at all.

West Kimberley Entered via Broome and Derby, the west has spectacular inland gorges, cut through the limestones of an ancient barrier reef, long since hoisted high above sea level. The river running through **Windjana Gorge**, composed of rocks that are part of a 350-million-year-old limestone shelf, is reduced to a series of pools in the dry season, while the mighty Fitzroy River manages to maintain an all-year flow through the much longer **Geikie Gorge**.

HOW TO GET THERE
Most traffic takes the long way round from Derby to Kununurra via the main highway. This gives access to Wolfe Creek Crater National Park as well as the magical Purnululu National Park (or The Bungle Bungles), though both of these extraordinary natural phenomena are better seen from the air. The shorter route is the Gibb River Road, rougher but more rewarding, with well-vegetated creeks, gorges and waterholes.

173

The Argyle Diamond Mine in the East Kimberley produces high-quality stones

A NEST OF RATS
Rottnest Island, meaning rats' nest island, was named in 1696 by Dutchman Willem de Vlamingh who found the place infested with what he took to be large rodents. The rats were in fact the hare-sized marsupials known as quokkas, a kind of small wallaby, found here on 'Rotto' and on parts of the mainland.

MARINE WONDERLAND
Shark Bay's UNESCO World Heritage status was bestowed for its remarkable natural beauty and significance. The Monkey Mia dolphins are the region's best-known attraction, but the bay also contains stromatolites—fossilized layers of blue-green algae, and the oldest form of life on earth—at Hamelin Pool, and one of the last-surviving herds of dugongs, or sea-cows.

Some of the hundreds of dolphins that inhabit the warm waters of Shark Bay

▶ Rottnest Island
155E2

Perth's weekend paradise, 19km (12 miles) off the Fremantle coast and reached by air or ferry from Perth measures a mere 11km (7 miles) long by a maximum of 4.8km (3 miles) across. It has a special charm, enormously enhanced by the lack of cars; bicycles are the main mode for exploring the delightful bays and white beaches along the rugged coastline. The extraordinarily clear turquoise waters are ideal for diving and snorkelling.

▶▶ Shark Bay
146C1

Divided into a series of inlets by peninsulas and islands, and with 1,500km (930 miles) of coastline, Shark Bay was named in 1699 by the adventurer William Dampier. The waters of the bay provide excellent swimming, fishing and other watersports, and there are spectacular dunes of red sand, high limestone cliffs and extraordinary beaches as well. Shell Beach, 60km (37 miles) long, is made up of countless shells to a depth of 10m (33ft); naturally compacted at this depth, this strange material can be cut into blocks and used in buildings. The little resort of **Denham** is the westernmost town in Australia; on the opposite side of the Peron Peninsula are the famous dolphins of Monkey Mia (see page 168).

▶ Southern Cross
146B2

The streets of Southern Cross, founded by gold prospectors in 1888, are still wide enough to turn a camel train. There are mementoes of the old days in the 1891 court-house, now a local history museum.

▶ Stirling Range National Park
146A2

A scenic highway threads through this range, 100km (62 miles) north of Albany, whose peaks rise 1,000m (3,280ft) above the surrounding country. As well as being southwestern Australia's highest mountains, with occasional snowfall, they are a botanical reserve of importance and great beauty, with over 1,200 wildflower species.

▶▶ Wave Rock *146A2*

Wave Rock is a surfer's dream turned to stone. More than 100m (325ft) long and 15m (50ft) high, the petrified breaker's resemblance to the real thing is emphasized by the vertical streaking, the result of natural chemicals in the granite reacting with rainwater.

Other curiosities near the little Wheat Belt town of **Hyden** (337km/210 miles inland from Perth) include further odd rock formations with names like the Humps and the Hippo's Yawn. In Mulka's Cave the visitor can view Aboriginal wall paintings.

▶ Yanchep *146A2*

Days out from Perth often take in the coastline to the north of the city with its fine beaches, sand dunes and chain of lakes just inland. Yanchep itself is a resort, but around it stretches the **Yanchep National Park▶**, with limestone caves, a lake, eucalyptus woods, koalas and a wealth of wildflowers in the spring.

▶ York *146A2*

With Northam (see page 170) and Toodyay, York is one of a trio of much-visited towns in the picturesque Avon Valley, 96km (60 miles) northeast of Perth. Western Australia's most historic inland town, York was founded in 1831, and many of its lovely old sandstone buildings have survived the ravages of time, including an earthquake in 1968.

The **Residency Museum▶** evokes the early days of life in Western Australia, as does the **Avondale Discovery Farm▶** at nearby Beverley, which also has a flora and fauna reserve and farm animals. More than 200 vintage cars, motorcycles and even some horse-drawn vehicles are on display in the **York Motor Museum▶▶**.

Wave Rock: another ancient geological curiosity

175

RIVER OF THE BLACK SWANS
The Avon is a tributary of the Swan River, named for the black swans that make it their home. Both rivers formed a corridor for early settlement, and the area around Guildford includes many historic buildings like Woodbridge at nearby Midland, built in 1885 and now restored and authentically furnished (open to the public). The Swan Valley is famous for its wine. A tour of the wineries is always a popular excursion.

Hotel sign in the small, respectable town of York

Northern Territory

Cape Van Diemen
Bathurst Island
Melville Island
Van Diemen Gulf
Gang Gunak Barlu Nat Park Cobourg Pen
Goulburn Islands
Cape Wessel
Wessel Islands

Clarence Strait
Howard Springs
DARWIN
Fogg Dam
Humpty Doo
Berry Springs Nature Park & Territory Wildlife Park
Darwin Crocodile Farm
Wildman River Res
Jim Jim Falls
Jabiru
Kakadu National Park
Arnhem Land
Arnhem Bay
Melville Bay
Nhulunbuy
Cape Arnhem
Gove Pen

Litchfield Nat Park
Adelaide River
Anson Bay
Daly River
Daly River Nature Park
Daly River
Pine Creek
Edith Falls
Nitmiluk (Katherine Gorge) National Park
Mainoru
Roper
Blue Mud Bay
Groote Eylandt

Joseph Bonaparte Gulf
Wingate Mts
Katherine
Cutta Cutta Caves and Tindal Caves
Willeroo
Upper Roper NP
Mataranka (Elsey National Park)
'We of the Never Never' Graves
Roper Bar
Port Roper
Limmen Bight
Gulf of Carpentaria

Keep River Nat Park
Timber Creek
Victoria River
Gregory National Park
Larrimah
Cox
Nathan River
Sir Edward Pellew Group

Top Springs
Daly Waters
Dunmarra
CARPENTARIA HIGHWAY
Cape Crawford
Borroloola

BUCHANAN
Kalkaringi
Newcastle Waters
Elliott
Wollogorang

Lake Woods
Renner Springs
Maryville
John Flynn Historical Reserve
Barkly Tableland

Tanami Desert
Three Ways
McDouall Range
Tennant Creek
Barkly Homestead
BARKLY
Mt Isa
HIGHWAY
Soudan
Georgina

Rabbit Flat Roadhouse
Devils Marbles Conservation Reserve
Wauchope
Hatches Creek
Lake Nash

TANAMI ROAD
584m Mt Theo
Lander
1140m Mt Leichhardt
Hanson
Barrow Creek
Tobermorey
Adam Range

Chilla Well
Yuendumu
Ti-Tree
Ryan Well
Atartinga
Sandove
Jervois Range

Lake Mackay
Stuart Bluff Range
Hann Range
Simpsons Gap
West MacDonnell National Park
Emily & Jessie Gaps
Frontier Camel Farm
Arltunga Historical Reserve
Ross River
Plenty

Ormiston Gorge
Standley Chasm
Alice Springs
MacDonnell Ranges
Todd
Hale
Hay

Gosse Bluff
Hermannsburg
Finke Gorge National Park
Henbury Meteorite Craters Conservation Reserve
Chambers Pillar Historical Reserve

Kings Canyon
Watarrka National Park
Lake Amadeus
Lake Neale
Petermann
Yulara
1070m Mt Olga
Uluru (Ayers Rock)
Uluru-Kata Tjuta National Park
Erldunda
Kulgera
Finke
Finke
Simpson Desert

WESTERN AUSTRALIA
QUEENSLAND

SOUTH AUSTRALIA
Adelaide

0   100   200   300 km
0   100   200 miles

THE NORTHERN TERRITORY With the thin bitumen ribbon of the Stuart Highway as its backbone, the third largest territorial area in Australia stretches from the country's desert heart, the 'Red Centre', to the coast and islands of the tropical north, the 'Top End'.

The cattle industry, once the basis of the Territory's economy, has been overtaken by mining (bauxite, manganese, uranium) and by tourism; more and more visitors are drawn here, not only to the mysterious landforms of the desert, of which **Uluru (Ayers Rock)** is just one, but to Darwin; to the natural riches of the north; and, above all, to the incomparable World Heritage wilderness of **Kakadu National Park**.

FIRST SETTLEMENT The first European sighting of the coast of the Northern Territory seems to have been made in 1623 by the Dutchman Jan Carstenzoon on board the *Arnhem*. However, the process of colonization did not actually begin until the 1820s.

The first attempts to found settlements came to grief; Port Essington (1824) on the Cobourg Peninsula had no fresh water, Fort Dundas (1824–29) on Melville Island suffered from attacks by hostile Aborigines, and Raffles Bay (1827), also on the Cobourg Peninsula, was abandoned after only two years. Victoria (on an inlet of Port Essington) was established in 1838, and despite cyclones and earthquakes, managed to last until 1849, when it too was given up.

The splendid natural harbour of Port Darwin was given its name in 1839 by Captain J. C. Wickham of the *Beagle* in memory of Charles Darwin, a member of an earlier voyage. However, it was not until three decades later, in 1869, that the site of the present capital of the Territory was surveyed and a start was made on building houses. The choice turned out to be a propitious one, and Darwin, which was originally named Palmerston, has survived and prospered in spite of numerous cyclones and Japanese air raids during World War II.

A ghost gum, recognizable by its white trunk

▶▶▶ REGION HIGHLIGHTS

ROAD TRAINS

The first car to cross the desert Centre took 51 days on its arduous trip from Adelaide to Darwin, and signalled the beginning of the end for the horses, camels and buffalo-drawn carts that had served the Northern Territory's needs until then. In the 1930s, a cumbersome A. E. C. diesel and trailer formed what was called the Government Road Train, hauling supplies to isolated communities. After World War II, Kurt Johannsen used an old army tank transporter to pull no less than eight cattle trailers. Today's road trains are limited to a maximum of three 'dogs' or trailers, a formidable sight as they roar along the highways of the Northern Territory, Queensland and Western Australia.

CONQUERING THE INTERIOR The interminable and arid spaces of the Centre resisted attempts to cross them until 1862 when, undeterred by five heroic failures, John McDouall Stuart finally blazed a trail from south to north; Stuart's route is followed by the highway named after him. Before the road was built, the famous Overland Telegraph, spanning the unmapped wilderness between Port Augusta on the coast of South Australia and Darwin, had been completed in less than two years. Linked at Darwin to the submarine cable from Java in 1872, Australia was connected with the 'grand electric chain that unites the nations of the earth'. The repeater stations, constructed along its 2,897km (1,800-mile) length at Alice Springs, Tennant Creek and other places, became focal points for travellers and townships later developed around these isolated outposts. Pastoralists then moved into the territory, and it became part of South Australia in 1863. The telegraph station at Alice Springs still stands, though the town itself has moved south.

INTO THE 20TH CENTURY In 1911, the Northern Territory, a drain on the meagre resources of South Australia, became the responsibility of the Commonwealth. Though self-governing since 1978, it has still not acquired full statehood, and some of its affairs (Aboriginal matters and uranium mining) continue to be handled by Canberra. For many years it stayed a backwater; few drivers braved the horrible surface of its unpaved roads and there were very few tourists. However, World War II changed all that. In a series of heavy raids, Japanese aircraft inflicted severe damage not only on Darwin but on the Australian psyche. Acutely aware of the country's vulnerability via the empty and remote north, government and armed forces paved the road from the railhead at Alice Springs to the coast, and built a chain of depots, bases and airfields, remains of which can be seen along the highway. The Northern Territory was hauled bodily into the life of the nation by these events.

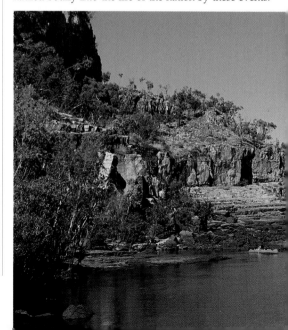

One of the lovely gorges cut by the Katherine River

National parks

Journeying along the Stuart Highway between the arid Red Centre and tropical Top End you experience some of the most dramatic contrasts nature has to offer.

THE RED CENTRE Geological processes have shaped the red rocks of the Centre, creating an almost abstract world of crater and boulder, jagged ridge and lonely monolith, starkly defined against a background of sandy plain or pebbly desert. Etched into this awesome pattern are the winding beds of watercourses, filled only when rare rainstorms rage. Ancestors of the present rivers were fed more generously, and they carved chasm, gorge and canyon niches in this hostile world for a surprisingly rich and varied wildlife. The rugged **MacDonnell Ranges** to the west and east of Alice Springs are breached by many a gap filled with ferns, palms and other exotic plants, some of them descendants of the flora that flourished on the shore of the vast sea that once covered much of central Australia. Waterholes persist here long after rivers have dried up, creating a refuge for both animals and humans.

Experiencing the desert is not difficult. Parks Australia North (Kakadu and Uluru–Kata Tjuta) and the Parks and Wildlife Commission of the NT (other parks) are improving facilities while preserving the landscapes entrusted to them. Their management of Uluru is a model of its kind.

THE MORE VERDANT NORTH Towards the northern rim of the Centre, permanently flowing rivers are a reminder of a more abundant, monsoon rainfall (up to 160cm/63in a year compared with around 12cm/4.75in in the south). Many rivers have their source on the high plateau of Arnhem Land; the Katherine River has cut a series of spectacular gorges in **Nitmiluk National Park**, while **Kakadu National Park** teems with wildlife. The Top End has some of Australia's remotest places, while Darwin has a superabundance of natural areas in its hinterland.

DARWIN'S TERRITORIAL WATERS
At Doctors Gully at the end of the Esplanade, thousands of fish, and no small number of tourists, come together at Aquascene during every high tide—the former to be fed and the latter to do the feeding.

179

RAIN FOREST AND RIVERS
An easy day's outing from Darwin, Berry Springs has both a nature park with natural swimming pools and the splendid Territory Wildlife Park. This tract of bushland and the aquarium is aimed at introducing visitors to the NT's varied wildlife.

Well off the beaten track down the Daly River Road, the Douglas River/Daly River Esplanade Conservation Area is a popular spot for barramundi fishing and boating, although the large number of salties (saltwater crocodiles) precludes swimming.

The remote Gregory National Park has a spectacular gorge and escaprments, and there are boat trips along the Victoria River.

Darwin

The capital of the Northern Territory clings precariously to the peninsula protruding into Port Darwin, a superb natural anchorage that is approximately twice the size of Sydney Harbour.

Darwin has almost disappeared from the map four times. Cyclones flattened the place in 1897, 1937 and again in 1974. In between, the aviators of the Imperial Japanese forces did their best to imitate nature at her most furious in the course of no less than 60 air raids. But Darwin's resilience is legendary; after each disaster, the evacuated population has returned to rebuild. In 1974, Cyclone Tracy

GETTING AROUND

The best way to orientate yourself is to take a trip on the Tour Tub, an open circulating minibus that allows you to get on and off at any point along its route.

destroyed nearly all the town's old buildings, including elegant old stilt houses; their replacements, although not as picturesque, still give Darwin a tropical feeling.

DIVERSE COMMUNITY Advertised as Australia's front door, Darwin has looked for much of its life more like the country's backyard. Its appeal is that it is on the edge, a place in touch with other places. Founded in 1869, it became a base for 'fabulous old-timers—pearlers, buffalo hunters, trepangers, prospectors, cattlemen and overlanders'. The city's population of around 108,000 is extraordinarily mixed; the number of ethnic groups varies between 49 and 61 depending on who is doing the counting. Many are Asians, and of all Australian cities, Darwin is the most conscious of the lands just to the north; Singapore is no farther away than Sydney, and Jakarta is closer.

Many visitors who pass through Darwin have other destinations in mind, either abroad or in the Northern Territory, many of whose attractions are within easy reach. However, they should beware the place's allure, based on a very relaxed, tropical lifestyle.

CITY SIGHTS AND ORIENTATION Small enough to walk around, the heart of the city has a number of surviving (or reconstructed) buildings from early days. Some of these face the parkland of the west-facing Esplanade; here is **Government House** (1883) as well as **Old Admiralty House**, a fine example of a tropical building on stilts dating from the 1920s. Among the grid of streets farther inland is the much rebuilt **Victoria Hotel**, the **Chinese Temple** or Joss House and, in the courtyard of the Civic Centre, an ancient banyan, the **'Tree of Knowledge'**, one of Darwin's most resilient landmarks. These venerable structures contrast strongly with the modern Northern Territory Parliament House, which can be toured. Other sights lie farther afield, many of them overlooking beautiful Fannie Bay to the north. Here is the MGM Grand Casino, close to Mindil Beach where a famous sunset market is held from April to October.

1883 tropical-style Government House, Darwin's oldest building

SHIP OF BREWS
Darwin's famous Beer Can Regatta, held each August at Mindil Beach, is one of Australia's most unusual festivals. This charity event, which attracts thousands of spectators, consists of beach and water races, involving craft made from soft drink cans. Beer cans were formerly used, but these days it's deemed more responsible to use the containers of non-alcoholic beverages.

CROCODILES

Meet the awesome crocodile, Sweetheart, at the Museum & Art Gallery

A FAST LADY
Darwin lies in the path of cyclones, none of which have raged as fiercely as Cyclone Tracy on Christmas Day 1974. In the space of four hours, two-thirds of the city's buildings were destroyed and most of the rest severely damaged. The death toll was put at 66. No one knows exactly how much puff Tracy had in her—the windspeed indicator at the airport broke showing 217kph (135mph)—but the peak velocity has been estimated at around 299kph (186mph). The disaster wasn't totally regretted. Pre-1974 Darwin was no showpiece of urban planning; rebuilding has been carried out along more orderly lines, with the provision of a satellite town, Palmerston, 19km (12 miles) to the southeast.

▶▶ **George Brown Darwin Botanic Gardens** *180C2*
Gardens Road, The Gardens (tel: 08-8981 1958). Open: daily 7–7
Admission free
Plants grow rapidly in Darwin's climate, and damage done to these fine gardens in 1974 (see panel) has been made good. The opportunity was taken to add new features, including collections of orchids, figs and ferns, and an exceptional array of around 450 tropical palms and cycads.

▶ **Fannie Bay Gaol** *180D2*
East Point Road, Fannie Bay (tel: 08-8999 8290)
Open: daily 10–4.30. Admission free
Although it has no history of convict settlement, Darwin nevertheless has an old prison, built in 1883 and in use until 1979. The museum has a gallows, used for the Territory's last execution in 1952.

▶▶ **Indo Pacific Marine** *180A3*
Darwin Wharf Precinct (tel: 08-8981 1294)
Open: Apr–Oct daily 10–5; Nov–Mar 9–1. Admission: moderate
One of the city's most popular attractions, this marine display in the lively Darwin Wharf Precinct focuses on a re-created coral reef. The informative **Australian Pearling Exhibition** is nearby.

▶▶▶ **Museum & Art Gallery of the Northern Territory** *180C2*
Conacher Street, Bullocky Point (tel: 08-8999 8201)
Open: Mon–Fri 9–5, Sat–Sun 10–5. Admission free
This modern complex emphasizes the unique geographical position of the Territory and its capital. In addition to an excellent collection of Aboriginal art and other items, there is a wealth of objects from southeast Asia and the southwest Pacific. The complex includes a maritime section with original seagoing vessels, among them sinister war canoes, dugouts, outriggers, a *lipa-lipa, proas* and the last of Darwin's pearling luggers, the *Vivienne*. However, pride of place goes to Sweetheart, a monster crocodile, which is now stuffed and harmless.

Crocodiles are compelling because many of us can't resist our morbid fascination with the havoc they can wreak. The crocodiles of the Northern Territory, Western Australia and Queensland have loomed large in the public mind not only because of the movie Crocodile Dundee, *but also because of their increasing numbers (a result of effective conservation measures), the opening-up of their habitat to wilderness tourism and the readiness of the media to dramatize any crocodile attack.*

Two kinds of crocodile live in Australia. Harmless to humans, the relatively small freshwater crocodile frequents rivers and billabongs between the Gulf of Carpentaria and Broome in Western Australia. Double its size (6m/20-ft specimens are not uncommon), and distinguished by a broader snout, the saltwater or estuarine crocodile prefers the brackish waters of tidal rivers, though it is quite capable of penetrating far inland as well as out into the ocean. It occurs from India to the western Pacific, and in Australia from the central Queensland coast around Rockhampton to the Broome area.

Salties prey on fish and animals of all sizes, including human beings. Many victims are taken unawares at the water's edge; the crocodile makes its approach underwater, then uses the massive muscle of its tail to propel itself from the deep like a Polaris missile. The prey is dragged underwater and drowned rather than immediately torn apart; the croc can stay below the surface for up to an hour. Male crocodiles lord it over a territory they defend from other males. Much of their time is spent lying log-like in the shallows, conserving energy that is expended in violent display needed to secure dinner.

Look before you dive Darwin's swimming pools and ornamental waters have to be checked before they are opened to the public. Swimming or paddling in areas frequented by crocodiles could well be fatal. Remember, too, that crocodiles are amphibians, capable of reaching high speeds on land. Always obey the signs forbidding swimming (though people sometimes take them for souvenirs!) and seek local advice if in doubt. The best way to see these intimidating creatures is to take a conducted tour in a steel-bottomed boat (one legendary beast—long since dealt with—developed a taste for the more chewy kind of outboard motor, so don't trail your hand in the water!). Craft of this kind ply Yellow Water in Kakadu and, nearer Darwin, the Adelaide River.

CROCODILES
The Darwin Crocodile Farm, 40km (25 miles) south of the city, is home to thousands of crocodiles reared for their skins. Closer to town, you can view crocs and other wildlife at Crocodylus Park in the suburb of Berrimah.

183

WARNING
Crocodiles respect neither man nor beast, so take no chances. Just because you can't see them, it doesn't mean they're not there.

Northern Territory

ALBERT NAMATJIRA

Born at Hermannsburg Mission in 1902, this member of the Aranda tribe became a talented watercolourist in the European tradition, his subject the stunning landscapes of his native MacDonnell Ranges. He and his work were acclaimed; he was presented to the Queen during a royal visit, and in 1957 he was given the extraordinary privilege (for the time) of full citizenship. But Namatjira was destroyed by the tension between white and Aboriginal society and by alcohol; imprisoned for supplying drink to a fellow Aborigine, his morale collapsed and he died in 1959 at the age of 57. His wonderfully fresh paintings can be seen in many Australian galleries. His representational, European style of painting has since been generally abandoned by contemporary Aborginal artists in preference to a more abstract, traditional form of expression, typified by so-called 'dot' paintings.

Alice Springs has a number of memorials to...

▶▶▶ Alice Springs
176B2

Smack in the middle of the continent, The Alice (as it is widely known) has transformed itself from a dusty outpost to an indispensable stop on the tourist itinerary. Equipped with all modern amenities, this pleasant town makes an excellent base for exploring the Red Centre.

The township began in 1871 as a convenient place for a repeater station on the Overland Telegraph between Adelaide and Darwin—it was named for local waterholes, and after the wife (Alice) of Sir Charles Todd, the Postmaster General of South Australia. Development was slow until the arrival of the railway from Adelaide in 1929, the famous but rickety *Ghan*. In World War II, the railhead acquired strategic value, particularly after the Stuart Highway leading on up to Darwin had been given its first coat of asphalt. But it was the advent of mass tourism from the 1970s onward that persuaded the town to provide comfortable hotels, sophisticated restaurants and even a tastefully landscaped shopping mall. All this came as something of a surprise to the old-timers, who not so long ago would ride in for an evening's drinking and hitch their horse to the rail in the main street.

The best place to get an overall impression of The Alice in its desert setting is to climb (or drive up) **Anzac Hill▶** with its obelisk memorial. The town stretches out on the west bank of the bed of the Todd River. The fact that it rarely contains any water has not stopped the hilarious Henley-on-Todd Regatta becoming a major annual event, with legs rather than oars supplying the motive power for the bottomless craft. To the south are the town, attractions like the Royal Flying Doctor Service base, the golf course and the long ridges of the MacDonnell Ranges, pierced by the Heavitree Gap, through which run road and railway. Beyond is the airport, and then the US/Australian Pine Gap communications base.

Although visitors come to Alice Springs more because of where it is than for what it is, there are a fair number of attractions in the town and its immediate vicinity. A few older buildings recall its beginnings; the **Old Stuart Town Gaol** is the most venerable of these, a jail dating all the way back to 1907. **Adelaide House** was built between 1920 and 1926 to serve as a hospital; it now houses memorabilia related to the early days of the Royal Flying Doctor Service. With settlements and homesteads hundreds of kilometres apart, doctors need aircraft to make house calls. For a short time in the 1920s the administration of the NT was split between Darwin and Alice Springs. The **Residency▶** dates from this period, and now houses a small but well-presented museum of local history. The town's main museum is the **Museum of Central Australia▶** at the Alice Springs Cultural Precinct; it has extensive exhibits on the art and natural history of central Australia. Also at this precinct is the **Central Australian Aviation Museum▶**, which celebrates early flight in the Outback.

Transportation and communications are one theme of Alice Springs, if not *the* theme. The place's *raison d'être* was the **Old Telegraph Station▶**, and its plain but evocative stone buildings still stand just north of the town. Both the **School of the Air** and the **Royal Flying Doctor Service▶▶** have bases in town that are open to the public, while off the Stuart Highway beyond the Heavitree Gap is the **National Road Transport Hall of Fame▶**. In pioneering days, the arid interior relied on camel trains for supplies; at the **Frontier Camel Farm▶▶** you can ride one and find out about them and their Afghan masters.

Alice Springs is one of the places where visitors can become better acquainted with the Aboriginal presence. Part of the town's living comes from money spent by Aborigines, even more from the merchandising of Aboriginal souvenirs, though you are unlikely to be able to buy a painting by Albert Namatjira (see panel opposite). At the **Aboriginal Art & Culture Centre▶** you can learn to play the didgeridoo, sample bush tucker and try your hand at spear throwing, or just absorb the culture through music, performance and visual arts. Another major attraction is the award-winning **Alice Springs Desert Park▶▶** with its native animals, walking tracks and Aboriginal presentations.

...and reminders of the Royal Flying Doctor Service

They both feed and entertain you in The Alice

THE STUART HIGHWAY

This 2,700km (1,678-mile) road unrolls its thin band of bitumen through the vast and deserted spaces of Central Australia between Port Augusta and Darwin. Known to all as 'The Track', it follows the route first traced in 1862 by the tough Scotsman John McDouall Stuart. For many years it was a notorious axle-breaker, but nothing was done until Australia's war situation became desperate in 1942 when, with US Forces' help, the road was speedily asphalted from the railhead at Alice Springs to Darwin. Several decades passed before the southern half of the highway was completely paved, and the adventure of gravel, rock and bulldust replaced by the relative predictability of bitumen.

186

One of the huge road trains that travel across the continent's north and Outback

How to travel

By air Darwin's international airport acquired a bright new terminal in 1991. From here there are connections to many overseas destinations, including direct flights to Singapore, Indonesia, Brunei and to all major Australian cities. Alice Springs also has a modern airport, again linked to a variety of Australian destinations. Connellan Airport, serving Uluru and its resort, has a more limited range of connections. If you are in a hurry, a light aircraft will take you virtually anywhere you want to go in the Territory; day tours are also available. The desert looks at its most dramatic from the air; try a hot-air balloon ride at Alice Springs.

By bus Long-distance buses link Darwin, Alice Springs, Uluru and other points in the Territory with major Australian cities. Tour operators offer any number of trips. Some day-trips, like Darwin–Kakadu–Darwin and Alice Springs–Uluru–Alice Springs, are not recommended for the faint-hearted—it is often better to arrange an overnight stop. Only Darwin has a public bus service.

By train The rebuilt line north from Tarcoola in South Australia carries the revived *Ghan* (see page 189), a luxury train connecting Sydney, Melbourne, Adelaide, Alice Springs and Darwin; this is the only railway within the Northern Territory. There are bus and air connections from various towns to the railhead at Mount Isa, terminus for the *Inlander* train from Townsville, almost 1,000km (620 miles) away on the Queensland coast.

By car From Darwin, the **Stuart Highway** runs south through Alice Springs to Port Augusta and Adelaide (3,050km/1,895 miles); at Three Ways the **Barkly Highway** leaves the Stuart for Mount Isa and on to Townsville (2,556km/1,588 miles); at Katherine, the **Victoria Highway** branches off towards the Kimberley and thence to Perth (4,081km/2,536 miles). Paved roads reach Uluru and Jabiru in Kakadu National Park, and all-weather roads will take you to most major tourist destinations.

▶ **Arnhem Land**   176E2

East of Kakadu, a rugged sandstone escarpment seems to bar the way to this mysterious and inaccessible area. Given the name of the Dutch ship whose crew were the first Europeans to sight it, Arnhem Land stretches spectacularly eastwards to form the western coastline of the Gulf of Carpentaria. Now in the hands of its Aboriginal owners, most of it can only be entered by permit, though a limited number of guided tours do take place from Darwin, Kakadu and Katherine, and you can also fly into the remote resort of Seven Spirit Bay on the nearby Cobourg Peninsula.

▶▶▶ **Uluru (Ayers Rock) and
     Kata Tjuta (The Olgas)**   176A1

Reproduced a million times on film, tape and glossy brochures, the great red monolith of Uluru has become one of the world's greatest tourist clichés, yet it still retains the power to stir the spirits of all those who visit it. Not surprisingly, Uluru, the Aboriginal name for Ayers Rock, has a unique spiritual significance for the Aboriginal people of the region, whose ancestors may have frequented the area for at least 20,000 years. A number of sacred sites around the base are protected, and they must not be entered or photographed.

The first European to sight the rock was the explorer Ernest Giles in 1872. In 1985 the land, which includes the World Heritage-listed **Uluru-Kata Tjuta National Park**, was ceremonially handed back to an Aboriginal trust on behalf of the traditional owners, then immediately leased for 99 years to the Northern Territory's parks service. Hotels and other visitor facilities are at **Ayers Rock Resort▶**, 18km (11 miles) away from Uluru itself.

The sediments that make up Uluru and the neighbouring Kata Tjuta were laid down some 500–600 million years ago and they were then tilted almost vertically by earth movements. Uluru rises 348m (1,142ft) above the plain and Mount Olga rises 546m (1,790ft), but their foundations go far deeper into the earth.

Continued on page 190.

The domes of Kata Tjuta, just waiting to be explored

ABORIGINAL PLACE-NAMES
While many Australian place-names were borrowed from the 'old country', the early settlers also used Aboriginal names. Parramatta was the first town to be designated in this way, and others can be seen all over the map, often sounding more appropriate than names recalling the villages, suburbs or shire towns of faraway England. Who could resist Woolloomooloo? Nowadays, many of these foreign names are being replaced with Aboriginal ones; The Olgas (named after a 19th-century queen of Spain) are now officially called Kata Tjuta ('many heads') and Ayers Rock is known as Uluru.

In such a vast country, the battle to overcome the tyranny of distance was a long and difficult one, and the role of the railway in shaping the country, helping it both to grow economically and to grow together politically, was of outstanding importance.

A LONG SHORT CUT
Once the Transcontinental Railway had linked west to east, those journeying from Europe who were in a hurry to get to Melbourne or Sydney would leave their ship at Fremantle and continue their journey by rail. In spite of having to change trains each time there was a break of gauge (at Kalgoorlie, Port Augusta and again at Albury in NSW), the advantage was that a day or two would be saved. The fare, just as on the ocean liner, included all meals—as it still does—but today you no longer need to change trains as the standard gauge stretches right across the continent from Perth to Sydney.

There is plenty of time to study the route

Gauging success The first iron road in Australia was a short line in Adelaide for horse-drawn traffic. The earliest steam railways were those linking Melbourne to its port (September 1854) and Sydney to Parramatta (a year later). But already there was trouble. What track gauge should be adopted?

The colonies initially agreed among themselves that the gauge should be George Stephenson's standard of 143.5cm (56.5in), but then a broader gap between the rails of 160cm (63in), as used in Ireland, was introduced. In the end each colony went its own way, Victoria and South Australia adopting the broad gauge and New South Wales adopting the standard gauge. Queensland and Western Australia came up with a different idea altogether, that of systems built entirely on the narrow gauge of 106.7cm (42in). Tasmania began with standard gauge, then converted to narrow gauge.

This was fine as long as each system remained self-contained, but eventually the tracks reached out to connect (or rather not connect) with those of other networks. Through-passengers had to disembark, goods had to be unloaded and re-loaded, and the most hated three words in all Australia at the time were supposed to have been 'All change! Albury!' the name of the station on the border between New South Wales and Victoria. In 1897, Mark Twain was more than vexed to have to change trains here, because it involved a tedious walk along a lengthy track.

Natural hazards Railways were often difficult and expensive to build in Australia, because of the distances that had to be covered, the variety of natural obstacles that had to be overcome and the high cost of importing rails and other materials. The capricious nature of the landscape didn't help, and flooding often occurred in places where no rain had fallen for years, washing the track away. To keep costs down, many countryside lines were built to a low standard, resulting in irksome speed restrictions. Bridges remained unbuilt; the train ferry that for years carried the coaches and wagons of Sydney–Brisbane trains over the Clarence River was replaced by a bridge only in 1932. Secondary lines were built not only to the 106.7cm (42-in) gauge but to an even narrower 76.2cm (30-in) standard, virtually a miniature railway of the kind that still chuffs between Belgrave and Gembrook in the Victorian Dandenongs today (the famous *Puffing Billy*). Narrower still—a mere 61cm (24in)—are the sugarcane railways that wander through the plantations of Queensland.

From time to time some parts of Australia have toyed with the idea of going their own way. Such a stance was taken up by Western Australia at the end of the 19th century, when it only joined the Federation on condition that it was physically linked to the rest of the country by a transcontinental railway (paid for by the Federation). It took years to lay the rails across the 480km (298 miles) of the waterless Nullarbor Plain, but the line was ready for traffic in 1917 and is now traversed by the world-famous *Indian Pacific*.

The *Ghan* A fascinating railway project was the South Australia–Northern Territory link. Shakily built narrow-gauge tracks snaked out from Port Augusta in the south and from Darwin in the north. The southern section was called the *Ghan* because it replaced the Afghan camel trains that had hitherto been the most effective means of transportation along the route. Reaching Oodnadatta in 1890, it took another 39 years to get as far as Alice Springs, and the top section only went as far as Birdum, 500km (310 miles) south of Darwin. Both lines were ripped up in the 1970s.

After decades of debate and delay the 1,420km (882-mile) northern section from Alice Springs has finally been completed, while the southern section was rebuilt many years earlier along a less flood-prone alignment. A luxury train, also called the *Ghan*, now provides one of the world's classic train journeys along this line, all the way to Darwin.

AFGHAN NIGHTS
An early passenger on the *Ghan*, Wilfred Thomas, settled down to try to get some sleep, but was amazed when his fellow-passengers—a tough-looking bunch of miners and stockmen—cleared the seats away brusquely, brought out the drink and some bagpipes, and then danced the night away together.

The luxury Ghan *connects Sydney and Melbourne with Adelaide and The Alice*

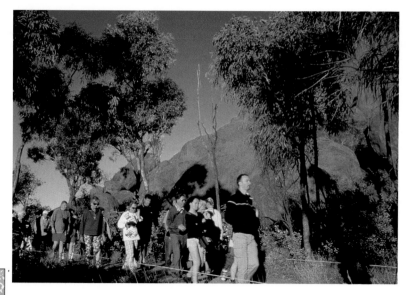

The Mala Walk starts from the Mala Walk sign at the base of Uluru; it is led by a Ranger, or you can do it by yourself if you buy a brochure at the Cultural Centre

AN OUTBACK DRAGON
The fearsome-looking thorny devil is one of the most astonishing denizens of the desert, well deserving its zoological name *Moloch horridus*. In spite of its bulbous spine-covered body and blotchy skin, it is an inoffensive creature, relying on its unappetizing appearance to deter any predator.

Continued from page 187.

Much is made of the mysterious responsiveness of both Uluru and Kata Tjuta to lighting conditions, and few visitors will want to miss the changes produced by dawn and sunset; the basic red is due to the presence of iron.

Most visitors rush to climb **Uluru**, but the expedition should not be undertaken lightly, least of all by the elderly or by those with a medical condition. Take the advice of Rangers and tour guides concerning timing, water supplies and the route (the only one) that must be followed. You might even respect the expressed wish of the local Anangu people (the Traditional Owners of Uluru and Kata Tjuta and the surrounding land) that Uluru should not be climbed, but experienced by a circular walk or tour around its 9.4km (5.8-mile) base. This reveals a wealth of fascinating detail, such as the strange, almost biscuit-like texture of the stone, and the way in which the almost vertical lower slopes have been eroded into deep furrows.

Of geologically related origin, the 36 domes of **Kata Tjuta** offer a quite different but no less fascinating experience, not least because of the rich vegetation and wildlife that flourish in the sheltered gorges between the individual summits. All those able to undertake one of the somewhat stony walks through the area should certainly do so, though perhaps the most spectacular way to view these sleeping dinosaurs (as they have been called) is aboard a light plane on one of the short flights that also takes in Uluru. As well as the isolated table mountain known as Mount Connor, which is perfectly aligned with Uluru and Kata Tjuta, this aerial perspective reveals the layout of the Ayers Rock Resort (see panel opposite). Its architecture and landscaping represent a remarkably sensitive response to its desert environment.

The visitor to Uluru will find an array of tours available, ranging from bus trips to a personalized commentary given while riding pillion on a Harley-Davidson. Aboriginal-led tours aim to bring small groups of participants into more intimate contact with the plants and animals of the desert, as well as with Aṉangu life and their Tjukurpa (Law). A visit to the **Uluṟu–Kata Tjuṯa Cultural Centre▶**, with its dynamic displays, artworks and video presentations, is a must.

▶ Bathurst and Melville islands   *176E1*
Lying off the coast to the north of Darwin, and separated from each other by the narrow Apsley Strait, these two large islands are the home of the Tiwi people. Lacking contact with the Aborigines of the mainland, they developed their own distinct culture, including the making of the extraordinary and highly decorated Pukamani burial poles. The British settlement at Fort Dundas, the first on the north Australian coast (1824–29), was a failure. A Catholic mission was set up in the early 1900s, but the islands have now been returned to their traditional owners and can only be visited on an organized tour.

▶ Chambers Pillar   *176A2*
This 50m (164-ft) high red and yellow sandstone monolith rises abruptly from its spreading foundation to make one of the desert's most striking landmarks. On the fringes of the arid Simpson Desert, the pillar, now protected in a historical reserve, was long used as a navigational aid by intrepid explorers, some of whom left their inscriptions in the soft rock.

▶ Cutta Cutta Caves Nature Park   *176D2*
South of Katherine on the Stuart Highway, these ancient limestone chambers linked by narrow passages are the home of the rare orange horseshoe bat, which was once believed to be extinct. Near by are the Tindal Caves, which have unusual sponge formations. The caves may be closed from December to April because of flooding.

GREEN ON RED
Deserts are fragile environments, whose ecological balance and visual appeal can easily be degraded when visitors arrive in large numbers. The collection of motels and other facilities that had accumulated at the base of Uluṟu was no triumph of design. Its replacement, the Ayers Rock Resort, is distinguished both architecturally and ecologically. Sited 18km (11 miles) away from Uluṟu, its visual impact on its unique surroundings is minimal, partly because of skilful landscaping using the characteristic landforms and plants of the desert. The hotel and other buildings of the resort have thick masonry walls for insulation, while shady verandas and eaves shield windows and walkways from the sun. The huge shade sails rising over the main hotel have become the emblem of the place, but they too play a role in energy conservation.

BARRAMUNDI
This fine tropical fish is Australia's most popular catch, making an excellent meal as well as providing good sport. Barramundi can grow to huge sizes; specimens 1.3m (4.2ft) long weighing up to 10kg (22 pounds) are not uncommon. They live in most northern aquatic environments, making their way to river estuaries to breed. The barramundi also has a feisty reputation as a fighting fish. Barramundi are still plentiful but catches are restricted.

Looking for the rare orange horseshoe bat in the Cutta Cutta Caves

The rounded granite forms of the Devils Marbles, around 100km (62 miles) south of Tennant Creek

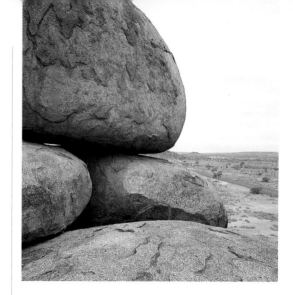

CASTLES OF CLAY

In a land of minimal moisture, there are no earthworms to turn the soil. This role is taken over in the Northern Territory and other arid lands by termites, which pattern whole landscapes with their extraordinary mounds (see below). Sometimes rising to a height of 3m (10ft), these insect fortresses are built from a mixture of soil, spit and dung. However hostile conditions outside may be, behind the rock-hard walls of the interior of the mound is a climate-controlled environment of 100 per cent humidity and a constant temperature of 50°C (122°F).

►► Devils Marbles Conservation Reserve *176C2*

Hundreds of granite boulders lie scattered across the plain beside the Stuart Highway just north of the township of Wauchope—some huge, some tiny and some perched in impossible positions. To the geologist, they are all that remains of the ancient mountains that once rose here, but to the Aborigines they are the eggs of the Rainbow Serpent, Wanambi. They are best seen in the early morning.

►► Finke Gorge National Park *176A2*

Access to the famous gorge in the West MacDonnell Ranges known as **Palm Valley** is along the rocky bed of the Finke River, normally dry but impassable after rain. In contrast to the desert is the lush vegetation thriving in the protected environment of the gorge. The 46,000ha (113,650-acre) national park's 3,000 or so cabbage palms are unique to the area, the descendants of prehistoric trees that grew on the shore of what was then a tropical sea. A walk to Kalaranga Lookout affords a great view of the rugged sandstone gorge, while the Mpaara Walk introduces the mythology of the local Aboriginal culture.

►► Garig Gunak Barlu National Park *176F2*

Now returned to its traditional Aboriginal owners, this national park covers the whole of the remote Cobourg Peninsula, protruding westwards from Arnhem Land, and its surrounding waters. There is splendid sailing and fishing, as well as the experience of utter isolation, since the number of visitor permits issued is strictly limited (contact the NT Parks and Wildlife Commission for details). The superb natural harbour of **Port Essington** was the site of Victoria, one of the early British settlements.

► Henbury Meteorites Conservation Reserve *176A2*

At the end of a dirt road off the Stuart Highway south of Alice Springs is a curiosity: A swarm of craters formed about 5,000 years ago when a big meteorite split into pieces on entering the earth's atmosphere. The largest crater is 180m (590ft) across and 15m (50ft) deep.

▶▶▶ Kakadu National Park 176E2

Some 250km (155 miles) east of Darwin, Australia's largest national park joined Unesco's World Heritage Area list in 1987 on account of the Aboriginal art sites it contains and its almost unbelievably rich and varied wildlife.

Kakadu extends over a number of distinct landscapes. The tidal zone along the shore of Van Diemen's Gulf is pierced by the estuaries of four great rivers, the East, West and South Alligator rivers and the Wildman River. Here the grey of tidal mudflats contrasts with the bright green of mangrove swamps, breeding grounds for the well-known barramundi (see panel on page 191). The flood-plains of the rivers become a vast freshwater sea in the Wet (November to April), teeming with migratory birds and other waterfowl, including egrets, brolgas, pelicans and jabiru. Salt and freshwater crocodiles lurk in creek and billabong. As the land rises southward, eucalyptus woodland develops, interspersed with termite mounds or dramatically interrupted by massive rock outcrops, fragments of the formidable sandstone escarpment marking the western edge of Arnhem Land. This rugged north–south barrier runs for 500km (310 miles), broken by gorges cut by the streams draining the vast interior, the scene of spectacular waterfalls in the wet season. Two of the best known of these are **Jim Jim Falls▶** and **Twin Falls▶**, in the south of the park, both with abundant tropical wildlife.

Natural galleries in the escarpment sandstone contain some of the country's choicest examples of early Aboriginal art. The most visited are those at **Ubirr▶▶**, where there are 'X-ray' paintings as well as other styles, and at **Nourlangie Rock▶**. The **Bowali Visitor Centre**, located near the main town of Jabiru and the excellent **Warradjan Aboriginal Cultural Centre** provide more insight into the area's indigenous history and culture. It is just possible to get some idea of Kakadu in the course of a day visit by air from Darwin (there are bus trips too, in spite of the distance).

ART OF THE OUTBACK

Aboriginal art is traditionally connected to ritual and ceremony rather than self-expression, and is ephemeral or renewable. Much of the art of Central Australia is abstract and symbolic. The artist's canvas could be a rock wall or the ground itself, with sand paintings executed in earth, pebbles, feathers and so on. The wall paintings at Kakadu National Park are representational. Some of them, depicting hunting scenes, are incredibly old, dating from the pre-estuarine period up to 23,000 years ago. The X-ray style, showing the internal organs and bone structure of fish and animals, dates from the estuarine period, which followed a rise in sea level some 7,000 to9,000 years ago. More recent depictions of Europeans and their accoutrements belong to the so-called contact period.

193

Dawn over Kakadu—a sight to remember

In the early part of the 20th century, it seemed as if Australia's indigenous people were doomed as a race. Their numbers had diminished drastically—from an estimated population of half a million at the onset of European colonization to perhaps 60,000 in the 1920s; and many of these were of mixed blood.

GOOD GRUB
While Aboriginal men hunted game with boomerang and fire, women and children foraged for smaller animals, lizards, insects, seeds and fruit. A particular delicacy is the witchetty grub, which is usually seared briefly in hot ashes before being eaten. Initiation into the delights of 'bush tucker' can be a fascinating experience.

194

These children live near a school; for those too far away there is always the radio-transmitted School of the Air

Christian missions established in the Outback destroyed the Aborigines' ancient spiritual links with the land, government 'Protectors' moved them around at will, and Aboriginal children were removed from their parents and brought up in homes or by foster parents. Devastated by alcoholism, exploited by cattle and sheep ranchers as a cheap workforce and consistently denied rights and privileges available to other Australians, it seemed to some as if it would only be a matter of time before mainland Aborigines suffered the fate of the Tasmanians (see page 241).

A genius not extinguished Today, the situation is more hopeful. A voice has been found, one moreover that is listened to and sometimes acted on by those in positions of power. The Aboriginal plight has been noticed by the white majority, thanks to protests like the 'tent embassy' in front of the Canberra Parliament, or the march of 30,000 people through the streets of Sydney, part of a boycott of the 1988 Bicentennial (or 'Invasion') celebrations, and the tens of thousands of people who took part in reconciliation marches in 2000. On a small scale, Aboriginal voices are heard over the air on Aboriginal-owned radio and television stations.

In the realm of politics, reforms have been carried out. The incredible situation in which Aborigines were not classed as citizens or even counted in the official census of population was rectified by the 1967 referendum that gave the Federal Government overall responsibility for Aboriginal affairs. One outcome was the drafting and passing of the *Aboriginal Land Rights Act* of 1976 that enabled Crown lands to be handed back to the 'traditional owners'. A dramatic illustration of the effect of this took place in 1985, when the **Uluṟu-Kata Tjuṯa National Park** formally became the property of the Uluṟu-Kata Tjuṯa Land Trust on behalf of the traditional owners. Entry to such lands is now only possible by means of a permit. Inspired by the success of the 1992 landmark native title claim by Eddie Mabo in the Torres Strait Islands, and the passing of the Native Title Act in 1993, Aboriginal people have since made numerous successful claims for ownership of former Crown Land around the continent.

As seen by others White attitudes have undergone change, even transformation. In an age of environmental devastation and loss of spiritual direction, the way in which Aborigines lived for tens of thousands of years in material and religious harmony with their surroundings has earned respect. Aboriginal art, both traditional and contemporary, is widely admired. There is a widespread wish, expressed by many, to make restitution for over 200 years of injustice. But problems remain, even if they no longer seem quite so insurmountable.

While some younger people of Aboriginal descent try to combine old ways of living with some of the benefits of European civilization, others fail to find a place anywhere and continue to live on the margins of society. Aborigines are far more likely to face a court for minor offences than other Australians; a shameful number of young blacks have died while in police custody.

It may be that Aborigines need to stand back from white values and return as far as possible to their traditional customs before the races can come together again in harmony, and the right of refusal of entry to Aboriginal lands should be seen in this light, rather than denounced as incipient apartheid. In any case, many Aborigines wish to share their heritage with their fellow Australians and with visitors. Contemporary Aboriginal art is widely available, while traditional rock paintings are best experienced in the company of an Aboriginal ranger. Music, dance and ritual are performed in many places, but the high point of many people's experience of Australia is a visit to an Aboriginal community (information is available from the Australian Tourist Commission—see page 266).

A RIGHT TO LAND
Since 1976, Northern Territory Aborigines have owned the land in what were formerly reserves and have been able to lay claim to vacant Crown Land. Many claims have been opposed, and even when successful do not necessarily inhibit mining and quarrying. But royalties have to be paid to the owners, and quite a few communities in areas like Arnhem Land now derive some income from this exploitation of resources.

195

Some communities are willing to share and explain their traditions

The total number of sheep in Australia today amounts to over 100 million, over three-quarters of them the resilient merino with a fleece of up to 2kg (4.5 pounds) in weight. Australia accounts for a substantial portion of the world's wool and is the biggest exporter of lamb and mutton. In some places the sheep/people ratio begs belief: At one time one million sheep roamed Kangaroo Island, for example, compared with only 4,000 humans.

196

RECORD SHEARING
Traditionally working in teams that moved from station to station during the shearing season, shearers honed their skills to an almost incredible pitch; in 1892 a Queensland man, Jackie Howe, set the record for hand-shearing, having shorn 321 sheep in 7 hours 40 minutes. Even with electric clippers, today's shearers find this difficult to match.

Will this be a new sheep-shearing record?

A tough breed One of the animals most closely identified with Australia, sheep were among the passengers of the first fleet, though 59 of Governor Phillip's 90 beasts soon perished. A certain Captain John Macarthur had better luck; he cannily bred Bengal ewes with English rams, then crossed them with Spanish merinos. This mixed breed flourished in the new environment, yielding a fleece of fine quality and good weight—making Macarthur a rich man and providing the foundation of Australia's wool industry, an important contributor to the national economy even today. In the 19th century, it was sheep as much as people that colonized the vast spaces of the new country; by 1900 there were nearly 100 million of them.

Sheep shearers Watching sheep shearers at their highly skilled work is quite a spectacle. The sheep are driven into the shearing shed, thrown to the ground by the shearer, and held fast between their legs. The electric clippers, which long ago replaced the more laborious hand shears, are run swiftly through the fleece, which is removed in one piece if possible. The heaps of wool are sorted according to quality and are then dispatched in huge bales.

▶▶▶ Kata Tju̱ta (The Olgas) 176A1
See pages 187 and 190–191.

▶ Katherine 176E2
This township is the middle of the vast and remote territory described by Jeannie Gunn in her classic 1908 novel of the Outback *We of the Never Never*. The area derives its name from the saying that those who live there can 'never never' leave. You can visit the Northern Territory's oldest surviving homestead, Springvale, but most of the town's 250,000 annual visitors come for the spectacular Katherine Gorge at **Nitmiluk (Katherine Gorge) National Park▶▶**, about 29km (18 miles) east. Rising in Arnhem Land, the Katherine River has cut a series of stunning gorges through the sandstone plateau, providing a refuge for a surprising variety of flora and fauna. The first two gorges can be seen aboard tourist boats, the defiles farther upstream in your own canoe. There are a number of walks from the information centre to points along the gorge.

▶▶ Kings Canyon 176A1
One of the most spectacular natural landscapes of Central Australia, this deep canyon (in **Watarrka National Park**, some 330km/205 miles southwest from The Alice), with its rugged sandstone cliffs rising over 200m (650ft) above the dry river bed, is becoming increasingly popular with visitors. A short walk leads up the floor of the canyon to a lookout point, but anyone with proper walking shoes who is reasonably fit should not miss the more challenging 6km (4-mile) walk up on to the plateau and around the rim of the canyon. Steep to start with, it gives panoramic views over the canyon and a distant glimpse of Ulu̱ru.

▶▶ Litchfield National Park 176E1
This tract of sandstone plateau and lush rain forest is becoming increasingly popular with both tourists and locals, not least because of the excellent swimming in the clear pools at the foot of its numerous waterfalls. The park also has many tall termite mounds and the free-standing sandstone pillars of the 'Lost City'. Access is via

Kings Canyon, rugged, but good walking country

197

A LIVING TRADITION
As a result of both increasing interest in indigenous Australian history and culture, and the initiative of Aboriginal people, several cultural centres have sprung up in the Territory. There is an excellent establishment in Kakadu (see page 193), as well as the Ulu̱ru-Kata Tju̱ta Cultural Centre, near the base of Ulu̱ru with traditional dance, art and craft demonstrations.

SPINIFEX
Early explorers cursed the spiky tussocks of spinifex as its spear-like blades impeded their progress through the desert. Spinifex grasses are often the only plants able to withstand the extreme heat and aridity of the centre, thanks to a deep tap root that manages to extract moisture from far below the surface. Growing outwards into hollow clumps, the plants provide a habitat for other forms of desert life, such as insects, lizards, skinks and even a species of pigeon.

the pleasant tree-shaded township of Batchelor, a couple of hours drive from Darwin.

▶▶▶ MacDonnell Ranges   *176A2*

These parallel ridges of red quartzite and sandstone extend their corrugations hundreds of kilometres across Central Australia, an impressive panorama of rugged natural grandeur when seen from the air. But this was home to the Aranda people until well after the arrival of the white man, and in the gorges cut long ago by the now infrequently flowing rivers there flourishes a lush vegetation of palms and ferns, descendants of the flora that grew on the shore of an ancient tropical sea.

Some of the most spectacular landscapes of the **West MacDonnell National Park** are easily accessible from Alice Springs via Namatjira Drive. Overlooking The Alice itself from a height of 940m (3,084 feet) is the distinctive peak of Mount Gillen. Only a little farther out at 18km (11 miles) from Alice Springs is **Simpsons Gap▶▶**, where the steep-sided gorge, pale sands and fine specimens of river red gums and ghost gums make an excellent introduction to the landscape of the ranges. The reserve is accessible by vehicle but, as always, the best way to explore is on foot, using one of several marked hiking tracks; there is also a special cycle path. Among the wildlife of the gorge is a colony of black-footed rock wallabies.

In dramatic contrast to the impressively wide gorge at Simpsons Gap is **Standley Chasm▶▶**, an incredibly narrow cleft between 100m (330ft) quartzite cliffs. For a short period around midday the sun fills the red walls of the gorge with vibrant light, a popular spectacle for visitors who have walked the kilometre (0.5mile) or so along the bed of the creek. At **Ellery Creek Big Hole▶▶**, high red cliffs frame the water-filled gorge, which is a popular spot for swimming and fishing. **Serpentine Gorge▶** consists of a narrow winding defile with semi-permanent waterholes

198

THE LARAPINTA TRAIL
This long-distance trail leads from the old Alice Springs Telegraph Station right into the West MacDonnells. Hikers can either walk its entire 223km (138-mile) length or undertake shorter sections with an overnight camp. Full details can be obtained from the NT's Parks and Wildlife Commission.

The blue lagoon of the Glen Helen Gorge

A noble face, first imported but now native

199

and ghost gums, and has been left deliberately undeveloped. **Ormiston Gorge and Pound►►** is the largest of the reserves in West MacDonnell National Park, and has permanent waterholes and magical ghost gums, while **Glen Helen Gorge►►** has rugged reddish-tinged cliffs contrasting with the blue water that forms a deep lagoon in the bed of the Finke River. Farther west is **Redbank Gorge►** with its chilly rockpools. Farther on still, Tylers Pass leads to Gosse Bluff, then back towards Alice Springs via the old Hermannsburg Mission; a possible detour is to spectacular **Palm Valley►►** (see page 192).

In the MacDonnells east of Alice Springs, **Emily and Jessie Gaps Nature Park►** has semi-permanent waterholes and Aboriginal paintings, while in **Trephina Gorge Nature Park►►** the pale stems of splendid ghost gums stand out starkly against the rugged cliffs. High above **John Hayes Rockhole►** is a vista of spectacular scenery and Aboriginal rock art. Beyond here, it is possible to explore further—to **Arltunga Historical Reserve** and **Ruby Gap Nature Park**, for example.

► Mataranka (Elsey National Park)   *176D2*
Just off the Stuart Highway, 97km (60 miles) southeast of Katherine, is the Mataranka Homestead and the thermal pool, a popular stop-off point. Every minute, 20,450 litres (4,500 gallons) of water at a temperature of 34°C (93°F) gush into a crystal-clear waterhole fringed by palm trees.

► Pine Creek   *176E1*
Ah Toy's store in this tiny Stuart Highway township is a reminder of the gold-rush days of the 1870s, when the Chinese population outnumbered Europeans 15 to 1. The old times are recalled in the **Pine Creek Miners' Park**.

► Tennant Creek   *176C2*
Legend has it that Tennant Creek came into existence in the 1930s when the axle broke on a wagon carting beer and building materials for a new hotel farther north. Moving on seemed too much bother, so once the beer had been drunk the building was put up here. Then gold was found and Tennant Creek became one of the roughest places along the track. Relatively calm now, the town has plenty of amenities for the passer-by. The **Gold Stamp Battery** still crushes the region's gold and has an interesting Mining Museum, and the 1874 **Overland Telegraph Station** and the 1930s **Dot Mine** are open to the public.

NOT A MIRAGE
Right up to the 1930s, camels played an indispensable part in opening up the middle of the continent. Explorers, surveyors, miners and pastoralists all used camel trains to transport food, equipment, building materials, barbed wire and metal ores. Their equally tough attendants all acquired the epithet 'Afghan', though many of them were from India. Turned loose when trucks, jeeps and planes took over their work, the camels adapted easily to the wild and today are numbered in the thousands. In captivity, they are successfully bred for export to Arabia, as well as giving many visitors the thrill of a humpback ride. The Frontier Camel Farm 6km (3.5 miles) south of Alice Springs is one of the best known of such establishments.

Idyllic Green Island

200

Queensland

Torres Strait

Thursday Island • Cape York

Jardine River Nat Park

E

Cape

Weipa •
Iron Range Nat Park
Portland Roads

York

Mungkan Kandju Nat Park
Rokeby Nat Park

Archer

Peninsula • Coen
Cape Melville
Cape Melville Nat Park

Gulf of Carpentaria

Coleman

Mitchell and Alice Rivers Nat Park
Lakefield Nat Park

Cooktown

Mitchell *Alice* *Palmer*
Laura

D

Staaten

Daintree Nat Park
Mossman
Port Douglas
Kuranda

Mornington Island

Wellesley Islands

Staaten River Nat Park
Chillagoe Mungana Caves NP
Mareeba
Atherton
Millaa Millaa

Gilbert

Karumba • Normanton
Ravenshoe

Burketown

Croydon
Georgetown
Yamanic Falls Nat Park

Great

Yappar
Greenvale

C

Lawn Hill NP

Norman
Burdekin

Gunpowder

Flinders

Cooktown

Camooweal
Saxby

BARKLY HIGHWAY
Cloncurry
Julia Creek
Richmond
Pentland

Mount Isa
FLINDERS
78
HIGHWAY
Hughenden

McKinlay

Barkly

(LANDSBOROUGH HIGHWAY (MATILDA HWY))
Kynuna

Tableland
Dajarra
66
Winton

Middleton

8
Lark Quarry Conservation Park
Bladensburg Nat Park

Georgina
Boulia
Aramac

Longreach
CAPRICORN

B

Mulligan

NORTHERN TERRITORY

Barcoo
Thomson
Barcaldine
71

Bedourie

Diamantina
Jundah
Isisford
Blackall

Simpson Desert Nat Park
Windorah

Bilpa Morea Claypan
Adavale

Birdsville
Cooper Creek
Quilpie

Grey

Lake Yamma Yamma
McGregor Range

Range

Bulloo

A

SOUTH AUSTRALIA
Thargomindah
Cunnamulla

Eulo

Hungerford
Paroo

MITCHELL HIGHWAY

1 **2** **NEW**

Queensland

▶▶▶ **REGION HIGHLIGHTS**

NEXT
20 km

SUGARCANE
One of the spectacles of Queensland is the fires that rage through the cane plantations in winter near towns such as Mossman (75km/46 miles from Cairns), when the dry stalks are burned off to get rid of debris, snakes and insects. At other times the tall green crop presents a peaceful sight, often combined on the coastal plain with tropical fruits like pineapples, mangoes, paw-paws and guavas. Sugar production goes back to the mid-19th century, when South Sea Islanders were brought in in large numbers as indentured workers (called 'Kanakas'). Many of Queensland's sugar mills can now be visited.

QUEENSLAND Second only to Western Australia in area, the Sunshine State straddles the Tropic of Capricorn between the New South Wales border and the Torres Strait separating Australia from Papua New Guinea. The immensely long and fertile coastline, with its beaches and island paradises, is mostly within sight of the hills and mountains of the **Great Dividing Range**. To the east, across the transparent waters of the Pacific Ocean, is the **Great Barrier Reef**, the largest structure in the world to have been built by living creatures. To the west, the subtropical rain forest covering the seaward slopes of the mountains gives way to plateau farmlands of gradually diminishing quality; here, where cattle stations sometimes provide the only names on the map, is some of the country's most authentic Outback, merging in the end with the sands, stones and spinifex of true desert. In the far north, the **Cape York Peninsula** remains one of the continent's strangest and most remote places.

Almost over-endowed with natural beauty and a benign climate, Queensland has become a popular destination with visitors from abroad as well as with Australians on vacation or in retirement. Together with a superabundance of mineral wealth, mined in such areas as **Mount Isa** (the world's largest city in terms of area), the growth of tourism has helped Queensland prosper when the economy of other states has languished. Agriculture maintains its importance; along the coastal plain it has created richly textured landscapes of tropical crops including sugarcane, which is delivered to mills by a network of narrow-gauge agricultural railways.

CONVICT ROOTS Queensland's recent history began with the establishment of a convict settlement at Moreton Bay in 1824. This dumping ground for particularly recalcitrant offenders was soon transferred to an upriver site near by, which was named Brisbane after the Governor of New South Wales at the time. In 1859, independence from New South Wales was granted, and the new colony was named for Queen Victoria.

The population increased and settlement spread; timber workers took the best trees from the rain forest, leaving farmers to clear the resulting scrub. Gold and other mineral finds helped open up the country; Queensland's richest goldfield was the remote, disease-ridden Palmer River, scene of a rush in the 1870s. Immigrant workers played a minor role in Queensland's history, but at one point the gold-digging Chinese on the Palmer outnumbered the rest of the Far North's population. Another immigrant group were the Kanaka—many thousands were abducted from their islands in the South Pacific and New Guinea to work in the canefields (see panel).

A high proportion of Australia's Aborigines lived in Queensland, perhaps more than 200,000 at the time of white settlement. Of a fiercer and more warlike disposition than their fellows elsewhere, they put up a spirited resistance to their dispossession. All their efforts were to little avail, however; by the turn of the 20th century the white settlers had reduced the number of these Aborigines to no more than 15,000.

Queensland has contributed much to Australian history—the state was the birthplace of both the Royal Flying

Doctor Service and Qantas, as well as the trade union movement and, eventually, the Australian Labor Party.

POLITICS AND PEOPLE For a generation, Queensland was governed by the ultra-conservative National Party, who were formerly known as the Country Party and represented rural interests. This organization was led from 1968 by the robust peanut farmer Sir Joh Bjelke-Petersen, a sworn opponent of moral permissiveness, conservation or anything that stood in the way of 'development'. Under his authoritarian rule, demonstrations were banned, books were censored and protected buildings demolished. Building speculators prospered and foreign capital was encouraged to share in the state's wealth, with few strings attached or questions asked. Sir Joh's demise was accompanied by numerous revelations of police misconduct and corruption.

The typical Queenslander is popularly supposed to be the most Australian of Australians. A macho frontier mentality lasted longer here than in the southern states, and until fairly recently, Brisbane took a positive pride in its decidedly provincial character. The state has changed dramatically, however, since the early 1990s and Brisbane is now a modern, vibrant city.

View from the world-famous Cairns–Kuranda train

203

Brisbane

Australia's third largest city, with a population of around 1.6 million, stands on the banks of the winding Brisbane River just inland from Moreton Bay. It used to be regarded as a provincial backwater and as recently as 1961 still had hundreds of kilometres of unpaved streets. Perhaps in order to combat this image, since the mid-1980s Brisbane has embraced the idea of progress with an enthusiasm that has transformed the city into a vibrant modern metropolis.

OLD-TOWN SIGHTS Not all traces of an older charm have been erased in the pursuit of modernity, however, and enough older buildings remain to tantalize the visitor with thoughts of the stylish tropical metropolis Brisbane might well have become. One such example is the corner of George and Alice streets where the **City Botanic Gardens** help frame the white stuccoed fronts of the **Queensland Club** and **Parliament House**.

A more positive face of modernization than the high-rise parliamentary annexe is across the river at South Bank. **Expo 88** was held here, leaving behind a legacy of parkland as well as an entertainment precinct and a number of cultural buildings of the very highest standard.

SUBURBAN SPLENDOUR The suburbs are among the best places in which to experience the city's special quality. Spread over a vast and largely hilly area, they consist almost entirely of single-family houses, and in areas like Red Hill, Paddington and Bardon, the Queensland stilt house can be studied in all its variety.

CITY ORIENTATION The heart of Brisbane's small city is easily explored on foot, although a nice idea is to take the free Loop bus, or the City Sights bus, which wanders around most of the sights, allowing you to jump on and off for a flat fare. A boat cruise to **Lone Pine** (see page 206) or historic **Newstead House** (see page 207) makes a pleasant excursion, too, while ferries link a number of destinations along the river bank.

The handsome 1868 Parliament House has been carefully restored

Walk

Brisbane's buildings and City Botanic Gardens

See map opposite.

Allow a half-day to explore the peninsula on which Brisbane is built.

Extending almost an entire block, the **Central Railway Station** of 1901 faces **Anzac Square** with its **Shrine of Remembrance**. At the corner of Ann and Edward streets stands the extraordinary **People's Palace** (now a backpacker hostel) with its verandas and cast-iron balustrades. The **General Post Office** is an imposing building; its arcade leads to Elizabeth Street, to **Old St. Stephen's Church** and to **St. Stephen's Cathedral** near the waterfront.

The riverside walk extends beyond the Edward Street gates of the **City Botanic Gardens**, flanked by the **Queensland University of Technology**. An intimation of the tropical paradise Brisbane might once have been is given by the lovely 1880s **Queensland Club** in its garden setting.

Opposite are **The Mansions**, striking terraced houses, now home to shops and restaurants. Just off Queens Gardens in William Street are the 1829 **Commissariat Stores**, one of only two convict-era buildings remaining intact in the city. On George Street, the Lands Building and old Treasury have been restored to become the Conrad Treasury hotel and Treasury Casino respectively.

Across the river, reached via Victoria Bridge or the pedestrian Goodwill Bridge, are the **Queensland Cultural Centre** and **South Bank**. A visit here could easily last a whole day; a quicker tour can be made using the Brisbane Transport ferry to return to the heart of the city.

Queen Street Mall is more commercial, though there are some fine older buildings. The walk ends in **King George Square**, which is dominated by the tall tower of **City Hall**.

Home of the Queensland State Parliament

SOUTH OF THE RIVER
South Brisbane's 17ha (42-acre) Parklands have a man-made beach and many other attractions (see opposite page), while the nearby Queensland Maritime Museum is also worth visiting. Also in this area is the vast modern Convention and Exhibition Centre.

PARKS AND GARDENS
Brisbane has a number of green spaces in its heart and immediate environs. The **Brisbane Forest Park** comprises 28,500ha (70,400 acres) of forests, hills and reservoirs, while the **City Botanic Gardens** occupy the tip of the peninsula formed by the great bend in the Brisbane River. There is a riverside walk, and the gardens form an ideal setting for the buildings of the Queensland University of Technology, among them the Old Government House of 1860. At the foot of **Mount Coot-tha** (244m/800ft), about 6.5km (4 miles) from the city are the splendid **Brisbane Botanic Gardens**, with stunning tropical greenhouses and planetarium.

▶ City Hall   204C2
King George Square (tel: 07-3403 8888)
Open: Museum daily 10–5. Admission free
In the late 1920s, a determined attempt was made to overcome Brisbane's provincial image by the erection of this colossal edifice. Inside, there is a museum, with plenty of exhibits celebrating the city's importance. Brisbane's Heritage Trail starts here, taking in the city's most important historic sites and buildings.

▶▶▶ Lone Pine Koala Sanctuary   *off 204C1*
Jesmond Road, Fig Tree Pocket (tel: 07-3378 1366)
Open: daily 8.30–5. Admission and cruise: expensive
This wildlife sanctuary offers an array of wildlife—wombats, Tasmanian devils, kangaroos—and the chance to cuddle a koala. The most enjoyable way to arrive is via a 90-minute cruise upstream from the city.

▶ Old Windmill   204C2
Wickham Terrace, Spring Hill
This is Brisbane's oldest structure, convict-built in 1829 and overlooking the city from the pleasant heights of Wickham Terrace. If its sails failed to work there was a treadmill, with plenty of convict feet to keep it turning, and more reliable, too! It was later used as an observatory.

▶ Parliament House   204B2
George and Alice streets (tel: 07-3406 7562 for tours)
Open: daily; tours from 10.30 on sitting days, from 9 on other days. Admission free
Opened in 1868, this fine French Renaissance-style building is still the home of the Queensland State Parliament. Tours are available at various times throughout the day.

▶▶ Queensland Cultural Centre   204B1
Melbourne and Grey streets, South Brisbane
Art Gallery: tel: 07-3840 7303. Open: Mon–Fri 10–5,
Sat–Sun 9–5. Museum: tel: 07-3840 7555. Open: daily
9.30–5. Admission free (charges for special exhibitions)

Brisbane's cultural heart is on the south bank of the river. Completed in 1985, this complex includes the Queensland Art Gallery, Queensland Museum, State Library and Performing Arts Centre, the latter with a 2,000-seat theatre and an equally large concert hall. Further development of the area up till 2006 will see the construction of the new Queensland Gallery of Modern Art, expansion of the State Library and the addition of the Queensland Sciencentre, formerly in the middle of town.

The **Queensland Art Gallery**▶▶ has a good selection of Australian and Aboriginal art, and a small collection of European painting, some of it interestingly arranged by theme rather than by artist or country. The contemporary Asian art collection is particularly good.

The exhibits in the innovative **Queensland Museum**▶▶ include dinosaurs, aircraft and sections on pioneering women and the art and customs of Melanesia, plus a major display on the history, art and culture of the Aborigines.

▶▶ Queensland Sciencentre — 204B2

Queensland Museum, Melbourne and Grey streets, South Brisbane (tel: 07-3840 7555). Admission: moderate

This interactive science and technology centre is one of Brisbane's most entertaining attractions. With around 170 hands-on exhibits, even non-scientific visitors will be captivated.

▶▶ South Bank — 204B2

South Brisbane (tel: 07-3867 2051)

Once the international crowds have gone, Expo sites often become forlorn places, but many of the pavilions and facilities erected for Brisbane's 1988 bonanza are still here, bringing life to this area of parkland. The attractions include a state-of-the-art **IMAX Theatre**, a kilometre-long (half-mile) floral canopied walkway (the Grand Arbour), Friday night and weekend art and craft markets, shops, restaurants, a Nepalese pagoda and much more.

NEWSTEAD HOUSE
Built in 1846, Newstead House (an elegant white mansion 4km/2.5 miles north of the city) is Brisbane's oldest surviving house. Now a museum of colonial days, it was once owned by Captain John Wickham, commander of the *Beagle* during its survey of Australia's coastline.

KOALA CAPITAL
Brisbane styles itself the 'koala capital', and the Alma Park Zoo at Kallangur, 30 minutes drive from Brisbane, and Lone Pine Koala Sanctuary (see page 206) are both good places to see these friendly marsupials.

207

Modern Brisbane is Australia's third largest city

Glass House Mountains scenery

Drive

The Sunshine Coast and hinterland

A full day's drive along Queensland's Sunshine Coast that also goes into the hinterland of farming and hill country west of the Bruce Highway.

About 60km (37 miles) north of Brisbane, the **Glass House Mountains** interrupt the monotony of the coastal plain. These old volcanic hills are best viewed from the old main road north of Caboolture as well as from the Mary Cairncross Scenic Reserve near Maleny. The **Blackall Range** panoramic drive gives access to this superb upland country of undulating hills and verdant valleys, tea rooms and craft studios. Just north of the little highland resort of Montville is the **Kondalilla National Park**, where splendid water-falls crash down through the rain forest. Equally spectacular falls can be experienced at **Mapleton Falls National Park**.

In **Nambour**, an area of tropical fruit production, a narrow-gauge sugarcane train trundles through the streets. A sequence of splendid beaches unravels along the Sunshine Coast north of Coolum to the highly fashionable community of **Noosa Heads**, while **Tewantin** boasts a couple of curiosities—a house built of bottles and the Big Shell. Back inland, the charming village of **Eumundi** makes a good stopping place, though it is packed on market days (Sat and Wed). The Bruce Highway is the best route for a swift return to Brisbane.

National parks

As may be expected in a state of its vast size, Queensland has an extraordinary variety of landscapes, many protected by designation as national or environmental parks.

Tropical coastline to desert heartlands Most visitors will become familiar with the reef and rain-forest parks of the tropical and subtropical coastline, but the spectacular and often unique parks of the interior demand attention too. More than 1,200km (745 miles) to the west of the coast are the monotonous sandhills of the **Simpson Desert National Park**, 'stretching interminably like waves of the sea' according to the explorer Charles Sturt, who gave up his attempt to conquer them. First crossed on foot in 1973, they still offer a challenge to anyone venturing into them today.

Farther east, the sparse vegetation of the desert gives way to grasslands, wattle scrub, eucalyptus woodland or scattered individuals of the strange Queensland bottle tree. Among the spinifex and rugged hills of the **Lark Quarry Conservation Park**, the footprints of dinosaurs that perished in a stampede 100 million years ago are preserved in mud that has long since turned to rock.

Farther east still, a broad belt of sandstone gives rise to spectacular scenery. This is where many of Queensland's major rivers have their origin; their erosive action has formed deep gorges in which a rich flora thrives, including the cabbage palms of **Carnarvon National Park**, also well known for its strange rock formations. As the land rises and rainfall increases, the blue-green of eucalypts gives way to the dark green of tropical rain forest, with its incredible wealth of species including ferns, climbers and other epiphytes. In parts of north Queensland, the World Heritage-listed rain forest descends to the beaches fringing the Great Barrier Reef, whose cays and islands are preserved as part of the **Great Barrier Reef Marine Park**.

Wild north to friendly south Cape York has some of the finest but least accessible of Queensland's national parks, where nature displays herself in all her savage unpredictability. In the wet season, rivers fill with fierce-flowing, silt-rich water, closing fords and cutting off communications for weeks on end, only to dry up into a series of isolated pools when the rain has finally stopped. Strange termite mounds stud the inland landscape, while mangrove swamps grow from the mud of the coastal plain. Brisbane must be one of the world's best endowed capital cities when one thinks in terms of grand scenery that is within easy reach of the town. A crescent of gloriously wooded highlands extends from close to the city boundary south to **Lamington National Park** on the border that lies between Queensland and New South Wales.

Brisbane's Lone Pine Koala Sanctuary is the state's best-known animal park, where kangaroos, Tasmanian devils and other creatures can also be seen

IN THE SOUTH
Near Warwick, at Cunningham's Gap in the Main Range National Park, there are fine views and a number of trails through rain forest and eucalyptus woodland.

Keep an eye out for the beautiful crimson rosella

The Pacific Highway to the south of Brisbane runs through eucalyptus country

A QUEENSLAND HIGHLAND LINE

Although there is now an alternative form of transportation (see page 220), half a million people travel the Cairns–Kuranda railway line every year. Few are disappointed by the spectacular 33km (20-mile) ride from coast to mountain rain forest. The line climbs from sea level to a summit at 328m (1,076ft) via a series of tunnels and sharp bends, stopping for a breather at the spectacularly tall Barron Falls. The railway was built between 1886 and 1891 to link the agricultural Atherton Tableland with the port at Cairns; it immediately put an end to Port Douglas as a harbour of any significance. The terminus at Kuranda, planted with palms and shady with ferns, would win any international award for the best-kept station.

How to travel

By air Queensland is unique among Australian states because it has three international airports—Brisbane, the Gold Coast and Cairns—with regular connections to many overseas airports. A variety of airlines links cities elsewhere in Australia with many places in Queensland, for example with the airports serving the Gold Coast (Coolangatta) and Sunshine Coast (Maroochydore). Given the large size of the state, internal travel by air is well developed, and may sometimes be the only way of reaching remote northern destinations during the wet season. Smaller aircraft, including helicopters and seaplanes, spin a web of services spanning mainland and islands; some islands can only be reached in this way.

By water Visitors are bound to find themselves afloat at some point in their Queensland holiday, even if it is only for a day-trip to part of the Great Barrier Reef aboard a high-speed wave piercer or a more humble craft rented locally. Most, but not all, of the islands are accessible by ferry or launch, which also carry vehicles to Fraser Island and a few of the Brisbane region isles. The best way of getting the feel of reef and islands might be to cruise; there are any number of operators competing for your business, some with sleek modern vessels calling at luxury resorts, others offering a more adventurous experience involving camping on uninhabited islands. Do not forget to take a cruise or ferry trip up the Brisbane River.

By bus Bus services link Brisbane with other Australian cities as well as major destinations within Queensland. Local services are variable, though well developed in Brisbane and on the Gold Coast.

By train Queensland has the longest rail network in the country. Services include two Brisbane–Cairns options: the twice-weekly *Sunlander* (which incorporates luxury *Queenslander*-class sleeper carriages), and the fast, comfortable *Tilt Train*, which travels via Rockhampton, Mackay and Townsville several times a week. Other services include the *Inlander* (Townsville–Mount Isa); the *Spirit of the Outback* (Brisbane–Longreach via Rockhampton); and the *Westlander* (Brisbane–Charleville). There are two rail curiosities to attract the adventurous: the weekly run from Cairns to Forsayth in the deep interior on the *Savannahlander*, and the *Gulflander* running on an isolated section of line near the Gulf of Carpentaria. The only interstate rail link is with Sydney.

By car The road system in the densely populated coastal strip is well developed, and reaches east–west across Queensland and into the Northern Territory via Mount Isa. Many places in the state are only accessible on unpaved roads. Cape York and other far northern places may be cut off in the wet season when fords become impassable and roads are swept away. Your own car, preferably a 4WD, will be an almost indispensable asset if you want to visit many national parks, though some sort of guided tour can be found for almost any destination.

▶ Atherton Tableland
200D2

From Cairns south for over 145km (90 miles) to near Innisfail, high tablelands rise steeply from the coastal plain. There are remnants of the once dense rain forest, preserved in several national parks and reserves, but the area's rich volcanic soils now mostly support sugar and exotic fruits. Southeast of Atherton on the Gillies Highway is **Yungaburra▶▶**, with extinct volcanoes and crater lakes.

▶▶▶ Cairns
201D3

Cairns is closer to Papua New Guinea than to most of Australia. The city, the key to far north Queensland, breathes in the balmy air of Trinity Bay. It helped open up the goldfields and tin mines of the interior, then became a major outlet for the booming agriculture of the area, particularly sugarcane. But tomorrow seems to promise even more expansive times; because of the proximity of the Barrier Reef, superb beaches, and the rivers and forests of the Daintree and the Atherton Tableland, tourism flourishes. Cairns International Airport, only opened in the mid-1980s, is now high on the list of Australian ports of entry in the amount of traffic it handles.

The town's founders laid out a generous grid of streets, whose width and relative absence of traffic contribute to the relaxed atmosphere. The waterfront complex housing boutiques, shops, the Reef Casino, cruise boat wharves and a luxury hotel add a sophisticated note, as do the ocean-going vessels of the super-rich in the adjacent marina.

Cairns Museum and nearby **Cairns Regional Gallery▶** give an insight into a past populated by Aborigines, railway workers, goldminers and Chinese workers. For a different experience, journey just outside town to the **Flecker Botanic Gardens▶**, with more than 200 varieties of palm trees and the tranquil Centenary Lakes. Also on the edge of town is the excellent **Tjapukai Aboriginal Cultural Park▶▶**, which offers a re-created Aboriginal camp, traditional dance performances and much more.

BUNDABERG
The name of this substantial town about 370km (230 miles) north of Brisbane is synonymous with its principal product—rum, distilled from the canefields of the coastal plain. Bundaberg is also the main gateway to the southern Barrier Reef. Mon Repos Conservation Park, a beach to the north, is a spot popular with turtles during their egg-laying season (November–February).

BIRDS AND BEACHES
The wildfowl enjoying the muddy flats of Trinity Bay in Cairns have won their battle against proposals to turn the flats into an artificial beach, but swimmers and sun-worshippers can head for the string of beaches stretching along the 26km (16-mile) 'Marlin Coast', a 10-minute drive to the north, each of them more paradisical than the last. From October to May, swimming is permitted only on netted beaches because of the presence of box jellyfish (see page 212).

211

The Esplanade and pier at sunny tropical Cairns

Drive

The Daintree and Cape Tribulation

If you can resist the temptation of the glorious beaches along the way, this full day's return drive from Cairns will take you over the Daintree River to tropical rain forest and coral reef.

The **Captain Cook Highway** is without doubt one of the world's finest coastal roads. Rarely overburdened with traffic, it runs inland at first from Cairns, rejoining the shore north of the exclusive resort town of Palm Cove. **Port Douglas**, the coastline's northernmost resort of any consequence, is home to the **Rainforest Habitat Wildlife Sanctuary**, an ambitious re-creation of the tropical rain-forest environment.

The canefields around **Mossman** feed the town's sugar mill via a stretch of narrow-gauge railway. A short detour leads to the rain forest of the Mossman Gorge in **Daintree National Park**, with its graded walking track, rapids and delightful swimming holes. At the turn leading to the ferry over the Daintree River the tarmac comes to a (temporary) end; non-4WD vehicles should proceed with caution

The goanna, or monitor lizard

or not at all in the wet season. The wide river is lined with mangrove swamp and is home to crocodiles.

Beyond the ferry begins the ecological wonderland of the **Cape Tribulation** section of the **Daintree National Park**, a remnant of the forests in which flowering plants first appeared on earth. The road lurches through the forest and across dry river beds, pale dust from vehicles coating the luxuriant vegetation with a thin film.

The **Heights of Alexandra Lookout** gives a superb view over the forest tumbling down to the sea. The best initiation into the complex ecology and sheer beauty of the World Heritage Area is at the **Daintree Rainforest Environmental Centre** with its boardwalk leading deep into this mysterious realm.

Even if the presence of highly toxic box jellyfish inhibits swimming in the sea, you should at least walk along one of the incomparable beaches of **Cape Tribulation**, several of which are easily accessible from the road. Beyond the cape itself, the 32km (20-mile) Bloomfield Track begins; it is only negotiable by 4WD.

The bottlebrush is native to Queensland

213

▶▶ Cape York Peninsula   *200E2*

Often described as one of the world's last wildernesses, this great peninsula tapers northward for hundreds of kilometres to its tip at Cape York itself, overlooking the island-studded Torres Strait. A total of perhaps 10,000 people are thinly distributed over this vast area, most of them Torres Strait Islanders and Aborigines, whose ancestors left a legacy of remarkable rock painting that is best seen around **Laura**. This little township straddles the lower end of the Peninsula Developmental Road, a less developed highway than its name implies, especially in the Wet when river crossings become impassable even for the most rugged of 4WDs.

In the Dry, the Cape becomes a fascinating destination for the more adventurous tourist. The rain forest along the Pacific coast gives way to savannah-like country farther inland, punctuated by the surreal turrets of termite mounds, some of them reaching an extraordinary 3m (10ft). The peninsula possesses some remarkable national parks—including **Lakefield**, coastal **Cape Melville** and the remote crocodile habitat of **Mungkan Kandju National Park**. The future of the peninsula probably lies in wilderness tourism; civilization's other activities, apart from bauxite mining at Weipa, have left little mark on the land.

▶▶ Carnarvon National Park   *201B3*

Much of this spectacular park is difficult to get to (and access is restricted during wet weather), but the extraordinary gorges cut by the Carnarvon Creek and its tributaries into the soft sandstone of the plateau can be reached from the Carnarvon Developmental Road between Roma and Rolleston. Here 200m(650-ft) high cliffs tower over cabbage palms, ferns, mosses and orchids. A number of caves shelter Aboriginal rock paintings. A footpath leads up the gorge from the ranger station, with side tracks leading to all the park's delights.

▶ Charters Towers   *201C3*

In contrast to the tropical environment of Townsville, 135km (84 miles) away, this upland town enjoys an invigorating climate. It has some of the best early Australian architecture to be seen anywhere (see panel).

▶ Chillagoe–Mungana Caves National Park 200D2

Around the old mining village of Chillagoe, west of Atherton Tableland, are extensive, spectacular caves eroded in the limestone by the headwaters of the Mitchell River. Not all are accessible, but the Donna and Trezkinn caves are artificially lit to enhance the drama and strangeness of the limestone formations. On the surface, the same rock has been weathered into equally peculiar shapes—turrets, pinnacles and forms resembling animals.

▶ Cloncurry 200C1

Once a bustling gold and copper town, Cloncurry sits astride the main road and railway line from Mount Isa to the coast, earning its living nowadays from sheep and cattle grazing. It was here in 1928 that the Royal Flying Doctor Service began operating (see panel).

▶ Cooktown 200D2

A late 19th-century boomtown in the rip-roaring days of gold strikes on the Palmer River, Cooktown was named for Captain James Cook. His ship, *Endeavour,* was beached here after she had been badly holed on the Barrier Reef. Though the peak population of 30,000 or more has shrunk to around 1,000, enough traces of the past remain to make Cooktown an attractive tourist destination. The Captain's enforced stay is recalled in the Victorian villa housing the **James Cook Museum▶**, as well as by his statue and by the annual reenactment in June of his landing. Cooktown is easily reached from Cairns by the inland road or, more picturesquely, by the mostly unpaved Cape Tribulation coast road. The town is also a useful base for expeditions into the Cape York interior.

▶▶▶ Daintree National Park 200D2

The outstanding international significance of the Queensland rain forest has been recognized by the designation of the Daintree and Cape Tribulation region as a World Heritage Area (part of the Wet Tropics of Queensland). A relic of Cretaceous times over 100 million years ago, the jungle of far north Queensland escaped the volcanic eruptions that destroyed other primitive forests in the region, and consequently has a unique ecological value. The tiny settlement of Daintree is on the banks of the Daintree River, famous for its mangroves and crocodiles. The rain forest can be visited on guided or self-guided bushwalks via river cruises or you can simply appreciate its wonders at the **Daintree Rainforest Environmental Centre▶▶**.

▶▶ Fraser Island 201B4

This is the largest sand island in the world, stretching 121km (75 miles) beside the south Queensland coast. With wonderful beaches, dunes rising to an extraordinary heathland, rain forest, mangroves and dozens of freshwater lakes, this World Heritage island attracts many visitors, though access is only by 4WD (there are no roads). A drive along the east coast takes you past the wreck of the *Maheno* and cliffs of multihued sandstone to the resort villages of Eurong Beach and Happy Valley. There are two other resorts on the island, as well as campsites.

IF DOCTORS COULD FLY
Set up in 1927–28 by the Rev. John Flynn, the Royal Flying Doctor Service (RFDS) began operations in Cloncurry with a plane supplied by the Queensland and Northern Territory Aerial Service (Qantas). The event is recalled in a memorial to Flynn, its missionary founder, and in the John Flynn Place Museum in Cloncurry.

SAVING THE WILDERNESS
Destruction of the Daintree by volcanic explosions and lava flows may have been avoided in the remote geological past; more recent threats have involved the dividing of the rain forest into handy packages for 'development' and the construction of the controversial Bloomfield Track. World Heritage designation has now rescued this irreplaceable tract of wild nature.

The island is easily reached by ferry from the mainland (Inskip Point, Urangan and Mary River Heads), or by air.

▶ **Glass House Mountains**   *201A4*

Inland from the Bruce Highway north of Brisbane rises a group of steep and strangely shaped peaks, the cores of old volcanoes. Given their enigmatic name by Captain Cook, they are popular with climbers; the inexperienced can best view them from the Old Gympie Road or from Mary Cairncross Scenic Reserve near Maleny.

▶▶▶ **Gold Coast**   *201A4*

Between Tweed Heads on the New South Wales border and Paradise Point in the north stretches a 71km (44-mile) chain of 35 glorious sandy beaches blessed by regular rolling surf and basking in regular sunshine. Everyone is catered for here: Swimming, surfing and sunbathing all have their place, but so do many other activities—golf and adventure sports like parasailing. There are any number of theme parks and similar establishments, among them the incredibly successful **Sea World**▶▶▶ at Main Beach, smoothly entertaining its tidal wave of visitors, and the popular Warner Bros. Movie World theme park.

At **Surfers Paradise**, with its lavish malls, excellent restaurants and good nightlife, and Jupiters Casino at nearby Broadbeach, you can enjoy this seaside Arcadia to the full. A somewhat quieter (and cheaper) ambience can be enjoyed to the south, around Currumbin or at wooded Burleigh Heads, where a discreet national park visitor centre introduces what is left of the coast's natural environment.

SAND FOR SALE
The sands of Fraser Island have a high mineral content that makes them very valuable in certain industrial processes. A notable victory was won here in 1977 by conservationists who succeeded in stopping sand mining and the consequent gradual export overseas of the very substance of the island.

GOLD COAST CONTRASTS
The sprawling Gold Coast is a textbook example of how not to plan an urban environment. The approach from Brisbane, an hour away, is lined with high-rise buildings, varied in shape and decorated in tasteful pastel shades. They jostle each other for a glimpse of the beach, which, because it is to the east and they are too close, is plunged into shade in the course of the afternoon. In stark contrast, the area offers a verdant hinterland (see Lamington National Park on page 220), and wildlife parks such as Currumbin Wildlife Sanctuary near Coolangatta.

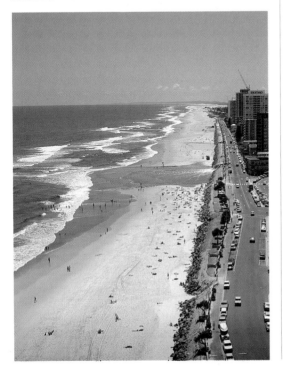

High-rise buildings loom over the beautiful beach of Surfers Paradise

Australia's greatest attraction, the reef stretches for more than 2,000km (1,240 miles) along the east coast from the Gulf of Papua to a point just south of the Tropic of Capricorn (off Gladstone).

REEF FISH

The reef is home to thousands of species of fish, from the greedy potato cod (see picture below), to vibrant parrot fish, graceful rays and poisonous lion fish. It's also home to many types of shark. Attacks are rare, however, and the sharks will probably be more scared of you than you are of them.

Giant potato cod expect to be fed and stroked at Cod Hole, 19km (12 miles) off Lizard Island and one of the world's best diving sites

The coral of the reef's outer rim forms a steep submarine escarpment, dropping abruptly into the abyss of the Pacific; only 30km (19 miles) out from Cairns, this Outer Reef gradually extends farther away from the mainland until, opposite Mackay, it is some 250km (155 miles) off shore. Landward is warm and shallow water, forming a kind of lagoon broken up by more reefs and hundreds of islands, some of them true coral cays, most of them detached fragments of the mainland, cut off when sea levels rose. They vary enormously in character, from exposed and sparsely vegetated cays of sand and coral barely rising out of the water at low tide, to reef-fringed mountain ranges covered in splendid rain forest.

Creatures of the deep Hardly another ecosystem on earth can surpass the reef for sheer beauty or variety. Responsible for its formation are humble polyps, tiny organisms with limestone outer skeletons that form a coral reef's basic building blocks. With wildly differing shapes recalling trees, plates, fungi and even brains, the still-living polyps vividly paint the underwater scene, to which is added a kaleidoscope of other living creatures. These include not only tropical fish of brilliant hue and intriguing personality, but also sponges, starfish, crabs, sharks, turtles, giant clams and an occasional dugong, a large and harmless creature also known as the sea-cow.

Another creature that is drawn to this watery paradise in large numbers is *Homo sapiens*, tourist variety. This medium-sized, sometimes amphibious mammal can be